The Jewish Library

5: PANORAMA OF JUDAISM

PART ONE

SONCINO PRESS
Books of Enduring Worth

Leo Jung GENERAL EDITOR
M.A. (CANTAB), PH.D. (LONDON), D.D. (YESHIVA), L.H.D. (NEW YORK)
RABBI OF THE JEWISH CENTER, NEW YORK

The Jewish Library

5: Panorama of Judaism

in two volumes: part one

by Leo Jung

THE SONCINO PRESS / LONDON AND NEW YORK

Made and printed in Great Britain by
William Clowes and Sons, Limited, London, Beccles and Colchester

TO THE SACRED MEMORY OF

CHAIM JOSEPH SONNENFELD · ZEVI PESAH FRANK ·

LEO DEUTSCHLANDER

Contents

Introduction

The Panorama of Judaism is among the best kept secrets of contemporary Jewry, not excluding social workers, Synagogue officers, and especially the youth. Judaism in concrete, needs to be conveyed in the most encouraging and enjoyable manner in order to win back to our faith and folk, the confused, rootless young men and women and in some cases, their parents. Problems of faith and science, in the light of modern thought, have become less significant. Likewise, comparison with other creeds or points of view, no longer presents difficulties. The bitterest and all too successful enemy of our Holy *Torah* is ignorance concerning its basic teaching and especially its social idealism.

If PANORAMA OF JUDAISM, in some manner can improve matters, I shall be happy indeed.

My warmest thanks to my daughters Rosalie and Marcella (Mrs. Leonard Rosenfeld and Mrs E. David Rosen) and to my friends Nima Adlerblum and Ethel Leibowitt for invaluable help in preparing the manuscript for press.

Leo Jung

Shevat 5733 – January 1973

Panorama of Judaism

part one

Contemporary History

Holiness and the Holocaust

Speak to the congregation of the children of Israel and say to them: Be ye holy, for I, the Lord your God, am holy.[1]

Rashi comments: 'this portion was offered before the whole congregation because most *Torah* principles depend upon it.'

Rashbam has a brief but very significant comment: 'Be holy – because the Lord gave them *mitzvot*, they are warned to sanctify themselves as they observe them.'[2]

Any careful observer of life will appreciate what is involved in this observation. The very multiplicity of commandments may cause a mechanical conformity to them. In popular language, one may not see the wood because of the trees. Their individual foliage may prevent the rays of the sun from warming, inspiring the observer.

The word 'holy', the term 'holiness,' evokes a curious reaction in modern man. There was a time in America, before the blessed day-school movement started, when parents whose boys could read a passage of the *Torah* were 'afraid' that the son might become a Rabbi or a Scholar. Even today, the word 'holiness' sounds somewhat outlandish to many people, evoking a hermit's hut, a sour physiognomy. One recalls George Bernard Shaw's acid description of a Puritan woman as very unpleasant and, therefore, considered most religious.

Those fears and prejudices are utterly un-Jewish. Holiness does imply reverence, righteousness, and *raḥamanut*. Fundamentally, it is a quality to beautify life, to make it physically wholesome and emotionally secure. In our daily prayer we assert, 'He has planted everlasting life in our midst.'[3] The tone and the motivations, the quality and the programme of our daily life in our mundane occupation, no less than in hours spent in blessed solitude or communal prayer, they all are meant to create *kedushah* (holiness). It means commitment to decency, kindness, patience, and wisdom. It means opposition to indecency, unkindness, impatience, and un-wisdom. It means sharing the protest against any oppression. It means improving the welfare of every human brother. The major opposition to holiness comes from modern heathens, who are dedicated to four idols: power, profit, privilege, and pleasure. To the bigoted white supremacists in the Southern States, no term is more vile than 'nigger-lover.' Among the Nazi hell-hounds, no *Schimpfwort* (bad name) was more offensive than 'Jew-lover.' Intolerant priests would hurl 'heretic-lover' as the worst term, meant to destroy a tolerant person. All these men with their ruthless folly and their self-destructive cruelty would smile at *kedushah*. To them the man in the pulpit must say Amen to every political unrighteousness. He must endorse the 'Klan,' the radical right, the howling gangs of misled religionists.

Against all that militates the *kedushah* which the holy *Torah* demands of us. There is a unique term in Jewish language and life – *kiddush Hashem*, the sanctification of God's name. It can be achieved by one sublime action of courage or self-denial as well as by the whole tone and calibre of one's life. It is a supreme virtue – *Kiddush Hashem berabbim*. Its opposite is the the most abject crime *Ḥillul Hashem berabbim*. (the public desecration of His Name).

The last decades have raised *Kiddush Hashem* from a private achievement to a mass virtue. The six million of our people who were butchered by fiendish Nazis are considered, both in the view of our great scholars as well as by popular emotion, as having sanctified the name of God. Of late, some voices have been heard, super-cynical, to doubt the justification of that title. They felt that a third of our people, tortured unto death, were like sheep being brought to the slaughter. There was something infinitely pathetic in their suffering but nothing deserving the appellation of *Kiddush Hashem.*

I put this question to my students at Yeshivah University's very significant branch – The Stern College for Women. I asked the students to offer an answer to that impious jibe. A young girl, not quite twenty, offered this comment: 'When our brethren and sisters went to the gas chamber and chanted *Ani Ma'amin* in the last moment of their life, defying the ruthless enemy and proclaiming their deathless faith in God, in justice, in moral values, they sanctified the Creator by their unbroken spirit.' Indeed, they proclaimed with their last breath the timeless commitment of the Jew to the religion of humanity. In the darkest hour of their life, their example spread light for all the world. While their bodies were helpless, their spirit soared and their last testament was the re-assertion of the prayer of the eternal people to their eternal Father in Heaven. The *Oyev tameh* (Unclean Enemy) died dishonoured, but the dying Jews built life everlasting.[4]

This is the meaning of *kedushah,* a faith transcending any environment, a devotion that ignores all difficulties, a conviction which establishes a path like a red thread through the vicissitudes of human progress towards a time when the cause of Israel will be recognized as the cause of all man, when *kedushah* will be the normal source of goodness, truth, and beauty, when the Lord will be One and His Name One.

Notes

1. Leviticus. XIX, 2.
2. a.l.
3. *Shaḥarit.*
4. See S. B. Unsdorfer, *The Yellow Star*; F. W. Foerster, *Die Juedische Frage*; Victor Frankl, *The Search for Meaning* (*Logotherapy*); Wells, *The Janowska Road*; Chaim Kaplan, *Scroll of Agony*; E. H. Flannery, *The Anguish of the Jews*; Dagobert D. Runes, *The Jews and the Cross.*

The Renaissance of East European Jewish Womanhood

Two words of late have made their entry in the United States of America. Two Hebrew words, conveying little to the average Jewish mind, but full of meaning when their import is grasped. *Beth Jacob* in English means 'House of Jacob.' House of Jacob has been a time-honoured Jewish appellation of Jewish womanhood. *Beth Jacob* hence is readily understood to have something to do with Jewish womanhood. It is the movement for the reclamation of the Jewish girl in Eastern Europe.

Does the Jewish girl in Eastern Europe need salvaging? Are there any dangers confronting her? Let me sink into anecdotage.

It was in Summer of 1927, on the way to Europe. Next to me on the deck sat a fine Gentile family, whose acquaintance I had made on the boat. They were father, mother, and daughter, who at once conveyed the impression of rare personalities. The daughter especially, a student, seventeen years of age, mercifully unrouged, serene, serious, withal buoyant, could not fail to impress herself upon any thoughtful person. One day, in the chair, she leaned over, her face full of joy: 'Rabbi, may I tell you something which gives me much joy?'

'Surely.'

'Well, I am waiting to finish my course at —— College and then, my parents promised, I shall have my ambition realized.'

My mind reverted to French finishing schools, to a winter debut, to a motor car of her own – to any and all of such things as might form the ambition of the average girl.

'Well, and what is your ambition, Claire?'

'I shall be going out (her face shone with rare spirituality), I shall be going out to East Africa to convert the heathen.'

That moment I felt unaccountably unhappy and Claire did not fail to notice it.

'What is it, Rabbi, that pains you?'

In my heart I felt unhappy because of the thought that we Jews had been dying for God, living for God for two millennia, but that our maidens did not dream of looking upon the spreading of Jewish ideals as their glorious major ambition, that it was a non-Jewess who had the imperative urge of spreading faith in God. I hastened to tell the young friend of my admiration for her spirit and my sadness at the thought that my own sisters, Jewish girls, were not alarmed by the thought of Godlessness somewhere in the far East or the near West...

The boat docked at Cherbourg, whence I went to England and Switzerland to join my family. But that thought still rankled in my mind. It disturbed the *revoir* with old friends in England, it disturbed an excellent crossing into France, it interfered with the blueness of the sky at Lucerne. And then I left for Poland. I had been interested in the *Beth Jacob* movement and the director had my promise of a personal visit.

The train brought me to my destination late at night. In the morning I left the hotel in the direction of the *Beth Jacob* Training School, which I was to examine. On the way I received my first shock. A Jewish woman came begging, a child at her breast, two stunted, wizened little children at her right and left. These tiny girls, corresponding in size to American youngsters of four, were eight and nine years of age. Her husband had been out of regular work for five years, they lived on less than bread, on potatoes and cucumbers, and rarely knew the luxury of bread and herring.

A friend led me round for the next two hours and I found the same story repeated and enacted throughout the city. I saw a Jewish family in a cellar, without windows, with candlelight to illumine the darkness, with rags as bedspreads, starvation in the children's faces. I saw grandparents, spectres of *les Miserables,* with every indication of neglect, despair in their eyes, crawling out of the dark houses, seemingly afraid of the very sun, lest he, too, suddenly withdraw his light to leave them cold and dismal, as they had been miserable and without hope for the dreary decade since the war. I saw young boys coming from the *Talmud Torah,* faces exquisite, but white, with the stooping gait of children mentally preoccupied, physically undernourished. And then I saw an unusually large number of young girls, standing in the street, sitting on the doorsteps, beautiful eyes, fine foreheads, but apparently without occupation, uninterested, yet with a certain longing that intimated a great emptiness, a craving for content.

Involuntarily I wondered what would be their destiny. Poverty and hopelessness at home, without any schooling to supply the vital need for romance, through which adolescents seek maturity. Deprived of the bigger joys of childhood and of the pleasantness of the minor vanities, even dresses and theatres and sport.

These girls, I felt, were in a position much worse than their elders. These girls will suffer from the pangs of growth, from surplus energies, from strange longings, superimposed upon the general repression due to abysmal poverty and abysmal neglect. These girls, before the war, had at least the advantage of the homogeneous Jewish *milieu* which, by its very life, though destitute of systematic schooling, had permeated the Jewish girl with a sense of decency and goodness and spirituality. These girls, after the war, are exposed to all the discomforts, to all the chaos, to all the destructive influences, born of decay and despair, the issues of bloodthirsty madness which still beset the nations of the world. These girls – beautiful, romantic, keen in mind, good of heart – are being burdened by great energies without outlets, by a hundred and one temptations and dangers.

Facts, sad and eloquent, had borne out my sombre thought. In 1927, in London, appalling statistics had been offered as to the number of girls from Poland who had been sold as white cargo by the unhung scoundrels of two continents. The newspapers had brought some reports of Jewish girls in the ranks of communism.

But all that, terrible as the figures are, refers to an almost negligible percentage of our people in Poland and Galicia. Much more terrible is the heart-sickening picture of thousands of young girls without a spiritual life content. The parents ground between the upper millstone of exceeding economic plight and the nether millstone of hatred and persecution, have no message for the children. They have had their life and the wild despair of their youth is a sin and a puzzle to them. Schools for girls were practically nonexistent.

Thus there grew up a generation of Jewish girls, rich in native endowment, ready for all the goodness and beauty of life, but doomed to inward emptiness and outward suffering. From year to year the leaders of our people in Poland watched with breaking hearts, without plan or hope, these awful conditions. Pogroms and government restriction, hunger and cold were the framework holding the utter tragedy of these young girls.

'We are without hope for the future. In the past it was the Jewish women who rose in times of emergency as saviours of our people. Out of Egypt and Persia, out of Hellenist crises and medieval bitter *Galut*, the spirit of Israel's mothers delivered us. But here, in this age, our very daughters, sullenly and madly, turn against us.' Thus lamented the fathers, the mothers, the teachers. Then came the inspiration of Sara Schenirer.

Frau Schenirer, by the accident of war, found herself in Vienna. There, one day, she heard a Rabbi explain Judaism as a system of life, as a way to beauty and goodness, as a divine plan of education. She had never dreamt of such possibilities; that all the laws and observances should have a meaning underlying them, that they should be weavable into a fine, inspiring, encouraging texture, that the *Torah* was indeed a book of life, a law of life, a guide to happiness.

'If I could bring this message to my sisters in Poland!' she thought. 'If I could explain to them what has been revealed to me, I could give them life content, I could bring them hope, courage, I could open to them a new vista.'

Sara Schenirer returned to Poland and collected into her home – she was the daughter of well-to-do parents – a number of these girls to whom she brought this unheard-of message. She met with touching response. Within a short time she had gathered a large number of girls, who, as she put it, were 'athirst, athrob, aglow.'

But there were no books. Her pupils knew only Yiddish and there were in Poland no Yiddish translations of the Bible, nor any satisfactory textbooks on Judaism and Jewish life. I had sent her some copies of Magil's Interlinear translation and the girls (I found out afterwards) copied into their writing books the translation of the *Ḥumash*!

In my files are some letters received by Mrs. Schenirer from girls in remote villages, whom the rumour had reached of the new undertaking. 'My saintly sister,' ran one of them, 'for heaven's sake take me into your school. I'll be happy to sleep on the floor and live on bread and water, but please, please, have mercy upon me, lead me to the fountain of life, take me in!'

Frau Schenirer's economic foresight did not keep pace with her noble intention. Within a short time she had five hundred girls around her, for whom she had no living quarters, no curriculum, no system, nothing, but the wealth of her love and affection.

Her work was taken up by the *Agudat Israel*, world-organization of Orthodox Jewry, which lent its best educators and organizers to the development of *Beth Jacob's* Teachers' Training Colleges and a system of elementary and high schools. The five centres (Cracow, Warsaw, Vienna, Bratislava, and Czernovitz) graduated a large number of young women prepared according to the best methods of modern pedagogy and inspired by fervent loyalty to our faith and by a proud sense of membership in Israel.

These colleges were responsible for the emergence of an inspiring type of girl-teacher, who not only brought the message of our faith to many thousands of girls, but also introduced modern methods of education and hygiene into the underprivileged homes and neglected areas of Eastern Europe. By 1938, 40,000 girls were enrolled in about 400 schools of *Beth Jacob* from Latvia to Roumania, from Lithuania to Czechoslovakia, and to the innermost recesses of Poland.

Beth Jacob in the War

The German occupation of Eastern Europe and its devilish plan of extermination well-nigh destroyed that great institution. Yet up to 1941, in the midst of famine and Teutonic mass murder, the light of *Beth Jacob* never failed! The famous letter of the 93 girls in the last *Beth Jacob* School in the Ghetto of Warsaw, which is appended, is an immortal document of the spirit of these young women who gladly preferred death to defilement by the Nazi beasts.

The Beth Jacob Movement Today

In the years after the war Beth Jacob organized and maintained a vast number of schools, kindergartens, children's homes, for those who survived the Nazi Holocaust, etc. From the European D.P. Camps, more than 4,000 girls attended the numerous Beth Jacob schools and institutions in Germany, Austria, Italy, France and Belgium.

With the destruction of the Jewish communities in continental Europe the main activities of the Beth Jacob movement switched to new centres of Jewish settlement: Israel and the United States of America. However, there are also a number of Beth Jacob Schools, High Schools and Teachers' Seminaries in England and some European countries, Canada, and even in South America.

Beth Jacob in Israel

The Beth Jacob movement in Israel was founded in the early thirties and in the beginning attracted only the old *Yishuv*. However, it slowly grew into one of the most outstanding educational networks, respected by the whole *Yishuv*.

The educational network of the Beth Jacob movement in Israel, beginning with the kindergartens and continuing through the seminaries for teachers, counts in its ranks over 30,000 students, distributed as follows:

(1) In the Beth Jacob elementary schools	18,000
(2) In the kindergartens	5,500
(3) In the high-schools and vocational schools	6,500
(4) Seminary students	900
Total	30,900

The Beth Jacob Movement in the United States and Canada

The Beth Jacob movement in the United States was founded in 1935, but it did not become a major force in the field of Jewish education until after 1945.

With the influx of new Jewish immigrants in the years following World War II, new Beth Jacob schools emerged in many Jewish neighbourhoods in New York, as well as in a number of other communities in the United States. It is estimated that approximately 30,000 Jewish girls have been educated in the Beth Jacob institutions in the United States in the last 25 years.

As of today, there are in the United States and Canada:

25 Beth Jacob Elementary Schools
10 Beth Jacob High Schools
3 Beth Jacob Teachers' Seminaries

with a total enrolment of about 22,000 students.

The majority of these schools are in the Greater New York area and the others are in Baltimore, Philadelphia, Chicago, Denver, Detroit, Los Angeles, Montreal and Toronto.

In all Beth Jacob schools, in whatever part of the world, the main purpose has been to train Jewish girls and women, to instil in them Jewish knowledge and to inspire them with love for Judaism.

A LETTER FROM THE MARTYRS OF WARSAW

Dear Friend in New York:

I do not know whether this letter will reach you. Do you still remember who I am? We met in the same house of Mrs. Schenirer (founder of the *Beth Jacob* movement) and afterward again in Marienbad. When this letter will come into your hands, I shall not live any more. With us are ninety-two *Beth Jacob* girls. Within a few hours everything will be over. Give our regards to Mr. Rosenheim (head of the world Beth Jacob movement) and our friend Goodman, both in England. We all met in Warsaw at our friend's Y——— and Y———'s son was also there.

We had four rooms. On July twenty-seventh we were taken out and thrown into a dark room, having only water. We studied the sacred works and got courage. In age we are from fourteen to twenty-two; the younger ones are afraid. I try to recall Mother Sarah's (Mrs. Schenirer's) teaching of the *Torah*. It is good to live for God, but it is also good to die for Him.

Yesterday and the day before we were given hot baths and we were told that German soldiers would come tonight to visit us. We yesterday swore to ourselves that we shall die together. Yesterday one sent us to a big house with bright rooms and nice beds. The Germans do not know that our last bath is our purification before death. Today everything was taken away from us, and we were each given one nightgown. All of us have poison. When the soldiers will come we shall drink it. Today we are together and all day we are saying our last confession. We have no fear.

We thank you, good friend, for everything. We have one request: Say *Kaddish* for us, your ninety-three children. Soon we shall be with Mother Sarah.

Regards from————————————of Krakow.

This letter appeared in the January 8th, 1943 issue of The New York Times.

Warsaw Ghetto Memorial Address

I

What has summoned us hither, brethren and sisters, is not an occasion for tears, no matter how hot. Life, national and individual, is too precious for sterile expenditure of time or energy. We must, for a moment, hold fast the memory of a frightful period in the history of human conscience, but we must live on in the broad vista of our own history – from *Avraham Avinu* (Father Abraham) to the *Yemot ha-Moshiaḥ* (the days of the Messiah). Between the two lies the glory and the tragedy of our people.

It is a moral obligation never to eliminate from our consciousness the mortal peril of Hitler's mad fury: the scientific devilry of that unclean enemy, his calculated mass murder, his fiendish system of torture, the whole witches' cauldron of the organized lie. For the good of the human family, to prevent such horrors for all future, that record of unrestrained barbarism must never perish from man's annals.

For our own spiritual resolves we must *not* forget the depth of our disillusionment with Western democracies, the deadly indifference of Christian 'humanitarianism', nor the shame of secular leaders turned into lackeys of evil, their followers shrieking their acclaim of the horsemen of hell. For ever we shall view with contempt all that cowardice and hypocrisy which in the years of our supreme agony had at best only *gedolim hikeke lev*, (great searchings of the heart) but knew neither justice nor pity for the Jewry of Europe. They moved no finger to help the people who had brought the accents of heaven to a heathen world, the programme for the humanization of humanity to conscienceless masters, the *neginah* (melody) of mercy to terrified slaves of power, no pity for our people who from the moment of emancipation had fought on every battlefield for freedom and more abundant life of all God's children everywhere!

Our pain would have been intolerable but for profound faith in the Rock of the Ages. *Hashem Yitbarakh*, we knew, would uphold our cause in the zigzag of human affairs (*Hashem yilahem lakhem ve-attem taharishun*). Our valiant battle for freedom of conscience would eventually challenge the noblest among the *umot ha-olam* (nations of the world), causing them to plough the furrows of the earth in slow progress towards the foot of Mount Sinai.

II

The ruin of Polish Jewry is searing, stunning, paralysing. The utter impotence that horrified us in those years, to save her thinkers and dreamers, her leaders and teachers, her heroes and martyrs, the passing years notwithstanding, has its steady impact on our homes and hearts. Who can forget the Jewish mothers, angels of *raḥamanut* (mercy) and *tzeniut* (decency), victims of relentless murders! Time cannot wipe off the memory of a million Jewish children, *al tig'u bimeshihay, elu tinokot shel bet rabban*, a thousand potential messiahs, thousands of mystics and teachers of morality, myriads of inspired artists and craftsmen! What melancholy pleasure it is to recall the great movements of Polish Jewry – the love of *Torah* and Zion in organized fervour, the passion for *Tsedek* (justice) and *Ḥessed* (kindness) in workers' councils, the sweet reverence and *Tzedakah* in the countless homes of *Stam Yiden* (average Jews)! Oh that we could re-enter for but a short hour the sacred halls of *Yeshivot* and *Bet Yaakov*, the houses of prayer and study, whose disciples have roamed the whole world as twentieth century prophets of our faith and the Jewish way of life!

III

But *Gam ki elekh bege tzalmavet* (Even though I walk in the valley of deepest darkness) there is more than gloom this hour. There is the imperishable glory of the last weeks of Jewish Warsaw. We Jews celebrate *Shabbat haGadol* (the great *Shabbat*) in memory of a human miracle, on the tenth of *Nissan* in the year of the Exodus when our forefathers defied at once the masters and the idols of Egypt. But in Egypt it was a people on the threshold of redemption. In the ghetto of Warsaw it was a doomed remnant that took up arms against Hitler's *Wehrmacht*. Such courage seemed madness to the few friends and to the masses of Nazi hellhounds. But it was real. In the shadow of agonizing disease and ravenous hunger it *did* happen. The terrifying visions of day and night were conquered by resistless spirit, by the glorious stubbornness of men and women with their backs to the wall. Long ago the Greeks had proclaimed: '*Ou gar adynasiais kreitton ananke* (No force is stronger than impossibility).' But the heroes of the Warsaw Ghetto defied impossibility. They rose above the limitations of common mortality. Their flame pierced the night of doom, its glow will be felt for years without end.

These folks, whipped, bled of all strength, created a new kind of *Kiddush Hashem*. To them Menahem Ziemba preached a determination which not only threw back the German battalions, but in the midst of cruelty, coldness, and corruption, they died fighting and fought dying, battling tyranny to the last ounce of their strength and the last moment of their life. These heroes were *Bassar mibessarenu etzem meatzomenu* (flesh of our flesh, bone of our bone). They have infused us with pride (*geon yaakov asher oheb*), not only God-approved, but a perennial source of ennoblement and invigoration. Their *Shir ha-Gevurah* (the song of their heroism) lives in our hearts. Their *ani maamin* (declaration of faith) shall forever inspire us. Their inexhaustible spiritual riches have become foundations of the blessed *moledet* as they have under-pinned the moral powers of Jewish communities in all the corners of the world.

IV

We stand here, *she-erit hapletah*, remnants of God's people. Our pain is too deep for words. Our pride is too sacred for expression. But Polish Jews have been also pioneers of prayer. Their *Ḥassidim* have taught us anew how to find God in deepest affliction, how to rejoice in His love whilst '"trembling" in fear of human perversity (*Gilu bireadah*).' So let our pain be eased and our pride be wedded to faith. Let our beseechment surge to *Avinu shebashamayim* (our Father in Heaven) to keep us aglow with the glory of their supreme spirit, to serve faith, people, and land, so that out of the depth of our pain and the height of our pride may be born a worthy generation of Jews fired by its dream of redemption for *Am Yissrael* (the people of Israel) and marching, building, fighting in the cause of universal justice and freedom.

Our heads are bowed in sorrow. We lift our hearts in faith. We pledge our hands for sustained work until the waste places of mankind are built up, until hatred and oppression cease, until the people of Israel can again serve their land and sit 'under the figtree and the vine with none to make them afraid.' *Shalom shalom laraḥok velekarov* (peace, peace unto him that is far, unto him that is near).

The J.D.C.'s Cultural Work

The three R's of the Joint Distribution Committee – Rescue, Relief, Rehabilitation – have brought salvation to our persecuted brethren, victims of man's inhumanity in two World Wars. Its programme has changed the horizons of Jewish life all over the world even as it has raised the moral level of American Jewry. As a forty-six years' veteran of Joint work, who has observed its operation in four continents, I am happy to add my humble note to the universal acclaim of the J.D.C. Only those who have seen the difference between Jewish life in Eastern Europe in 1917 and then in 1930, in Palestine of 1918 and then in Israel of 1967, have a grasp of J.D.C.'s miraculous achievement. Only those who have had some close knowledge of the dedication from Paul Baerwald and Edward Warburg, to Louis Broido, and of the total devotion from Bernard Kahn through Joseph Schwartz and Moe Leavitt to Charles Jordan, Sam Haber, and the Joints' staff – true ambassadors of mercy – are able to envisage its harvest, an unmatched sanctification of God's name – *Kiddush Hashem*.

There are three other R's of timeless significance which the J.D.C. has cherished and sustained through its cultural-religious work, rebuilding, maintaining, counselling, and aiding the institutions which served them.

The three R's of our faith are Reverence, Righteousness, and *Raḥamanut*: Reverence for God and human personality: Righteousness, positive in integrity of conduct, and negative in fighting oppression wherever it raises its ugly head: and the third R, the crown of Jewish life *Raḥamanut*, usually translated as 'pity' or 'compassion,' but etymologically meaning 'mother love,' the only utterly unselfish love in human relations.

Since 1926, I have been privileged to share in the work of the J.D.C.'s cultural religious committee. In 1941 the mantle, worn with great distinction by the sainted Doctor Cyrus Adler, fell on my slender shoulders. Horizontally, I was able to admire the Joint's work from Poland to Israel, from France to South America. Vertically, I found a resurrection of the Jewish spirit from Biyalistok to Casablanca and from Tehran, through Marseilles, to Montevideo.

Like other nations, Jews do not live by bread alone. What gave our people immortality was loyalty to the word of the Lord. The J.D.C.'s provision of food, medicine, clothing, and shelter has kept Jewish bodies alive, but it was the millions of dollars spent on Jewish education that helped revive the indomitable spirit of our people. J.D.C. fed a resurgent passion for worthy survival, for gradual self-help and, in particular, for the resumption of the millennial task of teaching our children God's way of life, His eternal principles: 'when thou sittest in thy house, when thou walkest by the way, when thou liest down and when thou risest up.' The resumption of study in half-destroyed communities, the re-dedication to spiritual values and to the *Torah's* social idealism, in Europe and all over the globe, have spelled the harvest of J.D.C. generosity and wisdom.

There have been heroes, saints, and martyrs in J.D.C. history and countless unsung servants of Israel and humanity in the offices, barracks, and workshops which the Joint has built or rebuilt in the half-century of its programme.

Some twenty-five percent of the J.D.C. budget goes to education, from kindergarten to high schools, from vocational guidance and youth centres to the academies of the *Torah* in Israel and the diaspora. The literature and the message of the *Yeshivot's* curriculum are utilized at Yeshivah University, through the Jewish Theological Seminary to Hebrew Union College. Their annuals, pamphlets, learned magazines, and mighty tomes have served as eloquent tribute to the perennial values of Bible, *Talmud*,

Midrash, and the noble library of Jewish philosophy. Let me state again what I have uttered before with mingled pride and regret: that the education work of the J.D.C., especially in the Holy Land, is one of the best-kept secrets in American Jewry. How many have a notion of an institution – at *Yad Benyamin*, in the *Nahal Serek* district of Israel, where all morning Bible and *Talmud* are studied and all afternoon electronic work is pursued, where after the conquest of difficult chapters of Holy Writ, parts of El Al planes are prepared for the Israeli airline? How many know that the young women in the *Beth Jacob* Girls' Teachers Training Colleges receive vocational guidance, to emerge at the end as pedagogues or secretaries or seamstresses or agricultural experts? How many know of the excellent books, magazines, pamphlets on education flowing from the J.D.C.'s headquarters at Geneva and hailed with profound appreciation by teachers and students all over the Jewish world?

The cultural-religious committee, interdenominationally Jewish, included in its membership Professor Tenenbaum of Columbia University, Doctor Eisenberg and Rabbi Rosenfeld of the Jewish Education Committee, Dr Solomon Freehof of Pittsburgh, Rabbi Kelman of the United Synagogue, Professors Lewin, Hoenig, and the late Moses Legis Isaacs of Yeshivah, Rabbi Mark of the Union of American Hebrew Congregations, Rabbi Simon Langer, most respected in France, as in U.S.A., and Rabbi Solomon Tarshansky, formerly of the Warsaw J.D.C. and now of New York. They represent academic skill, spiritual attachment, and all shades of Jewish religious opinion united in service to our people. Our consultant, Stanley Abramowitch in Geneva, keeps in creative touch with Jewish communities all over Europe and the Mid-East, and in constant dynamic endeavour with headquarters even as with the Cultural Committee. Doctor Aaron Greenbaum in Jerusalem, our representative in charge of higher religous education, has extended his labours to India and Iran. The experts on our committee have gone to various continents to deal with educational problems and occasional emergencies.

For years the cultural ambassadors of the Jewish Agency have been of great aid throughout. The sympathetic and empathetic co-operation of the J.D.C. directors in the numerous centres throughout the world has been a source of immeasurable encouragement and solid achievement.

The J.D.C. has been father and mother, physician, teacher, and friend, to millions of Jews. Its role as adviser, and sustainer of our people's mind and heart, from 1917 to 1971, has been for many years of basic significance in the twentieth century chapter of our history.

Among the many aspects of our Committee's work there are two deserving special mention. The first is the vocational guidance programme of the *Talmud* Academies of Israel. Let me briefly describe its goal and method. For millennia, *Yeshivot* have been schools of Jewish education, especially in the fields of Bible and Rabbinics. Most of their graduates become men of business or professions, with some choosing educational careers. In Israel there were many who had received fine intellectual training but who, for lack of post-graduate guidance and vocational planning, became a wasted human investment. Fervent scholars, they continued their studies, eking out a precarious living on the very meagre stipends the local institutions were able to grant them. These students, almost twenty-five percent of the enrolment, spent their life too often in unsupervised, hence sterile learning and dismal poverty. They became the intellectual proletariat of Israel. In 1951, on my plea, the J.D.C. initiated a special grant for vocational guidance. We established courses in pedagogy, in law, in arts and crafts. By 1969, forty percent of all *Yeshivah* students in the Holy Land were trained to become teachers, judges, agricultural or industrial workers, or government employees. The Paul Baerwald School for Social Work has catered to some of them.

The State of Israel is benefitting from their achievements; and these well-trained men, through J.D.C. care, are enabled to provide their families with elemental necessities. It has been a quiet revolution, meaningful in production of new precious personalities, participating in the upbuilding of the homeland.

The second aspect offers a sombre note; the Hitler horror has left countless Jews afflicted with traumatic fears. All over Europe there are some Teutonic victims, trying frantically to escape Jewishness by changing names, by intermarriage, by stubborn refusal to join the Hebrew community, by keeping their children away from Hebrew school or other Jewish contacts. Their attitude has challenged the wisdom, patience, and devotion of the J.D.C. staff. By now some countries have blossomed in a renaissance of Jewish self-acceptance, pride, and full resumption of social responsibility. But, as our reports indicate, there are others in which normally one-third and very rarely more than one-half of Jewish children are enrolled in Hebrew schools, are attending Jewish clubs or, with or without their parents, are joining Jewish centres. The therapeutic measures require expert skill and dedication. Slowly, often very slowly, they find the way back to our people.

Please, tell our folks all over the United States and in all countries of freedom how hard, wonderful, and successful J.D.C.'s work has been, how great the challenge remains, how, for the solution of the grave problem, we are dependent on the generosity of every Jew living in freedom! Tell them that we need heart, mind, and hand of every man and woman in our blessed country, as in all continents, so that we may achieve J.D.C.'s sacred goal: to rescue every Jew in danger, to relieve every poor, sick, friendless brother and sister, and to bring about their rehabilitation, body and soul, their sense of validity, security, and peace.

May I conclude with this charming message of a Ḥassidic saint. He said: 'I have learned more from a man in his cups at a wayside inn than from many a mighty volume. I saw him one dreary evening, his head buried in his arms, sobbing quietly. My heart yearned for him and I said: "What ails you, brother?" He raised his head, looked at me for a long minute and finally said; "Call yourself my brother and do not know what ails me?"'

J.D.C. is based on a passionate sense of brotherhood. J.D.C. knows what ails our people and serves, to aid them, cure them, and regain for them a sense of serenity, security, and dignity.

Federation at Fifty*

Sour Peter Stuyvesant never envisaged that the assumption of social service which he demanded from the Jewish refugees as the price of admission to the Island of Manhattan would in time develop into a most potent contribution to the general culture of our city – a contribution not only to the underprivileged of our group but to the courage and humaneness of its millions – from tycoon to the average merchant and wage earner, from the grey leaders of our people to the youth hungry for a high, warm, rich purpose to summon their buoyant energies.

To be hospitable to friends who can do without our hospitality is no great virtue. To prove a blessing to the unblessed is the supreme task of brotherhood. To enjoy freedom with the free, to promote happiness for the unhandicapped, is merely a civic programme, together with attention to red lights, the payment of taxes, and aesthetic awareness in private and public conduct. But to rise to the level of the prophetic mandate, to 'open the blind eyes, to bring out the prisoners from the dungeon and them that sit in darkness out of the house of confinement,' that has been the timeless task of the People of the Book, the constitution presented and urged upon all God's children by the kingdom of priests and the holy nation He wanted us to become.

*The New York City Federation of Philanthropic Societies (an address at its Jubilee Dinner).

The Hebrew Bible has no word for mendicant, no lingual precedent for *shnorrer*, its text speaks but of 'thy brother who has become poor' and to whom one's warm heart, ready hand, and generous spirit should offer wise and tender care. To the farmer and shepherd of old it meant tithing the harvest and extending a free loan. To the Hebrew in urban atmosphere it meant the gift of money and food and, on its highest level, the providing of occupation in honest labour. From our ancient homeland we carried, with the portable *Torah*, those principles and attitudes into the Ghettoes into which we were forced. The itinerant poor, seeking aid or employment, found the *Hekdesh* or hostel, to aid them in their quest. With emancipation, our folk brought the social idealism of our faith from continent to continent, experimenting skilfully and lovingly with scheme and technique to render brotherhood, helpful and affectionate, to those shut out from the normal comforts of the average citizen.

Federation of New York City, in its glorious record, is the twentieth-century chapter of a millennial way of life, the concretization of biblical precept and national asset.

Federation, for fifty steadfast years and with ever increasing wisdom and devotion, has indeed brought out those that 'sat in darkness from the prison of their despair,' bringing cure to the sick, food to the hungry, friendship to the friendless, hope to the souls in dismay. Allied to the highest endeavour of professional skill and technical excellence, from the wonders of modern medicine to the unprecedented assets of mid-century's technology, Federation, in our city – and through its example far beyond its frontiers – has written a living record of Jews on the height of Judaism. None is more imprisoned than a man without a friend, none more chained than he who, in the words of Robert Blatchford, feels that 'as far as the rest of the world is concerned I can die like a dog in the ditch.' Nor has any one given up faith in God who has not lost faith in man before.

But the work of Federation has deeper and wider significance. *Tsedakah tatzil mimavet*: Loving righteousness, say our Sages, delivers from death, it delivers from *physical death* the sick, the famished, the frustrated, the brother rescued from want, bodily or mental. But the practice of *Tsedakah* delivers from *moral death* the affluent, the average citizen, as he learns to assume his social responsibilities. In my troubled travels through four continents I have met, to my abiding shame, some hopelessly rich members of our faith who never knew the duty of proper giving, who never benefited from the happiness and peace of conscience which a decent discharge of religious mandate confers upon the giver. Those opulent persons, in the arena of primitive egoism, supported by some theology of their neighbours – comfortable to the rich – consider a man's poverty or riches the will of God which they may not interfere with. It has been the difficult but increasingly successful privilege of American Jews to overcome that curious mystique and to embarrass some millionaires of those countries into more decent contribution to the common good. These brethren of ours have taken many a 'blind rich citizen out of the darkness of his egotism, opening his eyes' to his spiritual and moral opportunities and inspiring him with a never-before-felt passion for sharing the work of rescue from fear and rehabilitation for a new life. None is more confined than the poor rich, on his knees before his safety vault, his shares, or baubles. None is sicker than the foolish hoarder of cash, which, in the words of Max Reinhardt, 'sneer and jeer in metallic contempt at him who cannot see beyond its glitter.' In our city, too, Federation, through the genius no less than the consistent dedicated work of its professional and lay leadership, has opened eyes, hands, heart, and brought undreamt-of peace and dignity to many who had become contributors and gradually disciples, champions, of its work.

'To open the blind eyes' pleaded the prophet-statesman Isaiah. That ideal is as timeless as it is universal. Kurt Lewin, decades ago, described a disease of Western Jews which has eroded the moral safety of many a home. My own experience, for almost half a century, has confirmed the solidity of his diagnosis. My own confrontation with post-war emergencies all over Europe has offered the vista of a coming dawn. Jewish self-hate, in many a country, has been the fruit of ignorance of Judaism and its philosophy of life, as profound as it is still widespread. In the emergencies of the last generation and in a sightless assimilationist rage, we have allowed our youth to be blinded to the spiritual and moral assets of our faith and folk. The confused student, madly bent on escaping what he considered the bane of Jewishness, knocking without sense or dignity on hostile doors, represented but the harvest of adult neglect. We have had a generation of the wilderness in America, uninformed, half-informed, misinformed. In the European scene a similar phenomenon prevailed. But the impact of the gruesome period of the Nazi hellhounds has caused a wondrous renaissance of the Jewish spirit all over that continent, from

Norway to Greece, with the exception, sad and deadly, of most of the countries behind the Iron Curtain. Rebuilt Jewish communities have engaged in rebuilding the moral health and spiritual dignity of our people by the establishment, promotion, and steady improvement, of Jewish education. Community effort, sustained by individual devotion, has knitted into creative unity the lay and professional leadership of free Europe.

Ḥinnukh, Jewish Education, providing an emphatic awareness of religious values, and a matchless training in self discipline, protects our youth from the tragic trivialities of L.S.D., the folly of Hippiedom and from the despair which propels the flight into extreme movements on the right or the left of modern political extravagancy.

The Jewish Day School has been eminently successful in teaching the American Dream on the basis of the Bible and both Sinai and Washington.

Education is not merely an orthodox principle. It is not a special conservative privilege. Nor is it a unique reform prerogative. It is a universal, vital necessity for a worthwhile survival of our people in dignity and sanity.

In this city, Federation has become increasingly aware and helpful in this field, too. Again, the impetus came from the categorical imperative 'to open the blind eyes, to bring the prisoners out of the dungeon of ignorance, to free them from the confinement' of rootless lives. Through the Jewish Education Committee, the New York Board of Rabbis, and cognate organizations, Federation has done much to free the New York youth from emotional and spiritual poverty, even as it has helped their parents, brothers, and sisters, to rise above physical, economic, and social serfdom. A few months ago, I was privileged to admire its benefactions as I visited up-state prisons, mental hospitals, and rehabilitation centres.

Heaven and hell, says the *Talmud*, have no limit, they are inexhaustible sources of human joy or misery. Dynamic brotherhood alone can build the bridge from the darkness of despair to the light of hope, from brooding resentment to cheerful co-operation. Federation has been, is, and shall be, the catalyst, the bearer of the great message, the challenger of human conscience and intelligence for a nobler, happier chapter in the world's greatest Jewish Community.

It is most meritorious to aid the sick. It is a priceless privilege to feed the hungry, to soothe the troubles of the aged, to retrain the handicapped.

It is the translation of God's command into the life-giving, life-blessing, life-saving programme of the Jewish people. Federation has every reason to be proud of its record. Federation has every right to urge the participation of every Jew, who can do so, in its sacred endeavour. Federation has every right to demand from all more generous, more steadfast, more enthusiastic co-operation. But Federation must also extend and heighten its endeavour, including a vertical and horizontal enterprise, to give every child in Greater New York a maximum chance of attaining or regaining a proud sense of belonging to the group which has proclaimed religious education as the vital pillar of its House of God, its community hall, of every family, and every individual.

May I wish to Federation, its leadership no less than its membership, the courage and the vision to make, through religious education, every New York Jewish soul safe, happy, and worthy, proud in the conviction that he must stay committed to the reverence, righteousness, and compassion which make for individual serenity and social peace in every community.

Tzadik yesod olam
an Exposition of *Tzedakah*

Justice

Long ago, Prof. William H. Kilpatrick Columbia's famous authority on the psychology of education, and I, lectured together at Williams College. We had occasion for confabulation on the proverbial 'Cabbages and Kings,' in the course of which he suggested that to establish the intellectual and moral condition of college students, the usual tests are insufficient, if not total failures. It would be wiser, he felt, to let students express themselves on matters which had not been previously discussed in class. I decided to try it out on my students in Ethics at Stern College for Women, a vital part of Yeshiva University.

One morning I offered the following challenge: 'I shall write a statement on the blackboard, and I want you to tell me within two minutes what is right with it, and within five minutes what is wrong with it.' Thereupon I wrote Thomas Babington Macaulay's famous dictum: 'Justice is only farsighted policy.' Two minutes later, one of the students raised her hand and said: 'Of course he is right. If one acts justly, one helps to create an atmosphere of fair play, and therefore, one has a right to expect just treatment from others.' I applauded that interpretation. Three minutes later, after a repeated challenge, a young sophomore offered this contribution: 'Of course, it is all wrong. Justice is not a matter of an investment, from which, as profit, fair treatment is to be expected. Justice is an unconditional principle. Not a matter of policy, but a categorical basis of life.' To my delight, she quoted the Biblical verse: *Tzadik yesod olam* – the righteous is the foundation of the world.

Tzedakah as Social Responsibility

May I emphasize that this perception applies not only to *tzedek* (righteousness) but in particular also to *tzedakah* (charity) which, in Hebrew parlance, means 'righteous discharge of social responsibility.' In the frame of Jewish thought, such attitude and action are unconditionally required. A decent Jew is meant to contribute a minimum of ten per cent of his income to the alleviation of poverty, sickness, or other distress afflicting his neighbour. Such aid should be independent of eloquent appeals, the previous enjoyment of a good dinner, or the quality and length of last night's sleep. The Hebrew phrase, *gemilut ḥassadim* (the bestowing of kindness), in the original is in the plural: *ḥassadim* – kindnesses, because the benefit of a charitable deed blesses not only the recipient, but especially also the giver. It frees the latter of an occasional guilt feeling as he is confronted by the sight of poverty and sickness, the saddest twin affliction of humans. A visit to the Mid-East, or to New York slums, often fills the perceptive person with an uneasy sense of such guilt at the realization that, without his fault, one's fellow man is deprived of basic comforts, and suffers, whilst the observer enjoys the boons of life.

The *Mishnah* says: *lefum tza'areh* – 'according to the pain involved is the reward one obtains for the performance of a *Mitzvah*.' Rambam (Maimonides), the greatest genius of our people in the last two thousand years, considers *Da'at Elokim*, the effort to attain – however limited – a knowledge of God through the study of Nature, His work and Revelation and His word the greatest *Mitzvah*. Such endeavour stands for constant determination to imitate, within the frame of human possibility, His justice and mercy.

The adored saint, Shneyur Zalman of Liadi, founder of the Lubavitch School of Ḥassidism, considers *Tzedakah* (the practice of charity) the supreme *Mitzvah*. He holds that more than intellectual achievement, it is the fruit of a warm heart's dedication to brethren in distress which crowns human life. That great Rabbi often left his court to visit the hovels of the hopeless. He suffered with every poor soul and went to all lengths to bring food, clothing, and cheer to the underprivileged.

I dare not dispute either of these great men, but my experience in half a century of public work has inclined me to believe that there is one virtue surpassing both intellectual effort and the charitable gift. It is the often painful but always glorious *Mitzvah* of *schnorrage*. Great benefactors often crown their own *gemilut ḥassadim* by a capacity for eminently successful pleading on behalf of *Torah*, Israel, and for God's children of every race, creed, and colour.

Accent on Personal Effort

Throughout our religious literature, urging awareness of our social responsibility, there is the accent on personal effort. Thousands of years ago, in the Holy Land, it was a committee of two men who collected funds for the charity box, and one of three who distributed it. Ezra, the second Moses, had ordained that the Jewish housewife bake bread early in the morning, so as to make it readily available to the poor. Personal service was both: challenge and bliss! This precious tradition often blesses our own times. I recall the eighty-year-old mother of a noted New York judge, whom I caught on a miserable, wintry day in Harlem, lugging two heavy baskets for a Rabbinic family on the fourth floor of a tenement. I promised not to betray her to her son if she promised to stop that beautiful service which endangered her health.

The humble charity box, the *pushkah*, found in countless religious homes, has, as yet, found no Bialik or Agnon to describe its quiet glory. The coin, which even poor housewives put into that box every Friday before kindling the Sabbath light, connected the Holy day with charitable effort and assured the light of God for the home. No Sabbath or *Yom Tov* was properly observed, unless a friendless person had been invited to partake of the meal. I remember how in our youth we children were vying with each other at the synagogue to find an *oraḥ* (a poor guest) to take home.

Tzedakah as Community Responsibility

There is a straight line from the Biblical 'If your brother waxes poor' to the Chamber of the Silent for secret gifts in the sanctuary of Jerusalem, to the famous *Responsum* of Rabbi Shlomo ben Adret emphasizing the obligations of loving, respectful, personal effort in charity. One of its most moving manifestations was this custom in German Jewish communities: after the funeral of a close relative, the *Fuersorge* (Jewish Social Service) always would send two charity boxes to the home of the bereaved, whether they were rich or poor. Of the boxes, one was full, the other empty. The affluent person filled the empty one. The needy one emptied the full one. Both boxes were returned to the office, and only the executive director knew who had benefited from, or added to, the gift.

The community records, minutes of meetings of Rabbinic and lay authorities in the ghettos of Europe, present a fascinating picture of a thousand years lived in political disability and social discrimination, but, the same time, on a level of morality which the neighbours could envy or defame, but never imitate. The Executive Committee (of the ghetto or *Shtetl*) – *Shivah Tuvai Ha'ir* – and the *Bet Din* (the Jewish Court of Justice) together issued orders, directions, or rules (*Takanot*) which governed commercial as well as charitable activity. In the course of my research, I came across a unique example of humaneness. It has to do with young girls, obviously of poor families, seeking positions in the city as domestic servants. Often they came from faraway villages, and they were subjected to the normal temptations and risks facing young womenhood away from home. In the community record, the 'Pinkas of Posen,' I found the following item: 'The Community Ordinance called for a special Board of Overseers (*apitropsim*) who were to be responsible especially for the moral, physical, and social security of these young women. That board insisted that the head of the household give the candidate for the job of a domestic servant a definite yearly contract in the form of an I.O.U. Unless guilty of inexcusable offence, she would thus be protected against arbitrary dismissal by the employer.' This is an outstanding example of a concrete, dynamic sense of social responsibility; indeed it reflects the unselfish kindness known as *raḥamanut* (mercy).

On Gratitude

May I offer a footnote on gratitude as the response of the recipient. Sustained gratitude is the hallmark of a fine person, but for more than a generation I have advised my students at Yeshiva University never to expect gratitude. That was to save them from disappointment, and when once in a hundred cases, a grateful person appeared, the surprise would be doubly pleasant.

These observations apply to all clients of social service. They are of particular significance for the victim of the *Shoah* (the horrible Nazi period from 1933 to 1945). For some of the inmates of the hellish concentration camps it is well-nigh impossible now to emancipate themselves from *she'ol tachtiyot*, their gruesome experiences. I have often heard a litany of self-commiseration, the manifestation of unhealed psychic wounds. These traumas also account for what looks like ingratitude but which often is but the precipitate of supersensitiveness, a sub-conscious resentment of the difference in status between the social worker and his client, which renders the latter upsetting or unpleasant. *Tout comprendre est tout pardonner* – all understood is all forgiven. These victims of man's inhumanity to man require guidance, *sekhel tov*, a sense of humour, patience, and never failing bonhomie.

There are a hundred and one ways in which throughout Jewish history, social service manifested not only efficiency, but respect, consideration, and the abiding endeavour to lead the client from want and despair to self-help self-respect, hope, and security in the family of Israel.

In Conclusion

May I conclude with this story, familiar to many students of our century's men of the spirit: The Ḥofetz Ḥaim, Rabbi Israel Meir Hakohen of Radin in Poland, the celebrated venerated teacher of the good life, once upon a time was visited by a woman whose husband had been buried a few days ago. There was actually no food in her house, winter was approaching and there were no garments for her children. Her situation was hopeless. The Rabbi consoled her and went out without delay on a programme of *schnorrage*. His immediate target was a man reputed for both his richness and heartlessness. He received the Rabbi very roughly and refused to help. That saint pleaded with him, and described the dreadful pain of the mother unable to feed her little ones, but the pachydermous *nouveau riche* stayed unimpressed. Indeed, when Rabbi Israel Meir repeated his plea, the ruffian boxed his ears. Thereupon, the sweet Rabbi said: 'That blow was for me, but what would you give me for the poor widow?' That answer is reported to have penetrated through the many layers of cocksureness and the hard curtain of gold to the spark of *raḥamanut* in the man's heart, which immediately prompted him to provide amply for the widow. The Ḥofetz Ḥaim had completed his mission of *schnorrage*, but even more, his outstanding personal example remains predominant, and the message of the Biblical verse *Tzadik yesod olam* eternalized.

Essays on Modern Problems

The Panorama of Religion*

Introduction

Let me start with the suggestion that the greatest danger to Religion flows not from attacks on its teaching, leadership, or faith. There is often, if not always, another side, at least a minimum chance of a good counter-argument in a fair dialogue. The crisis comes when religion seems to become irrelevant especially to our youth, when they follow other philosophies of life, other goals which seem more alive and worthwhile to them.

I *No Time for Polemics*

The famous Greek advice, *Anechou Kai Apechou* (bear and forebear), may for our purposes be fitly rendered: 'Endure cheerfully your colleague's long lecture and battle manfully to keep your own within decent limits.'

None of us, I believe, have time for, or interest in, polemics. The challenge to Religion is too great, serious, and urgent for the luxury of partisan arguments. For clarity's sake, let me say that I represent what is miscalled orthodox Judaism, what I'd like to call Judaism without adjectives. The term orthodox is of relatively recent vintage in our faith, and

* An address at the U.S. Veterans' Administration Workshop in Atlanta, Georgia.

insufficient. When coined 150 years ago it was meant to define classical Judaism and Jews who in theory and practice endeavoured to live up to it. In Judaism, *doxa* (opinion, doctrine, dogma) is important, but the major accent is on loyalty to the Jewish way of life, righteous and compassionate conduct.

In Judaism, God is not discussed but taken for granted. No cosmological or ontological proof for faith in Him is required. 'At the beginning God created the world' is at once the first verse of the Hebrew Bible and the basis of Jewish life and lore. God is the Creator, the Law Giver, the Merciful Father, who revealed the standards of the good life. The Sage of the *Talmud* said: 'The total purpose of all the commandments (ritual and moral) is to purify human beings, to strengthen their character, and to establish their unity.'

The fulfilment of the commandments is possible because man is endowed with freedom of will. Heredity and environment may narrow the margin of that freedom but can never totally obliterate it.

Every human being is created in the image of God with infinite potentiality for goodness, truth, and beauty. The ethical universalism of our faith includes every human being in the circle of its interest and grants him fundamental privileges as it imposes upon him basic obligations. Judaism, as well as the Jewish people, have never claimed monopoly of grace. In the view of our faith, there are seven laws or principles of law incumbent upon all mankind, called in rabbinic texts 'Children of Noah.' One of these principles is positive: the promotion of justice. The others are negative. They are: The prohibition of cruelty to animals, of blasphemy, theft or robbery, of homicide or murder, of idolatry and immorality. Any non-Jew believing in God and accepting these seven laws for his own conduct was admitted to citizenship in ancient Israel, was entitled to its social services, and was considered one of the righteous people among the Gentiles, who has a share in the world to come, in the words of Rabbi Eliezer, 'Even as a Jew.'

II *The Goal and the Survival*

Judaism teaches not mere tolerance, but basic equality. The Jewish people have not been promised military prowess or economic bliss but the sublime and often painful role of being a kingdom of priests: to teach by example. The whole nation, as God's messengers, are bidden to teach reverence, righteousness, and compassion. The Jewish people have been for millennia a minority. They must survive to fulfil their task in fullness of time. To survive, they received in the *Torah* a set of laws and principles which create a strong spiritual and ethical environment. The observance of the Sabbath, the dietary laws, the laws of family purity, and a programme of social idealism, foster adherence and coherence, for them to remain on a high, moral level and stay alive.

To survive worthily they must never lose sight of the Messianic vision and mission: 'To make the world full of the knowledge of God even as the waters cover the sea,' thereby to initiate an endless period of justice and brotherhood. Maimonides views Christianity and Islam as co-operative with Judaism in the humanization of humanity under the aspects of God. This is the philosophy of Judaism. Jews, on the height of Judaism, would have brought that golden age nearer. But our backsliding in the long ago, and man's inhumanity to man, have driven our people into the dead end of exile and ghetto, from which we have just emerged, bruised but sturdy to face the problems of our time. Very few Christians and no Jews have digested the horror of the Nazi holocaust. These scientific devils have driven more people to despair and to the denial of God than any philosophical problem. There was the tragedy of two world wars and the awful dilemma spelled by the atomic age: on the one hand promising the end of sickness and poverty and on the other hand, the prospect of killing hundreds of millions of human beings and leaving a dreadful remnant, mostly morons deformed in body and soul. All that has created a fearful scepticism, less wicked than sick, with helpless humanism and alas, often unskilful theology, unconscious partners in a moral and spiritual débâcle.

III *The Cancer of Ignorance*

Another source of evil has been profound ignorance of our faith: of its social idealism, of its freedom of interpretation, of its accent on right conduct. Once revelation is accepted, a large margin is granted to individual ingenuity. Indeed, the investment of the best minds and hearts in the classic texts of our faith is not only privilege but obligation. The social programme of Judaism includes every one of God's children in the ultimate scheme of justice and love. In the Hebrew prayer book the abiding refrain reads: 'Forgive us our lack of good deeds.' That is a sin far greater than our faulty thoughts or imperfect formulations of creed.

Two generations ago, the problem of Faith versus Science loomed large. Of late we have learned to perceive that religion fundamentally aims to teach us values, that science basically endeavours to establish facts. Where facts escape its quest, science employs the method of working theories for the advancement of its goal. Science and Religion hence are not in conflict, but represent separate ways towards truth. In a conversation years ago, Albert Einstein agreed that from a purely scientific point of view, religion was as good a working theory as causality. Causality, until recently a major divinity, has become a casualty in the writings of Germany's Heisinger, Cambridge's Schroedinger, and America's Sinnott.

During the years of my service in the Chaplaincy Commission of the Jewish Welfare Board, I used to spend two to three weeks a year visiting Army, Navy, and Air Force installations. On my last visit I heard that the recruits were impudent on Sunday, Tuesday, and Friday, and cowardly on Monday, Wednesday, and Friday. At the luncheon at the Pentagon on my return I mentioned this lamentable condition and offered the suggestion that two world wars of their parents and the shadow of another in their own time were sufficient to shatter the inner security of modern youth and therefore would create alternate moods of truculence and timidity.

IV *Democracy in Religion*

Democracy fundamentally implies the right to be different. Each denomination is endeavouring to emphasize *one* approach to God, and to develop it towards some goal of perfection. But each denomination shares in the great symphony of reverence towards our Father in Heaven, as part of the orchestra composed of various talents and fervours. It is only when each instrument is played in harmony with the great melody of universal worship that the denomination justifies its separate existence and proves a source for the common good.

Every minister who teaches an unfriendly attitude towards outsiders, undermines not only the spiritual foundations of all religion but the moral basis of Protestantism. Every rabbi whom two thousand years of persecution would turn bitter towards the non-Jewish majority, would be disturbing not only the spiritual foundations of all religion, but the moral basis of Judaism. Every priest who teaches an unfriendly attitude towards outsiders, endangers not only the spiritual foundations of all religion, but the moral basis of Catholicism.

The pilgrims who landed at Plymouth Rock fled hither from England where they suffered as religious outsiders. In this country, not only Catholics but also certain Protestant denominations have been minorities and have suffered on that account. The Jews, although not late-comers in America, have been afflicted with the pangs of a small group.

The strongest bulwark of the American dream is the freedom of the individual citizen. The Constitution has been buttressed by the convictions of the religious folks in the country. Its major hope resides in the organized power of parents and children who revere the Lord. If they are undermined by insincerity, the American dream may never be realized, and the divisive element in the populace may, God forbid, gain the upper hand. It is for that reason that all men of religion must fortify themselves against the illusion that they may gain any benefit from making scapegoats of minorities. They must ever rededicate themselves to labour for basic unity. At peace with themselves and respectful of the rest of the nation, all men of faith must join hands for a more abundant life.

Modern secularism attacks *all* religions. It is generally not the result of some neo-heathenism reimported from antiquity, but due to the failure of organized religion to promote a thoroughgoing awareness of human interdependence. Just as the stupid gods of the early Greeks created atheism and their followers forced Socrates to drink hemlock, so may much of current American disbelief – 53 per cent not affiliated with any kind of religious worship – be no more than a reaction to the social failure of organized religion. A decade ago, a one-armed soldier in a southern rehabilitation centre said to me: 'If I shall find the church preaching bigotry instead of love, I'll never again enter a House of Worship.' I can imagine similar sentiment among all our denominations.

V *Irreligious Religionists*

The misleaders of religious folks bring religion into disrepute and beget cynical iconoclasts. It simply will not do to call disillusioned men bitter names. Few can be won back, or will be impressed, by vituperation or anathemas. The so-called atheists often are merely people whose sanctuary of social justice has been defiled and who in their despair fail to see sacredness anywhere. In our denominational work we must give an example of what we preach in the best hours of our pulpit, to promote the happiness of the common man. Thus we could help to establish God's kingdom on earth.

There is a powerful sanity in our young people. They are ready for the good life. Our home-coming service-men have battled in a great cause. Years of personal comradely kindnesses have broken through heavy crusts of prejudice. American soldiers, beyond Catholic Mass, Protestant Worship, or Hebrew Service, have experienced the reality of God. There is a wonderful chance for harnessing this spiritual energy. All itinerant comedians and shapely actresses notwithstanding, deeper moral purposes have radiated themselves to our sons on the battlefields. In the post-war era, the veterans may prove to be the stabilizers of the home front, between the sweet immaturity of our children and the cold smugness of some of our elders.

What wonderful chance to burst the chains of prejudice and break the shackles of bigotry! By teaching love of one's neighbour even at the private seminar, in the intimate circle, and by speaking it in their own hearts, leaders of religion might change the course of modern American history from the rising flood of secularism to the still waters of true faith. As unconfined good spreads its branches, the practical righteousness of the forces of religion would make their roots grow deeper. In the process, religion would rise above its frequent offering of mere lip service to conventional good, to develop into thorough and dynamic God-consciousness. No more serving as a mere escape in tragic moments, religion would become a court of conscience, a school of noble and wise living.

VI *The Challenge to American Religion*

American industrial leaders do not admit of technical impossibilities. The ingenuity, daring and achievement of our engineers, managers, and labourers is stupendous. But in the sphere of religion we have not been the country of undreamt-of possibilities. Instead of resolute conquerors of the stumbling blocks of narrowness and unrighteousness, we have been masters of the smooth phrase, the polished platform, appeasers, the diplomats of theology, destructive of faith and love. That is why the majority of our adults are no longer affiliated with any religious group.

I believe with all my heart in the moral destiny of the United States of

America. I believe with all my soul in the need to fortify the American people with firm principles and unerring devotion. It is here that church and synagogue must play a vital role. Irreligious or non-religious people may be ethically noble or indifferent or bad. Modern youth questions their parents' conduct rather than their dogmas. The second generation is less worried about faith versus science than about church and democracy, and about the House of Worship and its part in the battle for social justice.

The voice of religion teaching faith in God *and* love for man has both appeal and authority. No matter how sophisticated some people think they are, they are rarely untouched by the summons to a consistent programme of justice and kindness. True religion still has its opportunity to influence young and old. Doctrines have their interpretations, platforms their professors, and religious conventions their managers. In its own sphere, each denomination could rally the faithful around its own flag, but above and beyond it, we all must work for promotion of universal peace and happiness.

We all know the task of religion. It is to give meaning to life, to create harmony among our instincts and thoughts, to build well-knit persons and harmonious communities. Through the concentric circles of denominational fervour and inter-denominational friendship, we could undergird the happiness of every citizen and the security of the nation. But religion must be as broad as it is deep. Creed is a matter of personal or historic experience, and by its nature is limited to a group. But faith in God is universal. As every denomination bases itself ultimately on the Eternal Father of the human family, none dare claim His exclusive possession. They deny Him as they confine Him. There is no worse blasphemy than that which reduces His mercy or care to narrow circles.

People can stand the aberrations of science. Science speaks in the name of man and man is mortal and fallible. They are reconciled to the recurrent failures of the democratic process because its chapters are written by human trial and error. But mankind views with horror and reacts with cynicism to organized religion speaking in the name of God and destroying His garden by open or camouflaged teaching of bigotry.

VII *A Major Source of Jewish Problems*

The profound ignorance of Judaism among American Jews has resulted in a generation of the wilderness who started by saying 'Why should I?'

and ended by 'Why should I not?' But the deviationists, as in every revolution, are an indication of something deficient or wrong in the *status quo*. When our people in hundreds of thousands fled Czarist Russia to escape planned pogroms and other cruel oppression, they came to the United States and faced the double pressure of immigrant plight and sweatshop conditions. It was almost impossible for them to provide good schooling, adequate synagogues, and encouraging patterns of community life for their youth. Hence the social idealism of our faith remained hidden to many of them. The rituals and ceremonies to which their parents still adhere, too often acquired no meaning for them, nor recruited their loyalty. It was only during the last forty years that the Jewish people in the United States have learned to develop better methods for directing their youth to the ancient faith. Now Judaism is on the march. Yeshiva University with its all-embracing programme, two dozen other *yeshivot* in our country, organized loyal Congregations with their care for young and old, the youth movements in schools and colleges among other efforts, have achieved fine results.

In America Judaism is experiencing a renaissance. In addition to countless afternoon classes, there are almost four hundred Jewish day schools in our country starting at kindergarten and moving towards a complete scheme of education embracing the Jewish tradition and American culture. The graduates are to make their major contributions to the United States through their personalities matured in this double orientation. To them the constitutions of Sinai and of Washington offer both inspiration and challenge. But I have found many denominations, including my own, occasionally afflicted by a vociferous minority going too far in the right direction, with excess zeal in the pursuit of one part of its programme, consciously or unconsciously covering a lamentable lag in the pursuit of another.

We have been sorely shaken by the murder of one third of our people. We have endeavoured to see in the horror of Nazism a warning for all mankind to battle hatred, bigotry, cruelty. By proper use of our free will we must oppose all wickedness, from the organized lie to the 'final solution' of the Hitlerite madmen. It has been difficult indeed to recover from the impact of the hesitancy, the often murderous indifference of people formally believing in God, which encouraged the Nazi Horror. We all need that quality of heart and mind which, with forgiving compassion, fosters the determination not to allow another global catastrophe to make of religion a matter of ridicule or a sorry shame. We need glorious, stiff-necked faithfulness in the Lord's programme of justice and love. Faithfulness, in the words of one of our Sages, is 'the quality of staying immovable even as nails driven into a solid wall.' Perchance, the genuine Ecumenical Monotheism of our denominations will hold the key to the solution of the problem at once of religion and humanity.

May I conclude by quoting a beautiful piece of ancient saga involving the education of Father Abraham, the first Hebrew who was God's first messenger to a heathen world. His hospitality was proverbial. One day he saw an old man struggling up the hill to his house. Abraham ran eagerly to meet him, guided him to the friendly table and treated him to a good meal. Then he bade him say grace. 'To whom?' asked the old man. 'To God, of course,' said Abraham, 'The Father of all of us Who causes bread to grow from the earth.' 'I do not know that God,' was the reply. 'I worship the fire.' Outraged, Abraham drove the aged heathen from his house. That night the Lord appeared unto him in a dream saying. 'Abraham, I have been patient with that ignorant old man for seventy years, could you not have stood him for one night?'

Intermarriage

I *Motive of Its Prohibition*

There is no law, civil or moral, obliging a Jewish person to marry another one of the same faith merely because he or she is Jewish. There is no Jewish race mythology excluding any one from love, life, liberty, and the pursuit of happiness because of the accident of his skin's pigmentation. There were some hopeless nationalists in ancient Palestine to whom an impatient or outraged prophet proclaimed: '"You are to Me," says the Lord, "no better nor worse than the coal-black Ethiopians."'

The *Torah* does not start with the history of the Hebrews, but with that of universal man, uncribbed by arbitrary discrimination. Jonah ben Amitai, a young man on the way from narrow faith towards the high level of prophecy, received a priceless lesson in the *Torah's* ethical universalism through God's message: 'Should I not have pity on Niniveh that great city, wherein there are more than six score thousand persons' – all confused heathens? The first Hebrew chose God and was chosen to be a blessing to all the families of the earth, or, according to Rashbam, to graft faith in God and man upon all of His children anywhere.

Why then, the emphatic rejection of intermarriage, with heathens, theists, deists, with non-Jews of all climes? The *Torah* supplies the single reason 'Lest thou make a covenant with the inhabitants of the land, and they go astray after their gods and they call thee and thou eat of their sacrifice . . . and make thy sons to go astray after their gods.'

No political or nationalist or social snobbery is involved in the prohibition of intermarriage. The motive is purely religious. We have died a thousand deaths, lived millions of heroic lives for our faith, have earned so many triumphs and scars in our historical migrations that no Jew may contemplate marriage outside the frame of Judaism. For intermarriage is one of the fastest ways toward the destruction of our people.

Intermarriage constitutes betrayal of countless generations to whom the *Torah* has been the most precious asset, at once a task and an assurance of eternality.

We Jews are conscious of the heavy calendar of religious duties, from *Kashrut* to *Shabbat*, from mandatory study of our sacred texts to social responsibility to be discharged by reverence, righteousness, and *raḥamanut* (*motherly love*). Our faith, the only tolerant one among all monotheistic religions, excludes no human being that is committed to a moral life. In ancient Palestine any such non-Jew was entitled to the privileges of citizenship as well as to the support of the community, financial, medical, personal, in times of distress or emergency. The *Ger Toshav* (resident alien) of Palestine did not have to become a Jew by religion to become a citizen. No non-Jew was threatened, theologically or otherwise, with a hot climate, *über hundert Jahr*, for failure to conform to the *Din Torah*.

II *Jewish Missionaries*

Jewish missionaries in antiquity were anxious to bring the heathen *taḥat kanfe ha-shekhinah*, to wean him from the cruelties, perversions, and superstitions of idolatry. The *sebomenoi* of Hellenistic times were pious, upright, God-believing men and women, treated with affectionate respect by Jewish scholars as well as by the common folk. The single exception occurred during the rule of the decadent epigone of the Hasmoneans, whom Herod and his coterie punished a hundred-fold for having violated the Faith of our fathers by forcible conversion of the Idumeans. The latter became ruthless haters of our people. From these formal Jews sprang the *Am ha-aretz*, an hypocritical, brutal group who treated their wives as chattels and hated the scholar and the pietist with the bestiality of Hitler's hellhounds.

Because of the constitutional liberalism of our religion there was no occasion for the missionary zeal which Christianity and Islam have displayed ever since they acquired power. Jews arranged no *auto-da-fés* and preached no spreading of our faith by the sword. We know neither gigantic expenditures on mass conversions, no neglect of local crudity, cruelty, or corruption for the ideals of a world-spanning crusade to add – *à la* revival-endeavour – *pro forma* Jews to our number.

Because we accepted, long before the rabbinic dictum gave it its classic form, the thesis that the pious persons among the nations of the world have a share in the world to come (with the notable addition, by one of our early zealots, of the words 'even as the Jew'), the curiosities of missionary effort were practically unknown in the community of Israel. When a non-Jew approaches a rabbi, without ulterior motives, out of pure love of our faith, and insists on his quest in spite of the clear warning that loyalty to Judaism implies for the newcomer heavy and continuous duties, then, if he undertakes to conform to these duties, he will be accepted into the fold and considered a full Jew, entitled to all the special love and helpfulness which we are bidden to extend to each other.

Any other motive is insufficient for admission to the faith of Israel.

III *Unfair to the Jewish People*

Intermarriage, in its train, has three unforgivable moral flaws: it is unfair to the Jewish people, past, present, and future. It is unfair to the non-Jew; it is unfair to the institution of marriage.

Immanuel Kant added to his timeless reputation when he thus phrased an ancient Jewish principle: 'Every man is an end in himself and must not be made a means to another man's end.' Surely, every religion is an end in itself and must not be made a means to any one's end. Religion is more than a set of affirmations, emotions, or ceremonies. It is a system of faith, thought, and action, tying up man with God and with his fellow-man; Judaism is the source of Jewish culture, from social ethics to the programme of Jewish life. Rarely does one's religious position start with oneself. In more than one sense we live on the ethical and spiritual capital of the past. It is parents and grandparents and sundry collections of relatives, who transmitted attitudes, intuitions, and trends that reflect and influence past reaction and present decision. To surrender all that to the suggestion of compulsion of love, from sex attraction to personality appreciation, not to speak of lower motives, is both morally wrong and hazardous. Intermarriage is unfair to the millions of Jews who, to preserve the nation – at once the people of the book and the ambassador of the One God – have wandered footsore from continent to continent and from century to century, enduring a thousand *Gehinoms* and ignoring a thousand promised *Gan Edens* so that, with Judaism, the Jewish people may survive.

IV *Unfair to the Gentile*

Intermarriage is unfair to the Gentile, who, impelled by the desire of marrying a Jewish person, is willing to give up what has united him or her with their own family. Their spiritual and ethical assets, to an overwhelming extent, were derived not from modern academies or the arguments of nuclear hostility, but from family worship, family feeling, understanding, and actions, for generations back. To join or be asked to join Judaism in *pro forma* fashion means to treat carelessly or contemptuously what normally has been the ultimate source of Gentile goodness, truth, and beauty. Any marriage, contracted on one single motive or ground, is bound to fail. Sex, mental brilliance, material advantage, do promise fulfilment, but, unsupported by deeper and more enduring things, have proven disastrous.

Every marriage knows its own problems and handicaps. The collision of two personalities of varied backgrounds rarely results in a sublimation of differences in a higher harmony. Much more often it proves a source of constant and increasing irritation, ending at best in a belligerent state of the union, or in the divorce court; or, at worst, in some mental institution, where rehabilitation on every level proves both most costly and uncertain. Intermarriage adds one more peril of contention or catastrophic explosion. Marriage, when successful, is the ultimate port of security and peace; when a failure, it lands both partners in deep unhappiness.

Dissatisfaction with one's own religion may send one shopping. If the new appreciation and love of Judaism *precedes* personal relation with a Jewish man or woman, there is hope for genuine conversion. From embracement of the Jewish way of life as the result of intellectual conviction, Halakhic commitment, and a desire to join the Jewish people, a precious personality may emerge. Many resultant marriages between such *gere tzedek* (proselytes of righteousness) and Jewish mates have been beautiful and enduring.

V *Remedies*

How can we reduce, if not completely overcome, the menace of intermarriage sought by Jews? It, very often, is the fruit of frustration, Gentile intolerance, or of profound ignorance of Judaism as Creed and Life which reduces one's allegiance to palatal habits, folksy superstition, and general superficiality. The problem can be solved by preparing a total educational programme from study to observance of Jewish law, to affiliation with Jewish goals and activities, and by consistent improvement of the patterns of Jewish individual and collective life. Thus would be created an abiding appreciation of the religious and social ideals and achievements of our people throughout the millennia of its existence. Jewish self-acceptance results from informed conformity to the *Din Torah*. Life, loyal to the *Mitzvot*, creates intuition and engenders enthusiasm. Freedom of interpretation in all non-Halakhic matters and a vision of the whole panorama of the Jewish world, from Abraham through *yemot hamashiaḥ*, keep the mind alert and emotions warm. All these facets of our living faith together will maintain evolutionary optimism, a combined love of humanity, and proud fealty to our own group. We shall thus be enabled to enjoy the contribution of other nations and to invest our assets in endeavours for the advancement of national and global welfare. We shall march apart in denominational enterprise and strike together for peace and prosperity everywhere. That type of collaboration without compromise has been of marked significance in some golden ages and silver periods of our history. It has alas, too often been disturbed or destroyed by religious or governmental intolerance, by wars, and the inevitable oppression in their wake.

In our time brush fires have been found very contagious. Today, the fact of human interdependence is being increasingly recognized. In a war-free world of tomorrow, each group or sect will be able to live in freedom, and develop its potentialities.

The frustrations, due to Gentile animosities and to some imperfections in Jewish life, have been largely responsible for the desire of some Jews to seek escape through intermarriage. These causes may gradually disappear through consistent communal endeavour. Our people will then rediscover the beauty and power of Jewish life and stay inspired by its combination of idealism and common sense. Ours are two concentric circles: an inner core of faithful Jewishness adorned by a periphery of dynamic sympathy for mankind's underprivileged. Our major contribution to America must be in the form and spirit of the Jewish religion, which means its culture, its philosophy of life. From the colourless abode of assimilation and from a diminution of Jewish life through intermarriage, we have neither message nor contribution to the U.S.A. or the American dream.

Intermarriage, a grave problem today, might gradually assume less dark hues as the united nations of the world, each true to its own religion and culture, will co-operate to abolish war, poverty and disease and to prepare for a happier period of human relations in all the continents.

The Sins of the Fathers

I

It seems perfectly superfluous to offer praise to the Ten Commandments. The whole difference between ideal and real in the life of mankind for the last thousand years may be attributed safely to the gap between the moral mandate of the Ten Commandments and sad reality in private and in public life. Kings, parliaments, local communities have almost accepted the fact that God stands for freedom and democracy and that religion which fails to preach and practice it must remain a sad and shocking failure. Had individuals as well as groups recognised the simple meaning of the obligation to shun every idolatry, every image of man-made gods, they would have not worshipped nationalism or other selfish philosophies of life; they would have prevented the murderous folly of the Nazis; they would have laughed out of existence the humanitarian pretensions of Communism. Instead of the constant tensions, the cold and hot wars of our century, the millennium would have been less of a mirage and on the way to becoming a blessed reality. The leaders of organized religion have almost never recognized the shameful folly of mouthing ideals, and of speaking the name of God in vain from pulpit to public assembly. Priests, ministers, and secular leaders have not as yet recognized the vital need of a Day of Rest on which people could forget the problems of money-making and dedicate themselves fully to family, friends, and nature. The weekday programme of global mankind would have benefited profoundly by the spiritual, emotional, and the purely physical relaxation of a weekly day of rest.

Out of such a philosophy of life would have come a normal parents-children relation. Children are most anxious to honour father and mother, to whom, under God, they owe life, body, and mind. Adolescence, grown in such an atmosphere, would normally consider murder, immorality, theft, and perjury as something too despicable to be considered and too much fraught with dreadful consequences for individual and collective life.

For all of these reasons, it may be taken for granted that in the best hour of their conscience, men and women of all races, creeds, and colours recognize the paramount significance and the vital potentiality of the Ten Commandments. Once they have been accepted they form an unutterable programme and direction of life.

II

There is one passage in the Ten Commandments which presents difficulty. It seems to be in clear contradiction with another Biblical principle and to put it mildly, its moral meaning does not seem to be clear. It reads 'I am the Lord thy God' *poked avon avot al bonim.* It is usually translated: 'Visiting the iniquity upon the children, upon the third and upon the fourth generation of those that hate me.' Against that there is a well known passage of Deuteronomy which reads: 'Parents shall not die because of their children nor children because of their parents.'

The solution of the problem lies in the double meaning of the word *paked.* It stands for both 'visiting or punishing' and 'remembering or considering.' The second meaning is obvious in Genesis XXI, I (*Hashem pakad et Sarah* 'and the Lord considered, remembered Sarah'). The application for our text is as follows: 'God in His mercy recognizes that the sins of the fathers both genetically and as a fruit of the environment from which the children suffer, have rendered it very difficult for the latter to walk His way.' Their own backsliding is to some extent undoubtedly due to the bad example of the parents. Our heavenly Father, in His mercy, considers the sins of the parents in order to judge with lenient understanding the faults of their children. Bad examples may affect three or four generations of a family and for them the Lord's grace remembers the difficulties which the conduct of their forebears spelled for their children. But good examples of father and mother strengthen the native will for righteousness and compassion in their children and leave an influence for good, even for a thousand generations. Hence: God shows 'Mercy unto a thousand generations of them that love Me and keep My Commandments.'

III

In the turbulent decades which are upon us, we are torn between condemnation of violent youth, and the whole philosophy of permissiveness that threatens to undermine the moral values which we have been taught and an understanding of conditions in the last generation which have brought about the spirit of rebellion and the cynical disregard of principles, procedures, and ideas that were sacrosanct to us through our youth, adolescence, and maturity. If the Imitation of God is the single goal of the good life, it is our moral, intellectual, and social obligation to apprehend the fact that the gap between ideal and real for the last generation is due to the frustrations, disillusionment, fringe of public and private hypocrisy, indifference, and selfishness. Considering it will prevent us from rushing into wholesale condemnation of the attitude and conduct of our youth.

IV

What is less evident is an awareness of the obligation of our youth to consider the grievous problems faced for the last few decades by their parents and grandparents which have confused them, weakened their self-discipline, and prevented their rising on the ladder of life towards the level which the *Torah* has urged for Jew and non-Jew. Just as we must not condone juvenile violence but none-the-less chastise, oppose, and try to overcome persons, movements, and conditions which have caused violence thus should we hope and pray that our youth will recognise the heavy pressures encountered by the establishment. Every purely negative programme defeats itself; mutual condemnation of young and old has no chance of a blessed harvest. Let us acknowledge the faults of the past, but put the accent on the challenges, and the chances, of the future.

Parents and children must know that the only way for them to achieve harmony and security is through the road of comradeship. Children must be willing to honour their parents, whose experience, in the face of disappointment and frustration, has endowed them with some wisdom. Parents must recognise that their children's opposition to some of the unpleasant aspects of our age may be justified and can be overcome by joint effort of old and young.

Even as the Lord considers the sins of the parents in order to judge mercifully the backsliding of the children, so must all think not only of the imperfection of past or present, but of the chances which consideration and fellowship offer for a happier chapter of human history.

'There is enough evil in the best of us and enough good in the worst of us that it behoves all of us not to speak about the rest of us.' What will help us out of the present misery is not mutual recrimination, calling the young wicked and the old insensitive, but a determination to try comradeship in sustained effort to improve life.

The noblest task of man is *Imitatio Dei*, the imitation of His moral qualities. Since freedom of will is the privilege of almost all human beings, theirs is the responsibility to fashion life in accord with the divinely revealed imperatives of justice and compassion. Even as the Lord 'considers the iniquity of the parents as a meliorating fact in judging their rebellious children' such a generous attitude is both duty and opportunity of all humans towards each other. It applies with particular emphasis to the Jewish people. The Gentile world has a devastatingly deplorable record in dealing with the children of Abraham: two millennia of ruthless persecution, from discrimination, to defamation, to exile, to pogrom, in which priests, kings, dukes, and the common folk have shared the guilt. Not only men of the cloth, but thinkers and writers, have, for centuries, ranted against our people, continuing the horrid message of theological bias. That list of thoughtless, heartless, Jew-haters extends from St. Paul to Luther, from Pascal to Voltaire, from the bishops of the Inquisition to Father Coughlin, to its gory harvest in the multi-million murders by Hitler's hellhounds. It would be easy to retain in our hearts eternal hatred of our persecutors. But that would not be Jewish. Ours is a more difficult and more worthy obligation: To consider the sins of those who incited the Christian and the Mohammedan in judging their present progeny. We are willing to consider the evil influence of past religious and civil authorities in all the continents, from the long-dead Assyrians to the Reformed churches of South Africa, whose total absence of a sense of humour allowed them in 1970 to describe as heathen the very Jews who brought God to the world and laboured, suffered for Him and served Him with deathless loyalty. We are ready to consider the moral and spiritual blindness of those who murdered, raped, and robbed the chosen nation and ready to ignore, as far as humanly possible, the horrors of past and present, if and as soon as the Gentiles are willing to rise above their wrongs and prepare for a comradeship in an effort to make religion universally concrete by fostering brotherhood, rectitude, and harmony in the confused and bitter world of today. Wherever and whenever the opportunity was granted to us to advance the cause of all His children, we Jews have co-operated with our Gentile hosts from working man to scientist, from teacher to banker, from rabbi to social leader. We have done so not in order to ingratiate ourselves, but as part of the *Torah's* programme of the good life, as the Jewish contribution to civilization and culture which our Father in heaven has demanded of us, from Sinai to Jerusalem.

We are waiting with bated breath for a more genuine and abiding change of Gentile attitude. We shall blessedly join their work for happiness, peace, and security of black and white, citizen and stranger, embracing America and the whole of humanity in a well-planned, generously and consistently pursued endeavour to bring light, peace, and security to all mankind.

On Visiting the Sick (Theological Roots for a Hospital Ministry – The Jewish Point of View)

I

The highest goal of the Good Life is the Imitation of God. More than a thousand years before Thomas à Kempis (15th century), wrote his famous essay, the Rabbis proclaimed the Imitation of God as a supreme human duty and goal. The text reads: 'As the Lord is gracious, be thou gracious; as He is merciful, be thou merciful; as He visits the sick, do thou visit the sick.'[1] This imitation of His ethical qualities is meant to affect all human relations.

The Hebrew Bible and the literature of the Rabbis know only one race, the human race. The earliest chapters of Genesis contain the statement that God made man – every man – in His image, and only one man so that none may vaunt superiority over his fellowman.[2]

Abraham, the first Hebrew, was commanded to live so 'that all the families of the earth may be blessed through him.'[3] In the Jewish code, the obligation rests on both the community and the individual to provide social service to every human being in its midst. These are the words of the law: 'The community must provide sustenance to the poor non-Jew, even as the poor Jew; it must provide cure for the non-Jewish sick, even as for the Jewish sick: it must provide a burial for the non-Jewish dead who has nobody to attend to him, even as it must do so for the Jewish dead in similar circumstances.'[4]

As its fundamental principle, the *Torah* states this obligation: 'Love thy neighbour as thyself.'[5] This is the universal, though not the only justified, translation of the Golden Rule. Students familiar with Hebrew usage know that the literal meaning of that famous passage is: 'Love thy neighbour, he is as thou.' The etymological meaning of the Hebrew word *rea*, usually translated as 'neighbour' or 'fellowman,' is revealed in *Psalm* CXXXVIII, 2. The poet addresses himself to God: 'Thou knowest my lying down and my rising up, thou understandest My *rea* (thought) afar off.' The Hebrew word for 'thought' has the same root-letters as the word for 'fellowman.' It means that every human is our fellowman because he shares with us basic thoughts, ideals, ambitions, fears, and hopes.

It is in line with these principles that the Jewish law imposes upon all its adherents the obligation of *Bikkur Ḥolim*, visiting the sick.

No iron curtain can keep our prayers from our Father in Heaven, says the *Talmud*. Nor can any crust of frustration, resentment, or despair forever resist the genuine endeavour to bring comfort and peace to any patient anywhere in His world. Nor should any denominational bias operate to prevent anyone of us from offering the healing boon of brotherhood to the sick, in body or soul, in any hospital of our country.

The American ideal presupposes such attitude, care, and concrete helpfulness from every citizen to every fellowman from New York to San Francisco, from Maine to Florida. For beyond our special devotion to the souls in our parish, we owe to Him a supreme service: our uncribbed humaneness, as men and women of faith, extended to all of His children everywhere.

II

I am sure that many a debating society would go out of existence if people knew what they were debating. Not only questions of semantics but especially of root meanings are involved. The etymology of a word, on the whole, is a safe guide to at least its original meaning, although in some cases its history reflects changing conditions and emphases. The Hebrew term for visiting the sick originally meant first examining them,[6] their situation, the ways towards their recovery. Then it means taking care of their particular needs and only the combination of both results in a proper discharge of that socio-religious obligation. It is to be crowned and concluded by a prayer to the Divine Supreme Healer for the restoration of their health.

Normally a physician, and a nurse under his control, attend to the physical examination and resulting effort at the cure of the patient. But the psychological aspect must not be ignored. It requires the special attention of a close personal friend or of a clergyman. The patient may have emotional and intellectual problems. As a psychophysical being, as a psychosomatic phenomenon, he knows many worries. Nobody is more alone than a man in pain. A vacuum is a potential source of trouble even to one in perfect physical condition. How much more to one on his sick bed, who easily succumbs to brooding, to despondency, eventually to unwillingness to fight for the preservation of his life! The patient must be led, by careful, sympathetic guidance, to look upon himself not as an object of charitable attention, but as a significant human being, in terms of modern thought, not as an 'It' but as a 'Thou.'[7] He needs the validation of his significance, of his individual worth, as a basic means of recovery.[8]

III

Very often the major service is the 'Ministry of Listening.' I have found many a person profoundly relieved because of my willingness to let him bestow upon me an hour or more of eloquent description of his physical suffering or of his anxiety. The very fact that somebody is ready to offer a willing ear to his complaints has a therapeutic value. Whilst one should not call on invalids who are not in a state or mood to receive callers, one must generally enter the sick room with the determination to place one's experience, one's human sympathy, one's earnest intellectual effort, at the service of the suffering friend. Indeed the Rabbis say the Biblical command 'To walk after the Lord your God' (which means to seek to imitate His attributes), includes the obligation to visit the sick.[9] Such a visit reduces suffering, removes conscious or unconscious resentment, and conquers dangerous apathy.

The first concern has to do with finding out whether everything that may be reasonably expected is being done for his, or her, cure. The second: to add to technical service the invaluable boon of personal, comradely attention.

In the sanctuary of Jerusalem,[10] there was a man appointed to pay steady, special attention to the sick. Says the *Talmud*: 'Even as the Lord aids him who suffers from disease, so may a human being help him to recover. Many people go to visit rich patients, go Thou to visit the Poor!'[11] 'God's mercies are upon all His works'[12] 'upon every human being, upon every living thing,' says the psalmist and emphasizes the message of the Book of Jonah.[13] Godliness must express itself in efforts to ease the pain and increase the joy of all of His children everywhere.

IV

There are intellectual problems which plague a man in the hospital and they require earnest and wise attention. 'Why do I suffer?' he muses or rages in the still hours of the night. 'Why are others enjoying good health, happy social life, whilst I suffer in solitude? I was taught that God is just, why does He afflict me so sorely? How can one justify one's faith in His mercy, whilst racked by pain?'

A few years ago, I addressed a dinner of an American Medical Association. At the dais, a mid-western professor sat next to me and suddenly he said, 'Rabbi, that was a fine talk. But how can one justify God's mercy in the light of cancer and other terrible, terminal diseases?' My reply was: 'Before answering this question, I should like to make it harder. How can one justify the merciful Eternal Father as one faces the horror of an earthquake with hundreds of innocent people, young and old, swept away?'

This may be the answer: In one of the earliest chapters of the Hebrew Bible, the Lord offers man the ideal life in the Garden of Eden, and imposes upon him the task 'to work it and to guard it.'[14] This earth was not handed to us on a platter as His unconditional perfect gift. It was offered to us rather as an opportunity for devoted co-operation. The Lord endowed man with mind and energy, and we are to use both, not only for our own good, but for the protection of our neighbour. The history of modern medicine has ample evidence to show that in the last few decades we have conquered many diseases which formerly were considered fatal. But consider this: In the year of that medical dinner, the national budget of the United States amounted to almost fifty billion dollars, to pay for some past and present wars and for prevention of a future one. In that year, our national expenditure for cancer research amounted to a comparatively paltry sum. Had we spent one tenth of one per cent of our national military budget for the study of that deadly disease, we might by now have known its nature and thereby provided a cure. But we were too busy attending to what we boast of as an ever-higher standard of living! Our social conscience was too underdeveloped for the community and the individual to pay generous and consistent attention to the challenge of this terrible disease. The blame is not on the Lord, but indeed on human lack of wisdom and sympathy.

Similarly, the grave problem of fuel scarcity of late has engaged the increasing interest of the United States' government and business. Some hope has been expressed that atomic power, before the end of the century, may enable us to dispense with oil as a fuel, and to remove the veritable danger of the poisonous atmosphere created by countless motor cars and by the smog of modern utilities. Yet, by the grace of God, there has been, from times immemorial a limitless source of fuel in the core of our globe, which, by the pressure of its very quantity, from time to time causes devastating earthquakes. It presents a supreme challenge to science. If by human ingenuity and persistent endeavour we could succeed in channelling that heat, it would provide sufficient fuel for everyone for all times, thereby solving one of the most acute problems, not only of income, but of the preservation of health and life itself. But we have been too busy in the pursuit of ever more luxuries, of surely non-vital political and social problems, to attend to this marvellous challenge: To change the power that causes periodic disastrous earthquakes into a potent force for immeasurable good in human affairs! Only in the last few years has our government begun to study the problem and to promote some slender research in that field.

Neither cancer nor earthquakes may be blamed upon the Merciful Lord of the Universe. Both would have been a matter of the dark past, if the conscience and intelligence of man had been concerned with them as seriously and consistently as their solution demanded.

V

Counselling is an integral aspect of visiting the sick.[15] From the patients I heard occasionally persistent questions as to God's goodness and to the whole problem of reward and punishment. These arguments do not derive only from envy of the neighbour who enjoys health and peace. It is the eventual impact of painful or loathsome disease which may drive the afflicted to despair and blasphemy. One must not condemn such outburst, difficult as it may be to restrain one's pious or righteous indignation. It is rather the reaction in form of friendly guidance which ultimately proves salutary. The Psalmist, the Book of Job, and many passages in Rabbinic literature have dealt with the timeless, interdenominational problem of 'the suffering saint as against the happy, triumphant evil-doer.' There have been a number of attempts at its solution, each significant in what is called inter-subjective discussion (discussion among people who share basic beliefs). One of them has to do with the ultimate happiness of the righteous in the world to come, which is to compensate him for his troubles during life on earth. But already in the *Talmud*, a Rabbi, asked whether the promise of eventual reward in heaven makes his suffering precious to him, said: 'I would rather have no suffering and no reward.'[16]

In an endeavour to find an answer, the Psalms[17] stress the shortlived success of the wicked as against the abiding serenity of him or her who has attained the nearness of God. The ultimate solution offered by the Book of Job is that there is no solution, for man's mind cannot ever know the mind of God, and hence lacks the wisdom, the vision, and the comprehension, of what befalls the individual. The cosmos shows His infinite wisdom and benignity; for the rest – faith is the answer!

VI

Yet there are some solutions that may complement the others. The real reward of a good deed lies in itself, in the thought which prompted it, in the will for good which performed it.[18] On the one hand, the *Torah* promises reward and threatens punishment,[19] on the other, the Rabbis in the *Mishnah* adjure us: 'Do not be like slaves who serve their masters on condition (or with the definite expectation) to receive reward, but retain an attitude of reverence towards Him!'[20] The Rabbis did not oppose the teaching of the Bible. They prepare us for a deeper understanding of its discipline. Reward and punishment *do* come, but they are not the final consequences of good or evil actions. Rewards and punishments, rather, are pedagogical devices to train us in the habit of doing what is good and shunning what is evil.[21] It is what old Aristotle calls the method of habituation, good habits creating a good character, which eventually results in a fine personality.[22] There are two considerations which I should like to offer to your kind indulgence. First: there is a difference between the perfectly justified hope in God's rewarding a decent life, and a mean slavish expectation of having sooner or later every good deed rewarded. I would call that the attitude of a tipster, a man performing small deeds for a tip. That is unworthy of human beings and offensive to a sense of reverence, because it reduces the Lord of the Universe to a kind of grocer, exchanging an article for a coin. The ultimate reward of a good life is the type of human being into which one develops. The ultimate punishment of an evil life is the type of human being into which one develops. That is what the Rabbis had in mind when they said that there is no reward, in this world, for a good deed – for every good deed.[23]

There is a second thought: If God were to reward every good deed and to punish every evil deed, His major purpose for man would be defeated, because with every good deed performed, there would be the expectation of an earlier or later reward; and that assurance of 'safe investment' would prevent us from doing what is good because it is good, and from not doing evil for the reason that it is evil. If God were to punish every evil deed, there would be many a human being with the blackest of hearts, yet restraining himself from performing things evil, not because he hates evil as he should, but because he is afraid of human or divine police. Therefore, as far as we can guess, so to say, God cannot reward every good deed, nor punish every evil one, in order to allow man's free will to choose what is good because it is good and to reject evil because it is evil.[24]

VII

Occasionally, modern psychiatry offers wholesome guidance. Some time ago, a young woman, whom I shall call Sophie, asked for an interview. She had heard my address at a famous eastern university. The child of agnostic parents, she found herself yearning for what she called 'a positive philosophy of life.' She came again and again and I endeavoured to lead her toward faith in God. For two years I lost sight of her and then she returned. I quote her, as far as I remember, verbatim:

'We have been married now for two years. Let me say that my husband is the finest of human beings. But we have been unhappy practically from the first day of our marriage. We are always quarrelling.' I agreed to see him, and curiously as well as innocently, he used the same words his wife had uttered: 'Sophie is the finest woman, but we haven't had a peaceful day, even during our honeymoon.' I elicited the following details from him: 'I would come home one evening and say to Sophie: "You are looking wonderful tonight, dear." She would say, "Only tonight – not yesterday, never before?" Whereupon unpleasant disputes would follow. Or I would say "This dress is very nice." And she would burst out – "How about the others? Have you no good words to say about my taste?"'

I realized now her part in the domestic drama, but not its causes. After that conference I invited Sophie to my study and for a few days I remained baffled. Suddenly, I remembered the methods of Freud and his disciples and I said to her. 'Sophie, I do not know your history at all. Please talk to me about your studies, your life in college.' She did, but it did not enlighten me as to the source of their constant unhappiness. Then I persisted 'Would you talk to me about your family, your youth.' She did and in the course of her rambling tale she mentioned: 'At home the boys were everything. Father would always express sanguine hopes about their success in life and about the comfort and pride they would spell for their parents. But girls were described as a source of perpetual anxiety, especially throughout their adolescence and until they were safely married. In a flash I saw the light. Sophie, for a long time, had resented this discrimination. She was too loyal a daughter to allow herself a reaction, in her heart or on her lips, against her beloved father, but she transferred her anger to the first male of her own life – her husband. When I explained it to her, she was furious, protesting most vehemently against my interpretation. She left me, bathed in tears and expressing her bitter 'gratitude for my attention.' Only two weeks later did she accept my judgment. After the next encounter with both of them, there began the first peaceful period of their life, which, as far as I know, has become permanent. This is how the work of Freud, Jung, Adler, and their disciples may impinge upon our work, my friends.

VIII

The problem of longevity interests many a veteran.[25] In the *Talmud* the Sage offers practical, ethical advice: He insists that a right social attitude creates inner peace which prolongs life; that generosity maintains a milieu of harmony and thus, of mental health; that pride which refuses an unnecessary gift is also an invaluable physical asset. Another scholar stresses the biological assets of loving patience at home, genuine modesty abroad, and generous consideration of one's fellowman's honour. A third one emphasizes the value of pervading reverence towards the sanctuaries of our faith, whilst another one warned that succumbing to fear and anger is a source of sudden senescence. Against the tensions of a busy life, the Sabbath rest with its profound relaxation is hailed as the day of a different attitude when we are relieved of the workaday troubles.[26] A final advice, which we may have to be careful in quoting, holds that wine helps to overcome fear. – In another passage the scholar is warned against our common sin: treating one's health with contempt.[27] Finally, as to the problem of love and marriage broached too often and alas, mostly too late, our sacred lore held this principle to be basic: There must be not only consent to marriage, but consent in marriage. His conjugal rights do not allow the husband to approach his wife carnally at will. He must woo her from the moment of marriage to the last hour they are granted together, for both to remain happy, worthwhile, and well.[28]

IX

The ancient and modern academies of *Torah* have known regular talks by the masters, moral and spiritual counselling. In some places they came every morning before the scholarly lecture or discourse; in others they preceded the term-curriculum or concluded it. The leaders of Ḥassidism, the pietist movement of the last three centuries, supported and provided such counselling. To them would come the poor in spirit, the sick, men and women burdened by all sorts of problems. As they approached these Saints, they knew them to be not only pious souls, but men of affairs, psychologists, experts in human relations, and authorities on family matters.

From the time of Moses to our own days, counselling has been a self-evident part of the *Torah* as divine direction, conveyed by the teachers to their disciples, and through them to men and women in the house of worship, in their home, in the hospitals, or wherever they were in need of warmhearted wisdom.

Notes:

1. *Shab.* 133b,
2. Gen. I, 27, *Midrash* a.l.
3. Gen. XII 2.
4. *Gittin* 61a.
5. Lev. XIX, 18.
6. *Ket.* 106a; *Ned.* 38b; *Baba Mezia* 30b.
7. M. Buber's famous formulation.
8. See Victor Frank's *Logotherapy*.
9. *Shab.* I.c.
10. *Bikk.* III.
11. *Ibidem.*
12. Psalm CXLV, 9.
13. Jonah, IV, 11.
14. Gen. II, 15. The N.Y. Times of March 22, 1966, reports an amazing pilot project suggested by D. M. Evans, a Denver, Colorado, consulting geologist.
15. See the article on 'Counselling' in my *Harvest*, N.Y. 1956.
16. *Ber.* 6a.
17. Psalms XXXVII and LXXIII; the whole of the Book of Job deals with questions and answers on this matter.
18. *Mishnah, Abot* IV, 2.
19. Deut. XI, 26f.
20. *Abot* I, 3.
21. Maimonides, introduction to *Sanh.* XI.
22. *Nichom. Ethics.*
23. *Kidd.* 39b.
24. J. Wohlgemuth, *Jeschurun.*
25. *Meg.* 28a.
26. See my article on 'What is Judaism' in Jewish Library II, 1930.
27. *Abot de Rabbi Nathan* XXIX, 6.
28. See 'Love and Marriage' in my *Heirloom*, 1961.

Some Problems of Jewish Ethics and Philosophy

The term 'dogma' belongs to the church, in the chapters of whose history it has had a colourful career: Individually, the acceptance of the dogma spelled the difference between damnation and salvation. Collectively, it thundered in thirty years of battle and burned its imprint on the pages of medieval and modern history. Almost all the continents have reverberated to the sound of its wars.

In Judaism, even in Moses Mendelssohn's famous dictum, dogma had no saving grace. Neither in catechisms nor in the folk-consciousness of our people, nor again in the code of Jewish law, did dogma play a role as constructive or as destructive as with our daughter-religions. Yet there have been fundamental doctrines and basic teachings of faith underlying the totality of Jewish life. From time to time they have assumed a *sine qua non* significance in accord with the philosophic temper and social imperatives of the day.

Maimonides, for instance, was severely criticized by Albo (*Ikkarim*, I, 16), for making a dogma of the incorporeality of God. This, in its turn, was but the reaction of Maimonides to excessively anthropomorphic tendencies and terms on the part of many of his predecessors and some of his contemporaries. Thus, also, are Crescas' celebrated animadversions against the Thirteen Principles of faith formulated by the great Moses to be understood as due to the fact that problems which appeared vital in the days of the *Guide for the Perplexed* and which therefore provoked the apodictic statements of Rambam, had well-nigh lost their meaning when Crescas wrote his *Or Adonay*. Similar observations are in place with regard to the reduction in number of Crescas' seven dogmas and to the criticism they are made to suffer in Albo's *Ikkarim*. Two volumes of the *Monatsschrift*, one or two of the *Jewish Quarterly Review* and at least five of the *Jeschurun* (edited by Joseph Wohlgemuth of blessed memory) dealing with 'Dogma in Judaism' and recording the opinion of experts and of *Torah*-true searchers, reveal the fluctuating character of the problem and seem to justify its modern formulation in the Wohlgemuthean direction: 'There is only one dogma – *Torah min hashamayyim* – from which all other doctrines stem.' And whether it is subjected to the Procrustean form of theological verbiage or not, it undoubtedly underlies the whole of *Halakhah* and *Hagadah* as well as of Jewish philosophical literature from Saadya Gaon to Rabbi Kook of blessed memory.

However, whilst we must be aware of the fact that individual dogmas lose relevance from time to time, we must hold fast to the ultimate doctrine of *Torah min ha-shamayyim*. Above everything else, we must be ever ready to prepare for a new analysis and a new synthesis in accordance with the best methods of philosophical, ethical, and scientific categories always avoiding the dangers of appeasement, never yielding to the pressure of contemporary, intellectual factions. Rabbi Yehudah Halevi, throughout his *Kuzari*, and Samson Raphael Hirsch, throughout his *Gesammelte Schriften*, have indicated that no comparison and no efforts of integration into any particular philosophy of life must be permitted to interfere with the authenticity, the independence, and the unshorn identity, of Judaism. In the highest sense of the word *Torah im Derekh Eretz* would then mean the study of Judaism, of its philosophical positions, its ethical imperatives, its social blue-prints for the purpose of expressing the *Torah*'s point of view, and of enriching, ennobling, and completing a contemporary thought, *Weltbild* (cosmic vision) and scheme of *Weltverbesserung* (world improvement).

In that respect one might say dogmas have changed in dynamic emphasis. As an example, immortality, resurrection, and cognate beliefs have become successively of paramount or of merely formal interest as the complex of thoughts and ideas closest to them have become peripheral or focal in the thoughts of the Jewish people, both rabbis and laymen. From another angle these so-called 'dogmas' were significant. They helped to capitalize the spiritual urges of the generation and to lend an acuteness and an up-to-dateness and therefore a relevance to the whole body of thought and practices connected with them. They helped to galvanize and to keep intellectually and emotionally vivid the *tar'yag mitzvot* and the philosophy of faith and life that they express. Last century the search aimed at synthesis, the old *Yeshivah* problem of science versus faith that occupied the stage. The more recent years, in accord with the views of especially Professor Max Scheler, have revived the general position and the particular demand of Yehudah Halevi for the self-sufficiency of Judaism and its rejection of the attitude that would lay stress on any *hekh'sherim* (endorsement) of the *Torah* by non-Jewish categories of living and thinking.

In some quarters revelation as a dogma is considered basic as the only doctrine from which all loyalty stems and through which the assurance of the meaning of Judaism gains dignity and endurance. Elsewhere, with our utter ignorance of the exact form the revelation assumed or the detailed way it came about, the doctrine of revelation was interpreted in its ultimate analysis as the belief that the *Torah*, in being divine, i.e., not the result of human fallibility, in its totality is basically and abidingly true. The continued effort at *da'at elokim*, the knowledge of the ways of God, as accessible to human minds, will be the hallmark of sound religious thinking, and of the awareness of our obligation to keep Judaism significant in the life of Israel and thereby valuable as an influence for good in the affairs of universal man.

Both for Jewish ethics and philosophy this assumption of an obligation is essential. We must maintain the laboratory of analysis and synthesis to which the best minds of American Israel will have to make their unceasing contributions.

One of the ultimate purposes of Yeshivah University might be a comprehensive and systematic *berur halakhah* (expounding of Jewish Law) that would endeavour to distil the social philosophy behind Jewish labour law, the Jewish principles of business ethics, as well as lay the foundation for a code of international law. Such constructive effort would be the concrete form of this century's contribution in terms of

Torah-guidance to the thinking and living of man. Yeshivah University, as it moves towards the fulfilment of its destiny, should be able to produce the staff, the secular specialists (educationists, sociologists, political scientists, economists, psychologists) who might help the dovetailing of the two aspects of modern philosophies of life, combining the advantages of the severe discipline of modern universities with the undeviating concreteness and directness of the divine *Torah*. What is missing in the modern world is not stimulation nor breadth of view but certainty, clarity, rootfulness. As *emunah* and *mada* are combined in the developments of such a body of thinkers and scholars, and of institutions and platforms resulting from their activities, we shall for once lift the promise of the *Torah* as a divine guide of life not only above the lowlands of homiletics, but also beyond the hills of academic cathedras into the pure air and the undoubted solidity of scholarly achievement, yet capable of coming down like the rains of heaven to fructify Jewish individual thinking and to ennoble the patterns of Jewish community work.

As far as modern philosophy is concerned, a similar effort will be found essential as against the unscientific finalities of the older Huxley and even the modern Sir Arthur Keith. The scientific temper has proved more cautious and the recognition of its inability to penetrate ultimate truth and the acceptance on the part of its true leaders of some distance off the goal of truth as the unavoidable point of resignation, presents a more hopeful aspect both of science and of the assertion of religion and its claim to be recognized as a working theory as good as any parallel effort. It is in this connection that Heisenberg's principle of indeterminacy which proved so seminal for Schroedinger and Sir Arthur Eddington has acquired great importance. Whereas one may not feel as sanguine as Eddington does in his statement that strict causality has been finally overthrown, at any rate it has been sufficiently shaken to render its attacks on religion much less potent than they were heretofore considered.

At any rate, Jewish philosophers and other teachers of Judaism may find it profitable to keep in touch with salient features of this discussion as it affects tangentially the whole question of faith and science. And just as Kant's interpretation of time and space has cut the Gordian knot of the vexed problem of *behirah versus ye'diah*, so should we ever be on the alert to discover both the way out and the synthesis which modern philosophies (Whitehead, Scheler, and the various schools in England and France) seem to offer. Yet, when all this will have been considered, we shall have come to the conclusion that any fruitful activity will have to be propelled by two considerations: (1) that no synthesis, no reconciliation, no interpretation of Judaism in the light of any philosophy will prove as useful as an ever-renewed effort to interpret Judaism on internal evidence out of the fulness of its *Halakhah*, and in concluding, (2) that the strongest contribution that Jewish philosophy can make to the re-Judaisation of our people and the gradual approach of the modern world to the foot of Mount Sinai, will come from a study of the message of the *Torah*, not in terms of ultimate philosophical categories, but of concrete directions as to the way man should go and the deeds he should do. And just as Yeshivah University one day was blessed by the vision of a scientific department which in a kind of progressive revelation would establish the significance of the laws of the *Torah* in the light of the best laboratories of the day, so should the study of the *Halakhah* beyond its ingenuities follow the classic pattern of the *Mishnah Torah*, to present to the world, God's philosophy of life, and set in its right place every aspect of human activity. Thus, like the Euclidean parallels, will the various approaches to truth be found to converge as a *Mizmor le Todah* (Psalm of Gratitude) in the infinity of faith. The new Israel, as, with the help of God and by the wisdom of our people there, it will create not only social forms by a philosophy of life that will be representative of the divine *Torah*, may prove the power-house and the fountain of erudition and a well of salvation for God's first-born, Israel, as well as for all His children everywhere. The Stagirite's old conviction will thus come true that man can be good and happy only at the same time.

Out of such an optimistic and dynamic view of religion will the next generation draw the strength to defeat the hopelessness of the *Kofrim* of our time, the so-called 'omnipotent matter' of Bertrand Russell and the dirge of disaster from Spengler to their last disciple. Only from the heights of Pisgah and with the vision of the promised land can we regain the power and the joy which justifies our philosophy and crowns it.

Woman's Threefold Role

I *Of Love*

For a right attitude towards her, there must be a proper appreciation of her function in love, in the home, and as educator – three concentric circles.

Love, the most abused and too often least understood of words, has never been more essential than today. Against the deadly menace of maximum destruction by atomic power, there is the maximum source of peace and security which marriage, based on love, offers. We all are in need of the warmth, the rousing effect of tender care, the sheer comfort, physical and emotional, flowing from trusted companionship. Nothing can better immunize us against the corroding menace of communal, national, and global conflict – (hate-ridden, envy-propelled, despair-sired) – as profoundly as a loving wife greeting our home-coming, an understanding husband offering his cheerful comradeship to the mate. The biblical expression 'wife of his youth' offers both challenge and counsel. Where there is selfless love, the wife remains throughout marriage the bride, the very sight of whom sets her lover aglow with joy and respect. Woman as lover would, by the grace of her intuition, know her husband's mind and heart, his problems as his harvests. The partners, by their love, would remain a perpetual source of mutual aid and encouragement. They would achieve a peace and security impervious to the noise and hazards of the political scene or the market place. Woman has native endowment for all of its implications, physical, emotional, mental. She, more than man, can build married life on what the prophet portrayed as its four pillars: righteousness, grace, compassion, and steadfastness. (Hosea, II 21.) Indeed, such love creates a human summit, it is the fruit of knowing God and loving Him.

II *Of Harmony*

In the gray confusion and ugliness of the super-busy life, the relentless drive, haste, and friction not only of the metropolis, but even of smaller cities modern man needs some vision of harmony, order, and a relaxing sense of beauty. The Hebrew word *Ḥen* implies all of that – combining sympathy, grace, and beauty. It requires art, endeavour, patience no less than perception. Woman's work, but also her wisdom, transforms an apartment into a home. Woman's unselfish dream goes beyond period furniture and the latest tricks of T.V. apparatus into the creation of an atmosphere, the antidote to the rash, brash, hurried, bumpful scent of the street, into the calming, charming colour scheme of her devotion. Cooking, too, is an accomplishment, with its ingredients of imagination, attention to detail, appreciative knowledge of foodstuffs, and consistent application. A good, cheerful, and cheering home is the achievement of woman's devotion and the rock of man's emotional wellbeing. The husband's success in business or profession may render her endeavour more pleasant, but the vital steadfast step-by-step progress towards the goal is her own challenge, plan of work, and eventual triumph.

III *Of Education*

Love is the basis of wholesome marriage. Grace and the accomplishment of harmonious home life express the wife's personality on a level at once practical and romantic. Both affect the relation between the mates and their heights and depths. Yet, in another sphere, woman's share is utterly more significant, indeed, the decisive element. With noblest effort, the father cannot be a major influence on the emergent character of his children. Because of the incessant demands of his office or store, he has neither time, nor mood, neither adequate patience nor sufficient intuition to be a useful educator, unless he were to give up his outside work and rely on endowment income. which might free him, releasing energy and granting time, yet not supply him with the wisdom that the loving mother acquires through pain and understanding, through compassion and dedication. The husband's heart (the Book of Proverbs asserts) trusts his wife, relies on her to be the potent influence on the children of their love. She teaches them by a hundred details of kindness and firm righteousness. They see her 'stretching out her hand to the poor' (ibidem XXXI, 19) and imbibe at her knee Jewish teaching of social responsibility. The old-fashioned *pushke* (charity box), into which the old-fashioned mother put her dime before *Lichtbenshen* on Friday night connected not only the Sabbath feast with mercy, but taught their little ones to include the poor, the orphan, the widow, the stranger (Deut. XV, XXIV) in their life's programme. The impersonal cheque mailed at stated intervals to organized charity robs the tender age of the sight, the solid experience of genuine *raḥamanut* and too often the absence of such training results in the ugly type of uncharitable sons of charitable parents: they have no feeling for the underdog and no desire at all to engage in personal effort to help him.

Woman's work is utterly irreplaceable for husband, home, and children. It offers an outlet for all her unspent energies, for her imaginative powers, for her maternal urges. Her aesthetic no less than her ethical urges can find happy fulfilment in her home programme. This generation has seen the ebb and tide in the affairs of progressive education. Thirty years ago it was the repressed children of an earlier age who, in heedless reaction, misunderstood its goal to be the youngster's self-expression, unrestrained by any earlier value or principle, forgetful of the fact that too often there was no precious self to be expressed. Of late the importance of self-realization has been stressed, and self-discipline as the harvest of wise pedagogy is being universally acclaimed. The home of wise affection – of carefully balanced granting of the child's wishes and equally devoted refusal of unjustified requests – again is the task, the blessing, and the abiding accomplishment of woman's genius.

These are the three roles of woman, trebly precious in our own days, imposing upon her effort, strain, the quality at once of mercy and judgment: She must be the husband's beloved lover, the home's practical, aesthetic engineer, the children's living example of goodness, truth, and grace. In the process her *ba'al* (husband) becomes *ishi* (her beloved man), her home a mansion of bliss, her children precious comrades.

Of Interpretation

Even beyond the century of their formulation, the Thirteen Principles of Maimonides have their significance. They helped to check the possibility of 'revelation' being adopted as a basic principle and then emasculated by unlicenced interpretation.[1] For it is easy to see that modern non-*Torah*-true Jews, too, may agree to revelation as a basic factor in Judaism and then water down that doctrine by dubbing and restricting it to progressive revelation, meaning the working out of the will of God in the development of human ability to see truth, and human determination to seek justice. Some modern dissidents, following closely on John Dewey's 'gracious permission' to use the name of God as the symbol of man's interest in the whole of humanity, are sprouting volumes and doctrines about 'The Meaning of God', and 'The Purpose of God', manipulating His sacred Name even as Plato did in some of his myths. Thus one could readily appreciate the salutary uses of a list of principles, doctrines, approaches,[2] which either by their massive weight or their irreducible meaning would prevent the gradual evaporation of a basic Jewish belief in a sea of individualistic ingenuities based upon the latest edition of Pitrim Sorokin's text books.

Maimonides saw the imperative need of fixing the basic contents of Jewish faith because he combined his belief in God with veneration for the scientific system of Aristotle. Faith in the *Torah* to him implied the recognition of its philosophy of life. Upon that scheme was the *Mishneh Torah* built, no less than the *Moreh*. But in his architect's blue-print of the building of Judaism he had left open a door to a rationalizing of Judaism, which, his own safety-device of the thirteen principles notwithstanding, might lead to a *Götterdämmerung* of Greek and Mohammedan categories, in which the principles of Judaism, however brilliantly stated, might ultimately be dissolved. Added to that was the partial overlapping of those thirteen principles which would be bound to lead to re-statement, to re-formulation, to increase or decrease in quantity and quality of such creeds, and render confusion widespread and abysmal. No wonder, therefore, that polar attempts were made. Maimonides, in his creeds, protected the *Torah* from philosophical formlessness by postulating certain inalienable cognitions, certain definite channels along which Jewish thinking shall go on, to remain Jewish. Conversely, it was inevitable that a limit be essayed to the rationalizing of the *Torah*. Such comment may have its logic applauded, its 'new light shed upon old matters' admired. But it may allow the invasion of Jewish thought by alien and hostile streams of thought, it may produce interpretation running counter to vital ideas. Hence the need to control the ultimate no less than the present course. Thus revelation and basic doctrines and rationalization in accord with both, may be viewed as the checks and balances which Jewish thinkers of Judaism, *Torah*-true philosophers, have evolved as a kind of *seyyog laTorah* in accord with the famous *Mishnah*,[3] and in agreement with the timeless stream of Jewish religious consciousness.

In a recent volume the late Isaac Heineman[4] dealt with a cognate problem, that of *Taame hamitzvot*. Many of the animadversions offered here can be easily projected upon that fascinating and not always unambiguous field. The *Ḥatam Sofer*,[5] in a practically unknown though very remarkable *Teshuvah*, took up, for contemporary review, the old Talmudic debate as to what constitutes the most important message of the *Torah* – alike for theological doctrine, philosophical approach, and practical significance. He reiterates in the cool prose of his *Responsum* what Simon Duran had stated in the introduction to this commentary on Job: That the *Torah's* full content, every passage, as derived from the same source, is the equivalent of the most eloquent social or moral principle. Hence every *law*, every incidental statement, every detail of its variegated content, shares the minimum and maximum of the divine book.

Thus the walls of the creeds were erected to protect the basis of revelation, and that basis was re-inforced to strengthen its walls by under-girding them.

Freedom of interpretation is not affected thereby. To the extent to which it is one of the things 'which He handed over to the sons of man' (or particularly: to the *shlome emune yissrael*), it could move all along the line from Saadya's audacious statement about reason being the only guide in interpreting Holy Writ to the deep *Kavanot* of Ḥassidic and earlier mysticism. The *Torah* thus would remain a triumphant constant, the source of all truth. Yet, as human beings sought for its between-the-lines meaning, its *drash*, *remez*, *sod*, to complement the *p'shat*, the *Torah* will stay at once in profound agreement with itself, and infinite in nuance and contours. Its light – *hamaor shebatorah* – illumines the highest flights, the farthest roaming of the minds dedicated to the pursuit of its ways. It mirrors in its eternally unchanging ocean the countless waves, the rise and fall, the quest for certainty, the resignation before the ultimate end, the theoretical *mahaloket ha-posekim*, the practical *mimnu vegamru*, the speculative no-man's-land of Jewish thought, the panorama, tragedy, glory, comedy, error, and achievement of its disciples.

Thus, to sum up: Maimonides, Crescas, Albo, and, on the other side, Jacob ben Asher, Duran, and Shneyer Zalman of Ladi, have together reared a platform, which absorbs there current cycles of rationalist ambition, mystic withdrawal, and halakhic austerity, a structure of synthetic strength, serving – *et vaheb besofah* – universal harmonization.

Shalom al Israel.

Notes

1. See the introduction to Joseph Kaspi's Commentary on the *Moreh*.
2. Maimonides' thirteen or Albo's three principles.
3. *Aboth* I, 1.
4. *Ḥatam Sofer al sugot haShass*, ed. A. S. Blumenthal, page 53a.
5. *Ta'ame ha-Mitzvoth BeSafruth Israel.*

Security, Security, Security!

I *Home and Heart*

Since the end of the Second World War, the word security has been on every citizen's lips. The heart of American men and women has been alternately disturbed and reassured and kept in a state of perpetual alertness about security. Measures have been taken from military and civil considerations, huge budgets have been passed, great industries established or promoted, experts have developed, columnists have become famous because of general pre-occupation with this thought of security.

For America is not only a land we inhabit, but an ideal we cherish, a dream the realization of which has been the major goal of the finest minds and souls on our continent.

We Jews have known a similar concern, the red thread throughout our history: for our *Torah*, the divine way of life, commencing with Abraham's pioneering out of Ur Kasdim and flowering – we know with a knowledge past words – in the eventual redemption of Israel in an epoch of universal justice and peace.[1] This national programme with its universal hope has been our most precious possession and its security, in the uncertainties of our march through the ages, has been the abiding concern of our prophets and sages, from Moses through Isaiah, Hillel, Saadya, Rambam, and Joseph Karo down to S. R. Hirsch and A. I. Kook.

The precautionary measures, the restrictions in the cause of greater freedom, the legal enactments, pedagogical devices, and moral admonitions for the single goal of preserving Judaism as the *raison d'être* of the Jewish people, are very large in number, in form, in approach, yet single-purposed in all climes and milieus. The technical phrase is: *gezerah*, usually translated as 'rabbinical enactment issued as a guard,' a 'prohibition or restriction.' Through such *gezerot* the ideal of the *Shabbat* as the day of rest has become concretized in an atmosphere from which the worries, strains, meannesses of the work-a-day world were ingeniously and consistently excluded. Through such *gezerot* the ideal of a family, in which husband-wife and parent-children relations are kept on a high spiritual and moral level, has been preserved; through such *gezerot* the whole of one's life has been held in a milieu of both freedom and adherence to divine standards.

II *Aspects of Gezerah*

Yet the *Talmud* abounds in warnings against raising these precautionary measures to the rank of ultimate values. 'Shall we enact a *gezerah* to prevent the violation of another *gezerah*?'[2] Do we require additional restrictions to safeguard earlier ones? This is the rhetorical question of the Sage. The answer, of course, is: No, one *gezerah* is sufficient. Similarly, the *seyag*[3] or fence around the law is a one time *ad hoc* enactment, such as the tithe to preserve (by deserving it) one's wealth, the vow to promote self-control, silence to protect wisdom. In *Abot de R. Nathan* (*ibidem*), the earliest commentary on the tractate of the *Mishnah* called *Abot* (meaning either 'The Fathers of the *Torah*' or 'Basic Principles of its Ethics'), ample illustration is provided of the evil consequences inevitable when restrictions are issued too often or in a manner too burdensome. Indeed, the supreme court, the *Sanhedrin*, is warned[4] against indulging in such effort, for if the community found the *gezerah* too hard to bear, that august tribunal would have to cancel its own enactment. Elsewhere[5] I have offered an illustration of the grave consequences of a one-sided, hence futile, attention to precautionary measures.

We in the United States seem to be passing through a period of such tragic error. No citizen normal in mind and devotion would acquiesce in any governmental carelessness as to the vital need of protecting the country against the sinister plans of her enemies. In the age of the atom bomb such measures must be costly, time-consuming, systematically organized, and universally maintained. What we must protect is the American way of life, with its emphasis on human dignity, freedom, and opportunity, upon the paramount importance of the individual who is the ultimate source of our country's strength. In the huge blueprints of Pentagon plans he seems of late to be occasionally forgotten. Only a healthy citizen can carry the burden of American destiny. Only a happy citizen will be able to resist the ceaseless attack on his loyalty, no less than on his common sense, by totalitarian schemers. To preserve his mental, physical and moral well-being, schools must remain a major concern of the country, from Washington to each of the forty-eight capitals.

III *Versus Social Infection*

To prevent the social infection of despair and cynicism in some corners of the republic – and such infections have been known to spread with lightning rapidity over vast areas – social welfare must never be permitted to recede from our private consciousness or public activity. Yet this is exactly what has of late been observed and lamented. Unless we are callous to the menace of inner corrosion due to inferior schooling and faulty social engineering, we must inform our city, state, and federal authorities of the people's determination not to permit such disastrous negligence. The Hitlers, Stalins, Huey Longs, and McCarthys of all ages have thriven on such errors.

The last two *Sidrot* of Exodus deal with the building of the *Mishkan*, the temporary sanctuary in the wilderness. Like the later Temple of Jerusalem, it was meant to symbolize God's presence in the community and family, to strengthen them against the allurements of heathen amorality or immorality, to keep up their courage and their desire to march towards the Holy Land.

In our days, organized religion, no less than individual piety, is challenged on all sides. Far-sighted men and women have recognized the need, all denominational varieties notwithstanding, of a closing of the ranks of all dedicated to faith in God as a means of eventual peace on earth.

IV *Mutual Aid*

Surely the time has come for leaders of religion to perceive the basic need to help each other in those vital areas all creeds have in common: faith in God, freedom of conscience, the translation of idealistic professions in the Houses of Worship into ways of life, methods of encouragement and co-operation, which will strengthen the faithful, bring the vacillating into the fold, and guide the unseeing towards His universal law of life.

It is doubly deplorable, therefore, that in a critical moment that attitude is found wanting. In Albany the Fair Sabbath Bill was offered to assure devout Sabbath-observing Jews an opportunity to keep their places of business open on Sunday. In the majority of cases these shop-keepers are small people, whose loyalty to the divine Sabbath is punished by the obligation to keep two days of rest. This is a radical interference with freedom of religion, inasmuch as these citizens, against the dictates of their conscience, are compelled to forgo economic activity necessary for their livelihood. On the grounds of the American way, no less than on those concerned with Jewish law, this inequity ought to be removed. Christians who have supported the bill have recognized the righteousness of the cause. It is deeply to be regretted that a powerful authority in the Catholic field has denied the Jewish Sabbath-observer his American rights and has organized a public resistance that has defeated the proposed measure. Every defeat for religious Jewry is a defeat for religious Christians. Houses of Worship in this country and elsewhere are built best and most enduringly on a terrain of freedom. Houses of Worship and the faith they represent can be built only together, on the foundation of mutual fair play and understanding. The few shops opened when the law is passed, will not endanger the Christian Sabbath, but they will help to underpin the religious foundations of our country.

V *On the Old Continent*

Bigotry in Europe has not brought success to the powers of the church, but has split it from within and created widespread cynicism, nihilism, atheism. How does Scripture put it? 'Oh that they were wise to understand their own latter end.' If Jews close to the great leaders of their neighbours' organized religion were true to their own faith, they would ignore the minuteness of their own political chances to draw the vision of cardinals, bishops, and lay readers to the inevitable evil which intolerance for millennia has been begetting in many climes and ages – deplored and regretted too late, and too costly for the comfort of all concerned. By all means, said Isaiah: 'Enlarge the place of thy tent, lengthen thy cords, but strengthen thy stakes.'[6] We underpin the tent by justice, fair play, appreciation towards those with whom in individual approach to God we may disagree, but whom in their reach for Him, we should aid. The orchestration of the universal worship calls not for interchange of instrument but for the harmony and self-discipline of every participant in that symphony.

The last verses of Exodus have been subjected to dedicated search and interpretation. Rashi and Rashbam have endeavoured to hold fast the central ideas of the Great Architect as they appear in the sober detail of the chapter. The *Torah* states[7]: 'And Moses was not able to enter into the tent of meeting because the cloud abode thereon and the glory of God filled the tabernacle.' Rashbam comments: 'At first the glory of the Lord rested upon the Tent of Meeting, then on the Holy Ark between the *Cherubim*.' Man's first thought places God in the building; the House of Worship seems an end in itself. The prophets fought this common illusion[8]: 'The Temple of God, the Temple of God that is their sole thought.' In grim pre-vision they described the destruction of the building since, by Israel's base conduct, its moral foundation had been shattered. Their disciples, the Sages of the *Talmud*, proclaimed that the glory of God rests in truth upon the Ark containing the Tables of the Law, the divine revelation and direction. . . . But the ark was protected by the mysterious *Cherubim*, 'wings spread upward, their faces towards each other.'[9]

VI *Interdependence*

The ultimate destiny of every House of Worship depends upon the character of the worshipper. Multi-million dollar buildings might be whited sepulchres of the spirit, that is a truism, just as is the emphasis on simplicity as a supreme value. But even simple tabernacles may be empty of spirit, even gorgeous halls of worship might be blessed by it.

The criteria of spiritual – truly religious – harvest are two: if the spirit moves ever upward, towards God, eternal values, unconfined vistas, then the basis has been created, the great chance offered. But it would remain an opportunity lost, an empty noise,[10] a meaningless expenditure of time, matter, and energy unless the 'faces turned towards each other,' unless that upward compelling force moves in the field of human interdependence, bent not on schemes of selfish exclusive salvation, but upon the achievement of a free world, the horizon unlimited, whence comes and which produces the 'land full of the knowledge of God even as the waters cover the sea.'[11] For, as the Book of Kings has it, the ultimate covering the ark are the *Cherubim*, upward in flight, facing the neighbour. Outside the sanctuary, it is feeling, planning, acting towards the fellowman in accord with the teaching of the Tables and the sanctity of the altar that will build up the world's ruins.

The ultimate security of the human family rests not upon mutual fear of war, nor upon general hope for a disease-less, strifeless human society, but upon the inner horizons, the inner vision, the self-discipline of the men and women that comprise its adult power and of a youth trained in the patterns and ideas which school and society hold before their eyes.[12]

Notes

1. Isaiah XI, 1–9.
2. *Betzah* 3a.
3. *Abot de Rabbi Nathan* I, i.
4. Rambam, *Hilkh Mamrim* II, 2
5. *The Rhythm of Life*, p. 58.
6. Isaiah LIV, 2.
7. Exodus, XL 35.
8. Jeremiah VII, 4.
9. Exod. XXV, 20.
10. Jerem. XLVI, 17.
11. Isaiah XI. 9.
12. *Midrash ha-Gaddol a.l. Exodus* XL, 38, end.

Things that Matter

I *Of Integrity* (*Temimut*)

1

The dictionary quotes accepted interpretations of the word 'integrity.' Popular opinion would bestow it upon a man or woman of honesty. But the Hebrew word *temimut* has a wider and deeper meaning. The *tamim* partakes of perfection: his righteousness, as his kindness, is neither accidental nor shallow. They flow from the depth of a personality which, all human frailty notwithstanding, seeks, in steady devotion, to live in accord with God's principles of *tzedek* and *ḥessed* (justice and grace).

2.

It is almost impossible to overstress the decisive quality of integrity. Wise parents, in their educational plan, should give it priority, both in their oral teaching and in the pattern of their own conduct. In every aspect of life this virtue is the major source of comradeship: in profession, in business, as in marriage, it offers the only abiding bond of fellowship.

3.

We may, for a moment, be overwhelmed by massive learning, by great respect for human intelligence; we may for a time, watch with amused tolerance the antics of a ruthless careerist. But we do cherish the *tamim*, a man of integrity.

Particularly in matters of Jewish life no one can show us the way to God when his own attitude leaves doubt in our mind as to his true character.

The *Torah* bids us *tamim tihyeh*,[1] to seek integrity so that we may be accepted by Him. The same applies for enduring success with our fellow man, still more for our peace of mind.

In the house of prayer, in the market place, in the bosom of the family, only he who 'speaks truth in his heart'[2] is God's gentleman.

II *The Lowest Level*

1.

Rasha means a wilful, wicked man. But he is not the lowest type. His background often explains, if it does not excuse, him. For, conceivably, he could be a victim of a poverty-complex, the undigested experience of early privations, which makes him greedy and violent in his passion for riches.

Or, subconsciously, he may be impelled by an inferiority complex, which renders him arrogant, ever suspicious, and contentious. Both, however, may occasionally be troubled by the voice of conscience, and therefore may gradually attain moral normalcy.

2.

The lowest type of humanity is the hypocrite. Doubly low when he mouthes patriotic phrases, insists on prompt payment of dues to an institution of organized democracy, ostentatiously conforming to symbol and custom. But 'in his heart' he says: 'There is no God',[3] no judge, no retribution. Hence 'his deeds are corrupt', abominable.

3.

Of all persons the basest is the hypocrite and of all forms of this social plague none is more despicable than he who cloaks his wickedness in 'loyalty' to a religious group. Several passages in the *Talmud* express abhorrence of a person who hides his inner foulness behind pious protestations. It is an obligation to unmask him *mipne ḥillul hashem*,[4] because he misleads the unwary and profanes God's Name.

4.

Two thousand years ago this was paternal advice to a budding prince:[5] 'Don't be frightened by zealots, they may be honest! Don't be dismayed by heretics, they may be religiously illiterate! But beware of the hypocrites who engage in evil work and claim the reward of the righteous!'

III *The Irresistible Force*

1.

Our generation has almost absorbed the threat of atomic warfare. Apart from very few frightened sectarians, no group of cave-dwellers in flight from hydrogen bombs has yet emerged. Five millennia of warfare have had their impact, armistices have shown resistance to war and yesterday's victims have launched victorious attacks on their oppressors. For every death-dealing tank, chilling the heart of the imaginative, other machines of destruction have offered defiance and menace.

2.

Totalitarian movements, as well as globe-spanning monopolies disturbing the citizen's peace, are resisted through democratic federation and through united effort of labour and consumer. In private life, too, a self-seeker calls forth a search for methods to secure one's rights. Every home tyrant arouses resentment and produces countermeasures. In the long run, partnerships are dissolved, marriages end in divorce, in reaction to the corrosion of confidence. Thus evil is resisted and self-defeating. The pathways of history no less than the records of families eloquently attest this fact.

3.

But none can enduringly resist goodness. It is a powerful catalyst, dissolving the crust of bitterness, penetrating the cynic's defences, bridging the chasm between genuine benignity and unhappy suspicion. Of the qualities of a rich personality (*eshkol*), goodness is the crown.[6] Indeed, as a motive of charitable enterprise it is life-saving (*tatzil mimavet*),[7] both for the recipient, whose despair is ended by true brotherliness and for the giver, who is blessed by the serenity of a happy conscience.

In the hierarchy of values none is greater, stronger, more sure of ultimate success than the force of goodness invading one's brother's problems and helping to solve them.

IV *'Klein Aber Mein'*

1.

On the way from St. Moritz to Maloya there stands a little house, whose owner, with Swiss sturdiness, inscribed *Klein aber mein* on its wall. They mean in English: 'Small but my own!' The pride and joy of having a place of his own adds stature to a man rooted in his country's soil.

These words have stayed with me for days now, ever since they struck my eye in the vehicle taking us towards the Italian border.

They have a message for every alert Jew and Jewess in our day.

2.

Israel is no bigger than the smallest state in our country. But it is the only place which welcomes with open arms every Jew from every land of oppression.

Israel has scant two million inhabitants, but is hospitable to every soul, from radical *ḥassid* to the religiously illiterate, excluding nobody because of accidents of geography or the pigmentation of his skin.

One-half of its population, only a few years ago, escaped the murderous fangs of human beasts, but that small country has sent its pedagogic, technical, and social service experts to the African continent, just emerging from centuries of subjection and exploitation.

3.

Israel, as yet financially insignificant, too poor to provide free high schools for its youth, has precious academies, universities, institutions of research to plot a more abundant life for people everywhere.

That young republic, scarcely *Bar Mitzvah*, appointed for its capital the cradle of all religion, Jerusalem, the City of Eternal Peace. In its streets the prophets' timeless truth was ever again proclaimed. In its fields the battles for human freedom were waged, from its hills the Psalms' mighty music brought the melody of divine mercy and human dignity to the world.

4.

As a minority whose rights are guaranteed by the Constitution of the United States, we feel profoundly at home in our America. As citizens of the world, we appreciate Great Britain's democracy and France's passion for liberty. But, above and beyond all that, we know Israel's *Torah* as the perennial source of morality and as the fountain of our peace and joy.

What American Jewry contributes to Israel, in aid, in pride, in encouragement, is but the concretization of a declaration of loyalty to their spiritual homeland.

5.

To every one of us, as we think of Israel in hours of prayers, in U.J.A. enterprise, in the fellowship of friends, in the still moments of lonely thought – there ought to sound the deep, happy sentiment: Israel, Israel, Israel – small but my own!

Notes

1. Deuteronomy XVIII, 13
2. Psalm XV, 2
3. Psalm XIV, i
4. *Yoma* 86b
5. *Sotah* 22b
6. *Ibid.* 21b
7. Prov. X, 2

Freedom of Religion

From the dawn of civilization a prayer has sounded, rousing the hearts of men and banishing darkness and superstition: 'Hear, oh Israel, the Lord is our God, the Lord is One.'

It was a battle-song, the confession of faith of God's first-born people. The rosebuds of its babes formed its first choir. Slowly, first faintly and then with a thundering crescendo of force and colour the echo came back. Out of Greek scepticism and Oriental helplessness, before malign fate developed the soul of the human family, came the melody of its heart. United in God were the aspirations of man. In the East sang Lermontoff about prayer *Yest sila blagodatnaya* ('There is a blissful power in the harmony of living words and an ineffable sweet message breathes in them'). *Mit Gott fang' an, mit Gott hoer' auf, das ist der beste Lebenslauf* ('Start the day with God and complete it with Him, for this is the best way to live') piously sang the people of the country once civilized. The country that was once the fortress of liberty, equality, and fraternity added as its note *Aime le Dieu de tout ton coeur et ton prochain que toi-même* ('Love the Lord with all thy heart, and thy neighbour as thyself'). The Rock of the Ages has been adored in the countless Houses of Worship of England and America. Their noblest spirits, at the highest peaks of national endeavour, thrilled with the voices of the Holy Book.

Religion expresses an approach to the ultimate verities as well as the most intimate sentiment of gratitude and reverence towards the Father of all life. Religion changes men from a mere intellectual animal into a figure of historical meaning; from self-contained, self-narrowed men and women into an army sworn to break every chain and to labour unceasingly in the furrows of the future.

Religion ties us up not only with God as the Father of human destiny but with our human past and future; not only *vertically* with parents and ancestors whose life vibrated His message, but *horizontally* with all classes, all creeds, all races, God's children in every corner of the world. There is no source besides religion, whence can flow the ideal, the dream, and the firm determination to make this world a happier place for all. The message of Religion is not of Paradise in dim pre-historic ages. Religion inspires us to envision the beckoning days of the Messiah when 'No nation will lift up sword against nation; when they will do no evil nor deal corruptly on all My holy mountain, for the earth will be full of knowledge of God even as the waters cover the sea'.

Freedom of Religion is as elemental to the happiness of the individual as to the humanization of humanity.

Free religion not only fills us with dreams and hopes but inspires us with dynamic challenge. The music of divine worship must include the groan of every oppressed soul whom we must seek to redeem as well as the song of exultation in the heart of the impassioned soldier of freedom. Free Religion is mirrored in the fearless calm of our children's trustful eyes. It speaks in our conscience as we commune in the solitude of night with our Father in Heaven.

The core of all true religion is the fatherhood of God and the brotherhood of man. If it is in the totality of the various expressions that the culture of an age reaches its highest level, so in the hearts of the righteous of all the nations does the symphony of God-consciousness reach sublimity.

But religion must be untrammelled. Only as a sovereign voice will it win the heart and hand of man towards the God-blessed and self-achieved heights of a warless, fear-emancipated, and want-redeemed society. Any shrinking of religion, of its tune or portion, narrows the generation's outlook, any confining of its message impoverishes the whole country.

Religion undisturbed in its vision, unthwarted in its effort, is the strongest reservoir of moral strength. Only from men free in their faith comes the deathless determination and courage to fight the battles, face the perils, win the victory, from evil. Free religion teaches men and women to move from local patriotism to national loyalty, thence to international peace and security. Freedom of religion is basic not only as a moral postulate but as the expression of supreme statesmanship, the strongest foundation of democracy. Two thousand years of ceaseless struggle for freedom of conscience has taught Israel unshakeable faith in Freedom of Religion and deathless valour for its struggle against slavery and darkness. The Hebrew prayer-book proclaims 'To Thee bends every knee, by Thee swears every tongue', interpreting the dark yearning of even the heathen in his search for the reality of God and the meaning of life. How much more does this concept embrace every believer in the one Father of mankind!

Democratic America stands and falls with the dignity of the individual. Not only man, but his soul, must be free. Not well-fed slaves but free men and women enjoying unharassed the harvest of their labours are the hope and the basis of American culture.

The American armies on the far-flung battlefields of the United Nations, for their morale depend upon the serenity of each man, the soldier who has made his peace with God and thereby has conquered inward hollowness and doubt. The American people, to achieve complete and abiding peace, to overcome sectional prejudice, foolish bigotry, and self-destructive greed, need the vision of religion free in its way towards God and united in its faith in the ultimate decency of things. To none more than to Americans is freedom of religion the very breath of national life. It was no political ideal that was the making of America. It was the voice of religion that summoned the pilgrims to their perilous voyage. It was not in the name of secular nationalism that America invited the brave and the forlorn of the world to her hospitable shores. In the name of God did America become the Statue of Liberty, the haven of refuge, the light of human eyes. Organized religion must never surrender its privilege to serve as the undergirder of America's foundations.

The glory of America is her constitutional guarantee of freedom of religion. The power of the Atlantic Charter lies in the hearts of men who derive strength from its pledge to extend freedom of religion to all nations and individuals. It is the principles of biblical justice, equality, and brotherhood through which we can secure liberty and opportunity for all. The peace of tomorrow is based on the convictions of citizens loyal to democracy, enthusiastic soldiers of liberty who worship the Rock of the Ages in humility. They bend their knees but to Him in gratitude and march united in prayer and labour towards the abiding happiness of all their brethren.

Modern Woman in the Arena of *Tzedakah*

I *Through the Millennia*

Eighteen hundred years ago, the *Talmud* declared it the task of woman to justify love by purity, possession by charity, and life by spirituality.[1] According to our Sages, any man who has no wife is no proper man; he lives without joy or blessing, without goodness, direction, and without protection.[2] The same applies to any community, bereft of its women's co-operation in its affairs.

In recognition of her vital significance to the nation, the Jewish woman was awarded a unique privilege, unachieved yet in America, Britain, France, or any other country. According to Jewish law, there must be not only consent to marriage, but consent in marriage. Woman's personality, no less than her person, is to be respected. Her path was to be one of grace and goodness. She was warned of the danger implied in any vacuum – moral, spiritual, or intellectual. Especially was the wealthy wife urged never to delegate her precious own job to others; but to fill her life with worthwhile work, because – the ancient text reads – laziness leads to the deadly malaise of boredom.[3]

Woman has the gift of intuition, of innate wit, and wisdom, above the labours of logic and beyond the circumlocution of lawyers or psychological indigestibles. Her greatest asset is *raḥamanut*, unselfish kindness. That word, usually translated as 'compassion' or 'pity,' means literally 'mother love,' total dedication to her child, whom she serves with all she knows, has, and is, to guide him from helpless infancy to self-sufficient maturity.

Among her assets is the wonderful gift of irony. Do you remember Judge Deborah's scathing indictment of the tribe of Reuben, to whom, in the mortal danger of her people, she had in vain been pleading for quick aid.[4] She chastised them thus: 'In the divisions of Reuben there were great searchings of the heart.' In the parlance of a 1966 leader, she would have said: 'When we cried to you in our agony, you decided on prolonged discussion. There were great resolves of the heart, but no saving action.' Some such incisive rebuke may prove useful at all times.

II *Her Task at Mid-Century*

The modern woman must teach bureaucrats to stay aware of the limitations of bureaucracy, or the programme of charity will become a soulless affair. Social work, as vital as ever, needs to be guided by woman's prudent affection, so that it may move beyond statistics and questionnaires, to the root of the human problem involved, and towards a wholesome, abiding solution. You do not need Albert Schweitzer to teach you respect for all life. Long ago the Book of Psalms proclaimed that 'God's mercies are over all his creatures.'[5] So ought our mercies to be – over the charming and the sullen, the accomplished and the coarse. For nowhere in the Constitution of the U.S.A. or in Hebrew lore have I found it said that only rich folk have the right, occasionally, to be unpleasant. Poor people have the same privilege and woman's tact and sense of humour are wanted for dealing gently with such victims of their troubles.

It was the Jewish woman in the long ago who, in the rare case of someone sentenced to death, offered him a cup of drugged wine before his execution, so that his suffering would be shortened.[6] It was the Jewish woman, proud of her descent from the people, called *raḥmanim b'ne raḥmanim* – merciful, the children of merciful ones – who translated her heritage into endless and infinite acts of kindness. In twentieth-century Germany, it was the Jewish woman who taught the *Vaterland* practical methods of loving kindness, such as aid to expectant mothers, child care, and the hundred and one ways of *Tzedakah*.[7] In Eastern Europe, she attended quietly and tenderly to the forgotten scholar and the joyless orphan.

Federation has offered to her American sister a glorious opportunity to carry on this timeless task, to invest heart and mind, ingenuity and warmth, in the quest to bring light to the blind, cure to the sick. Isaiah put it thus: 'Is it not to deal thy bread to the hungry and that thou bring the poor that are cast out to thy house; when thou seest the naked that thou cover him, that thou hide not thyself from thine own flesh?'[8]

III *Man's Worst Crime*

In our days, man's worst crime has been deadly indifference to his brother's woe. We weep for one-third of our national strength that, but for the murderous apathy of modern nations, could have been saved. But Jews, in accord with their classic tradition, as soon as the ghetto walls were breached, fought on the barricades and on many a battlefield for justice and mercy for all peoples and creeds.

These times again are marked by profound unrest, fruit of the double impact of atomic science: its wonderful promise, its ghastly menace. It has bred a universal insecurity and multiplied the normal tensions of life a hundredfold. It is woman's chance, individually and collectively, to accept the discipline of organized charity, to smooth the furrowed brow, to wipe tears off human faces; to bring cheer, fruitful advice, and help to the underprivileged, to engage in her life-saving endeavours with the humble mercy which is her greatest asset.

There is a fashion whose proud messenger I should commend you to become, whose dictates every wise heart and acute mind should accept: Make '*tzedakah*' a self-evident mark of distinction and, therefore, a matter of fine moral fashion. In the seventeenth century, after the profligacy of the English Restoration, Addison and Steele taught a chastened people that vice was both low and shoddy and that decency had grace and charm.[9] You must stress the fact that niggardliness is aesthetically repulsive; that the most exquisite gown or perfect filigree jewel will fail to erase the marks of meanness from a face.

IV *Jewish Cosmetics*

Indifference is bad form, selfishness is ugly. There must be a decent proportion between what luxury one allows for oneself and one's family and what comforts one offers to the hungry or sick, to the lame, the blind, the orphan, or the helpless aged.

We have never been taught that poverty is a virtue, nor have we ever accepted that fatalistic doctrine – very comfortable to the selfish affluent – that somehow God wants some people to be rich and others to stay poor. The evolutionary optimism of our faith opposes any such life-denying doctrine. Rather is it our obligation to help handicapped wage-earners, to aid folks regain their economic status, their self-respect, and their joy of life.

The Hebrew language does not include the word *schnorrer* in its vocabulary. Our *Torah* knows only the fellow man in trouble and the 'brother in low estate.'[10]

For many years, your hundreds of expert volunteers have assisted Federation's staff in every aspect of their work. Thus, the major results of modern science – the findings of depth psychology, no less than the assured results of medical and economic research – have been integrated in the conferences, discussions, and the practical work of your perennial programmes of loving kindness.

Our Sages hold that at the age of forty one reaches understanding.[11] During the forty years of your organization, you have led charitable enterprise with enough understanding, intuition, and common sense to bring the message of your amazing achievement into every corner of Greater New York. The work of the Women's Division of Federation is a translation into concrete of the social ethics of our faith and the finest assurance of longevity, youthfulness, and *joie de vivre*.

A noble sage, in a charming essay on Jewish cosmetics,[12] described the impact of a merciful life on the eyes and face of a woman. It is the combination of wisdom and goodness, of resourcefulness in the cause of mercy, that lends a woman an irresistible grace – what Plato called *kaloskagathos*, beauty in goodness, goodness in beauty. My own observation has taught me that nothing helps one more to stay young and serene longer than preoccupation with tender benefactions. There is no greater horror than a mannish woman. But to cultivate the qualities, abilities, the ethical ideals of her way of life, is both beautiful and fruitful. A wise woman will want to develop the infinite potentialities for grace, wisdom, and goodness that the Lord has bestowed upon her.

For the next decade, spread the truth that all expected federal and state aid notwithstanding, the escutcheon of New York Jewry will not be stainless until every Jewish child is provided with food, clothing, shelter, and especially Jewish education; until in every Jewish home the pangs of hunger and the sorrows of sickness are banished. May you be enabled, for many years to come, to bring that message into every home and heart of our great city.

Notes.

1. *M. Shabbat* II, 6.
2. *Sotah*, 48a.
3. *M. Ket.* V, 5.
4. Judges IV, V.
5. *Ps.* CXLV, 9.
6. *San.* 43a.
7. *Jewish Library* III, *The Jewish Woman in Germany.*
8. Isa. LVIII, 7.
9. T. B. Macaulay, *Essays.*
10. Lev. XXV, 25.
11. *Abot* V, 24.
12. S. R. Hirsch, *Gesammelte Schriften*, III.

Three Covenants

A modern Hebrew poet has called Jewish survival 'God's greatest riddle.' Voltaire has seen it as the ultimate proof of the existence of God. Both the religious literature and the simple attitude of the Jewish people have shown also to marvelling Gentile generations their self-evident, unshakeable, millennial conviction that there will be endless chapters of our people's history. From the Euphrates to the Hudson, from Rome over Berlin and Moscow, the alert reader will find the same message.

From years of yore we have received the assurance from God's spokesmen, the prophets of Israel, that He will protect us from both man's inhumanity and the cruel accidents of history. The faith in His providence has proved the unfailing light in the darkest nights of *Galut* and persecution. *Zarim omrim en tohelet vetikvah* ('Only persons estranged from both faith and folk have ever doubted this immortality') says the *Siddur*. The poet in his prayer implores the Lord: 'Pray, do not give those utterly strange persons (*akhzarim*) control over us, for they are sunk in the contemporary scene, dismayed by one or the other of the countless handicaps on our march through history.' But our *Torah* envisions an eternal partnership between Him and His people in the annals recording progress of human history towards the peak of Mount Sinai, and simultaneously towards the infinite field of peace and security to be achieved by universal justice and mercy.

As we study the structure of Jewish individual and collective life, we discover the nature of our contribution towards the achievement of the God-revealed, happier chapter of human affairs. It comes in the form of three covenants between Him and Man, between man and woman, between parents and children, transcending the domestic scene and embracing, in its ultimate scheme, all of the 'seventy nations' of mankind. The word 'covenant' is defined as 'an agreement entered into by two or more persons or parties, a compact; God's promise of blessing to be fulfilled on the performance of a condition.' There are three covenants charged with that task, undergirding its slow realization, in ever closer coherence and interdependence. These three covenants, together, form the moral framework of Judaism, maintain the sense of Jewish life, and assure a fruitful future of our people. Frame is 'the constitution of a thing, the supporting and formative parts of a structure.' The Hebrew equivalent, *missgeret*, means 'fortress, fastness.'[1] Judaism, as the *raison d'être* of the Jewish people, is held together by three pledges and secured by their concretization. The goals involved are the Jewish personality, the Jewish family, and the Jewish commitment to universal human history. Each of the pledges is uttered at crucial moments in personal history.

I

The word *berit* (covenant) to the average Jew is identical with circumcision, but the latter, in truth, is but a symbol of the covenant between Abraham (and his flock) and God. The *Torah* says:[2] 'It (the circumcision) shall be as a sign of the covenant between Me and you.' The essence of the covenant is:[3] 'That he command his children and his family after him to observe the way of the Lord, to act kindly and justly.' The spiritual and moral education of the children is the task of the parents. It may be viewed as 'bringing out'[4] faculties dormant in the child's nature, or as a training,[5] through habituation, in the self-discipline which, eventually, shapes a good person. Father and mother, in fealty to the covenant, must stay ever aware of that obligation, both to encourage and to correct. Above all, they must speak, act, live so that their example will arouse abiding affection, respect, and a strong and consistent challenge to move towards the image of the good life they have presented to the infant and the adolescent. Their children are keener in observation and more ready for emulation than the average adult imagines.

Heredity is our lot, a major, but not a decisive, influence. For we can shape the environment within expandable limits. The child's Jewish personality, steeped in reverence, trained in righteousness, crowned by compassion, should be the normal harvest of parental endeavour, and gradually of the autonomous impulse for the good life in its career from infancy towards maturity. What commences as a parental command, thus becomes the programme of adolescent self-direction towards the family ideal of goodness, truth, and grace.

II

'It is not good for man to stay alone.'[6] The longing for comradery is universal, from fellowship at a ball game, through the attachments of teenage, the pursuit of a social atmosphere of encouragement and comfort. The psychophysical constitution of humans leads to the search for an *Ezer Kenegdo*[7] (a team mate), whose perpetual presence, whose love and devotion, will keep life beautiful. At the entrance to the enchanted castle of the lovers' dream and hope, a resolve must be asserted, the covenant: 'Become thou my wife according to the religion of Moses and Israel, and I shall serve thee, honour thee, and provide for thee according to the principles of a Jewish husband who shall serve, honour, and provide for his wife in sincerity.' The blushing bride in turn accepts the challenge of becoming an *Eshet Ḥayyil*, a good wife, loving, devoted to strength, peace, and joy in the life before them. The marriage, in Hebrew *Kiddushin* (a sacred programme), stays based on their covenant, the preamble and the constitution, the blue print for the home to be built. That home shelters their deepest dedication, as it fosters emotional stability, ethical consistency, and intellectual satisfaction. But its prowess has more far-reaching results. The Jewish home underpins the survival of the Jewish people.

A mighty king's dream and a statesman's interpretation thereof, in the long ago, have spelt out that message. What Nebuchadnezzar saw was: 'An image mighty, of surpassing brightness. Its head of fine gold, its breast and arms of silver, its belly and its hips of bronze, its legs of iron, its feet part of iron and party of miry clay. Then a stone smote the image upon its feet and broke them in pieces, whereupon the iron, the clay, the bronze, the silver and the gold, broken in pieces together, became like the chaff of the threshing floor and the wind carried them away so that no trace of them was found . . .'[8]

The king of Babylonia, to whom Daniel interpreted the vision of his dream, owned an empire. Its fame had spread all over the world. Its colleges spread golden literature. Its army and navy helped establish the silver of an inter-continental trade. Its industry built chariots, museums, palaces, great markets, and the modest homes of the populace. But other empires of similar greatness and apparently indestructible power had vanished from the concert of the nations! Daniel's master, anxious and alert, sought to avoid such disaster for his own realm. 'A man's dream is but the reflex of his thoughts during the day,' say the Rabbis.[9] The vision of this night perturbed as it confused the king of Babylon, but Daniel interpreted it lucidly and persuasively: 'The ultimate security of any nation or kingdom derives not from its colleges, impressive as they are, nor from its armed forces, be they never so formidable, nor from commerce and industry, however well-functioning. The ultimate basis of the whole structure is the family, the source and laboratory whence the citizen's personality emerges. Unless the family is sound, strong, wholesome, all other agencies must fail. If, instead of iron or stone, the homes become miry clay, the men and women they rear will be inferior and thus will lack both strength and wisdom for a wholesome national life. With moral flabbiness, universities become waste places, industries mere camps of class struggle, army and navy domains of corruption, the government impotent, the whole nation eventually a victim of the first aggressor. The mighty, though invisible, 'stone of historical necessity' smites yesterday's mighty image, its fragments scatter, its place knows it no more.' Only a good family can sustain a people. Only a marriage based on genuine devotion and mutual respect can build such a family. The preamble of the *Ketubah* (the Hebrew Marriage document) and its detailed mutual obligations create the sustained spirit and the unalterable dedication whose harvest is happy, complexless, trauma-free children, ripening into the nation's loyal adults. The promise under the *Ḥuppah* (marriage canopy) is the second covenant undergirding our people's moral security and physical survival.

III

What Judah had vowed to his father, every parent, in so many words or in wordless determination, has proclaimed to the Lord as his major aim in life:[10] 'I shall be surety for him; at my hand shalt Thou demand him. If

I bring him not unto Thee and set him before thee, all my life shall be failure before Thee.' Thus did generation after generation seek the assurance of a worthwhile future through the dedication to timeless principles and ideals: to bring the children ever back to their Father in heaven, to let them become sharers of the nation's religious and moral ideals. Thus did the good Jew lay the foundation of their education, watch for the wonder of their growing, bestow all his love, all his wisdom, upon their burgeoning personalities. Father and mother were waiting with bated breath for the moment when their children would take the torch from their own, wavering hands to march on towards the Lord's way of justice and mercy.

IV

Life may be a challenge, a dream, a programme, a course, but it knows its limits. The moment comes when we have said our last prayer, offered our last counsel, when we are feeling the ebbing of our strength and welcoming the peace everlasting of a good life and a sturdy faith. It is then the third covenant is made. The wisdom of our tradition inhibits public display of bereavement. No incense, no flowers, nothing that may hide the stern image of death is allowed by our code. Father or mother have entered into the very fabric of our life, what they have bequeathed to us lives on as the deepest asset of our heart and mind. Because we have learned to face the realities of our existence, the inevitable loss of our dearest ones, no psychopathic complex burdens our later years. We have seen the beloved face frozen in the stillness of death, the hands cold, the body motionless. We have accepted the Lord's decree but, at the same moment, we are conscious that the parent's soul or personality will never be lost to us. We are suddenly penetrated by the challenging conviction that what father and mother lived for, must not die with them, that upon us descends the burden of the noble effort, the good fight, the march without end which on their highest level their years gave to us.

Then we pronounce the third pledge: *Yitgaddal veyitkaddash shmeh rabba* – to think, wish, act so that 'His name become ever more sacred,' ever more significant in the life of all around us, of Jews and non-Jews, to the end of days. That prayer contains no word of bereavement, no expression of sadness, no other-worldly fancy or vacation-dream. 'I want to be sanctified in the midst of the children of Israel'[11] has been from the time of the divine behest, sanctified by the character of individual and collective life dedicated to the pursuit of reverence, righteousness, and *raḥamanut* (unselfish love), which His *Torah* teaches. To sanctify His name in the great world by becoming His ambassadors, teachers, priests, warriors for a universal happiness has been the timeless condition for every Jewish generation to deserve the acclaim of 'His special treasure.'[12] That pledge made on behalf of the surviving family, has been the pledge of every generation of loyal Jews in ages of dread persecution as in periods of peace and security. That pledge, uttered in the congregation of fellow-Jews, is to have its echo beyond its confines in a dynamic cooperation of all democratic groups in every continent. However, it is only through the total programme of the *Torah* that Jews can reach the level of a 'kingdom of priests and a holy nation,'[13] capable of inspiring 'the way of the Lord,' the rule of justice and mercy, for the benefit of His children everywhere. Uttered at the moment of shattering disaster, it has proven a source of sustained life.

V

None of us has started the course of Judaism, We are heirs of a millennial tradition and of a task unlimited as to time and place: 'To set the world aright by the kingdom of God Almighty'[14] means to stay glued to the vision of a warless, envyless, hateless, humane society; to stay stubbornly devoted to an uncribbed vista, to a non-deviating loyalty, in the faith not only in God's moral rule of the cosmos, but of enough good men and women ultimately to help bring about 'heavenly days upon earth.'[15] No persecution may dim our view, no prosperity weaken our resolve, no smugness deaden our passion for the good life, the peace, and the happiness 'at the end of days.'[16]

Thus the three covenants, at the dawn of infancy, at the entrance to the gate of love, at the bitter hour of parting, singly and jointly, give meaning to our record. They provide foundations uncrumblable to family happiness and prepare for the moment in the history of the human conscience when 'the earth will be full of the knowledge of the Lord, when none will deal evilly or corruptly with his fellow man'[17] when an astonished and enraptured age will witness the glory of human potentiality in a world of peace and happiness.

The three covenants have formed a meaningful whole that has stood many a strain. *Veḥut hameshulash lo bimeherah yinatek* (the threefold cord will not easily be broken).[18] Faith, folk, the *moledet* (the homeland) – the threefold cord will not be broken. Three concentric circles: the family, the nation, mankind – the threefold cord will endure forever.

Notes

1. II Sam. XXII, 46; Mic., VII, 17.
2. Gen. XVII, 11.
3. *Ibid.*, XVIII, 19.
4. The original meaning of '*educere*', the Latin root of 'education'.
5. *Ḥinnukh*, the source of all dedication to ideals, whence *Ḥannucah* was achieved.
6. Gen. II, 18.
7. Gen. II, 18.
8. Dan. II, 31–35. Cp. Christopher Hibbert's *The Roots of Evil* (Little, Brown, 1966) for the modern appreciation of the crucial role of the family.
9. *Ḥullin*, 92a.
10. Gen. XLIII, 9.
11. Lev. XXII, 32.
12. Exod. XIX, 5.
13. *Ibidem.*
14. *Alenu* prayer in the *siddur*.
15. Deut. XI, 21.
16. Isa. II, 2; Mic. IV, 1–4.
17. Isa. XI, 9.
18. Eccles. IV, 12.

Art in Religion

Normally, one would think of sculpture, of paintings, of skilful weaving, or embroidering, as one reads or hears of 'art in Religion.' Some would remember that the *Torah* prohibits any pictorial presentation of the Deity,[1] for He is above any physical condition, a free spirit without body and the limitations of a body,[2] having nothing that could compare to Him in the world of senses. Devotional literature, too, is art, but it is not normally thought of in this context.

Art is 'the skilful and systematic arrangement or adaptation of means for the attainment of some end.' It is 'the practical application of knowledge or natural ability, the embodiment of beautiful thought in sensuous forms.' For all these tasks, religion offers opportunity. The use of art is mandatory and promises results not only for the enrichment of museums, but also, in all, and especially in religious, education.

For Judaism to become 'a covenant for their generations,'[3] for us to transmit its moral and spiritual values to our children, faith is not enough, integrity is not enough, kindness is not enough. Every generation has its own semantics. Words and ideas assume different meanings because of the subtle or radical events in personal history.[4] What is essential is the presentation of both the world-view and the daily programme of our *Torah* in a manner thought out enough; broad enough with all its depth, deep enough with all its breadth. Only then shall we get the attention, and the acceptance, of our sons and daughters so that what commenced as something father and mother espoused develops into a way of life for our children to endorse, acclaim, and stay devoted to.

I *Art and the Sabbath*

The Sabbath is an institution based on faith in God as the Creator of the world and as the source for standards of human conduct. In terms of our *Siddur* that is simple enough. Paternal example does have some effect on children's life. But the world outside the home, both Jewish and non-Jewish, does not favour a seventh day of perfect rest. It is inconvenient for mundane affairs, from income to sport. It sounds to the mind of the mid-century adolescent like a call to that curious thing: 'ritualism.' The major aspects of the Sabbath remain hidden from the wisdom alike of profound sophomores and ignorant adults.

How can one convey a sense of its beauty, and power? Sermons, however eloquent, are part of 'institutional religion,' insufficiently popular with twist and beatlism, and the whole circus of 'youth's revolt.' Let us discuss but those aspects which are accessible to moderns. Its personal and social implications can be conveyed successfully through the 'art in Sabbath observance,' in the home, the community, and, as a natural consequence, in the world without.

II *The Two Sabbaths*

The word *Shabbat* in the *Torah* has two meanings. It refers either to the seventh Day of Rest,[5] or to the week.[6] The first applies to the prohibition of work, the establishment for twenty-four hours of an atmosphere of physical relaxation and spiritual renaissance; the second to the work-a-day week. The first, as the postulate of our religion, stresses the relation with God, who established the *Shabbat* rest for master and slave, even for the beast of burden; the second, as a postulate of our religion, demands honesty, fair play, compassion in our relation with our neighbour. These two Sabbaths are interdependent. From a genuine attachment to the Creator flows a consistent right attitude towards all His creatures, human and animal. To achieve a harmonious attitude in both aspects of Jewish life is a major goal of all religious and moral education. Too often, excessive accent on the one has served to hide or to excuse non-conformity, or compromising half-conformity, to the other. The wisdom of our

Sages penetrated such fruitless disguise. In terse admonition they said:[7] 'If the children of Israel observed the two Sabbaths (the seventh Day of Rest and the programme of the mundane week), redemption would be their immediate reward.' The Sabbath has to do not only with prohibition of work, but with a message, affecting the six days between one *Kiddush* and the other! As with any other law of the *Torah*, the Sabbath has moral purpose beyond ceremonial ones, indeed the latter crown the former. The *Torah* enjoins:[8] 'The Children of Israel shall make the Sabbath.' 'Make it' in addition to 'observing it.'[9]

III *Parental Art*

The Lord in His compassionate wisdom imposed the Sabbath, a day of emancipation from tensions both physical and emotional. The Jew is bidden to 'make it.' His co-operation is essential for the success of that divine venture. This challenge, to become[10] *Shuttaf bema'asseh bereshit* (a partner with Him in primary creative work), requires loyal observance, consistent pattern of *sh'mirat mitzvot* (keeping the commandments involved.) But beyond that, it requires the manifestation of art, 'the skilful arrangement of means for the attainment of the end.' Piety of the parents is not enough. Enchanting Sabbath cuisine may meet with the youth's sincere acclaim, but will prove insufficient to bring about his own enthusiastic conformity. The weekend often finds an adult exhausted, hence impatient, in Sabbath dress but in a week-day mood. The art of the Sabbath observer must marshal all mental and moral forces for a deliberately planned and cheerfully sustained Sabbath of harmony and loving-kindness. It must not become or appear as a day of mere prohibitions and frustrations, of endless 'no's. The creative genius of the parents, assisted gradually by the emulative trend of son and daughter, must devise and ever improve a Sabbath programme of family intimacy, holiday spirit, co-operative planning – *oneg shabbat* – so that for both generations the day will be one of undiminished joy, towards which they all will be looking longingly[11] as the culmination of love and understanding, as the bridge to unite 'both sides of the river.'[12] A real Sabbath exerts influence throughout the week. Wise ingenuity, buttressed by abounding goodwill, will produce that work of art, the contemplation, collection, and impact of which will shed its light on many days. As a result, the seventh day Sabbath and the six days working period will share in the supreme goal of all religion: the creation, through careful training in an encouraging *milieu*, of fine personalities. Every week then offers both opportunity and challenge in climbing a rung on the ladder of Jacob's profound dream. While the ladder rests firmly on earth, the top reaches the level of heaven,[13] with His inspiration guiding one's steps throughout life.

A hostile witness testifies to the fact that the Sabbath, lived in accord with *Torah* and Rabbinic teaching, indeed bestows upon the Jew the promised boon:[14] 'Anyone who has had the opportunity of knowing in our own day the inner life of Jewish families that observe the Sabbath of the fathers with sincere piety and strictness, will be astonished at the wealth of joyfulness, gratitude, and sunshine, undreamt-of by the outsider, which the Law animates in the Jewish home. The whole household rejoices on the Sabbath, which they celebrate with rare satisfaction not only as the day of rest, but rather as the day of rejoicing. Jewish prayers term the Sabbath a "joy of the soul" to him who hallows it: he enjoys "the abundance of Thy goodness!" Such expressions are not mere words, they are outcome of pure and genuine happiness and enthusiasm'. (Prof. Rudolf Kittel, not unsympathetic to Hitler's Germany).

IV *Kindle the Light*

The *Mishnah*, in a short passage, sums up both process and goal:[15] 'On the eve of the Sabbath, with darkness setting in, a man shall say three things in his house: "Have you given the tithe? Have you arranged the *Eruv*?[16] Kindle the Sabbath lamp!"' Says the *Talmud*:[17] 'These things must be said with sweet reasonableness to be accepted.' 'Have you given the tithe?' challenges every believer to examine his response to social responsibility during the past week: Have you given from what you have earned, from what you know, from what you are, the tithe of help, encouragement, personal service to those in need? Has the seventh-day Sabbath spirit been strong enough for you to live up to these obligations during the work-a-day week?

Through the *Eruv* one includes in one's Sabbath programme some who were outsiders before. The Question reads: 'Have you, by example, admonition, selfless effort, brought during this week into the courtyard of the Lord someone who had been strange to it before? Have you brought: *Taḥat kanfe ha-shekhinah* (under the wings of His presence) a soul destitute of religious vitamins, ignorant, unhappy, frustrated, whom through genuine *Raḥamanut* (unselfish kindness) you may have won over to the peaceful "army of the Lord?"' These challenges may startle the person who never perceived the total programme of the two Sabbaths. They should be met with brave response by one to whom *Torah* is a perpetual promise and task. Only when one can, in good conscience, answer both calls in a positive manner, has one's week been truly lived. Only then may one deserve to kindle the Sabbath light, only then one deserves and receives the full boon of the Sabbath. Thus ritual and ethical are united as means and end, thus Sabbath rest leads to the high level of the week's moral life. Thus religious art partakes alike of the divine and human. The tithe is our answer to the brother's material need, the *Eruv* to his spiritual anaemia. Art in religion uses all human resources, all high ideal and happy charm, all moral commitment and humane perception, to the end: *yom shekullo shabbat umenuḥah leḥaye olamim*: a period suffused with the Sabbath spirit, hence of rest, peace, security for years without end.

Notes

1. Exod. XX, 3.
2. Rambam's Thirteen Doctrines.
3. Exod. XXXI, 16.
4. *Responsa Panim Meirot.*
5. Gen. II, 3.
6. Lev. XXIII, 15.
7. *Shabb.* 118b.
8. Exod. XXI, 16.
9. *Ibidem.*
10. *San.* 38a.
11. The mystic, through philologically correct interpretation of *Vayekhal* Gen. II, 1.
12. *Meg.* 6b.
13. Gen. XXVIII, 12.
14. Soncino *Talmud*, Sabbath, p. XV.
15. *Shabb.* 34a.
16. A symbolical act, to establish a geographical community for the Sabbath, thereby permitting the carrying of objects from one dwelling to another.
17. *Ibidem.*

The Art of Giving

Nothing of any significance is ever achieved without a generous spirit to prompt vision, action, and contribution of gift or service. No sanctuary, no national shrine was ever raised unless there was an outpouring of genuine devotion in planning and execution, with a persevering dedication to overcome normal and unexpected handicaps. Charity is due to more than sentiment; it is the fruit of social awareness and responsibility. In the frame of Jewish thought charity is a legal as well as a moral obligation.

I

Says the sacred book of the *Zohar* (Spiritual splendour): '*Hy man debayee leishtatadala bemitzvah, itzterikh delo yishtaddel beh berikanaya uvemagana*[1] (one who would endeavour to perform a good deed, must beware against doing it in a miserly, vain manner).' That book of remote mysticism and profound moral actuality in its terse language bids the Jew perform every *Mitzvah* in manner ever appropriate to the task involved.

It urges that we share our possessions with the poor, bestowing sympathy and empathy upon the sick and the friendless; that we give generously, fast, and graciously. For charity is more than a commandment, more than a civic enterprise. On its high level it is an art. There is a confluence of source, impulse, and skill, to render *tzedakah* both noble and effective. A gift benefits the recipient or cause, but it will also bestow blessing upon the giver. The Hebrew for 'loving-kindness' – *gemilut ḥassadim* is in the plural (implying two persons bestowing kindnesses). Much as the gift may do for the needy, it does infinitely more for the giver. The rich bestows the gift of money upon the poor; the poor bestows the boon of moral value upon the rich. Every generous, gracious gift refines him or her who offers it. *Tzedakah tatzil mimavet*[2] (charity delivers from death), *Shemesh Tzedakah umarfeh bikhnafeha*[3] (the sun of kindness has healings on his wings) read the texts of our holy literature, emphasizing the therapeutic and, indeed, the life-saving, quality of that *mitzvah*. The beneficiary is not the distressed person alone. To him or her a neighbour's interest proves wholesome and encouraging, as it wards off despondency and deadly despair. That someone is anxious to wipe tears off the sufferer's face, to inspire him with fresh hope, is a blissful encouragement, a powerful antidote to the evil effect of great or prolonged unhappiness. But there are many persons whose selfish way of life lands them eventually in a dead end of frustration. The egoist's cynicism eventually results in disgust and self-contempt. Life to him has nothing more to offer, pleasures have a bitter, stale taste. He is in danger of moral and spiritual demise. But any act of generosity, his single genuine immersion in other people's problems, the deep satisfaction from having restored joy and peace, health and courage, to one on the brink of disaster, may give new meaning to the life of the *Ba'al Tzedakah* (one who performed that kindly act); thereby saving him from moral death. (*Tzedakah tatzil mimavet*).

Many of us occasionally suffer from 'brown hours', when, under the impact of a sensitive conscience, we are prone to belittle the record of our life, to doubt the moral worthwhileness of our personality.[4] In such mood, the memory of charitable purpose truly served and its blessings achieved, will prove cheering and will prevent pessimistic self-appraisal. That may be the true meaning of the popular proverb: *Tipshim notnim, hakhamim lokhim*:[5] 'it is the unwise who stress their having given; the wise know that when they give, in truth, they receive.' The foolish are unduly impressed by whatever kindly act they have performed, looking upon their contribution as a magnificent display of generosity. Wiser folks know that every good deed refines their character, strengthens their will for charitable work, returns to them, in inner felicity, much more than they have spent in gold, silver, or other commodities.

II

What prevents a person from giving charity? The Book of the *Zohar* emphasizes: 'It is the unclean spirit of selfishness,' *Ruaḥ messa'avah*,[6] in control of all miserliness and smallness of mind and heart, at once child of apathy, and father of indifference. Indeed, that ugly spirit marks the face of persons addicted to its evil influence. The warmth of human sympathy lends grace to the homeliest face, whereas selfishness seems to freeze the features in unnatural rigidity. The eyes of a kindly soul shed warmth and beauty; the tight lips of the miser add to the repulsive aspects of existence. The charitable soul prolongs its life, the avaricious one hoards gold and loses vitality. The *Torah* speaks of the 'gifts of gold, silver, and brass' contributed to the sanctuary of the wilderness. The Rabbis saw in that enumeration a classification: gold is the most precious metal, so is the gift of a man in good health, happy and successful, who feels the obligation to share what the Lord has bestowed upon him; so is the gift offered cheerfully, flowing from dynamic love of one's fellow-man. Silver, next in value, symbolizes the grant in the twilight of middle age, when the first shadows of decline invade a person's mind; so is the gift offered as social obligation, as prestige value. Brass is the contribution made grudgingly, slowly, in an almost whining spirit out of mixed fear and superstition, an eleventh hour offer in the hope of ultimate reward or escape from punishment. Gold is the gift of youth and joy, silver the contribution of later years, whilst an eventual postponement of generosity to the direction of a last Will and Testament has a brassy taste and tone. As one gives one receives. Therefore, the *Torah* reads:[7] 'That they take the contribution' for the sanctuary, when one would have expected 'that they give their contributions.' 'Teach them,' the book urges, 'to give of their material possessions that they may take moral and spiritual boons!' The ultimate reward of the good deed lies in the improvement, refinement, perfection of personality which results from that fine habit.

III

There are, as you may know, in every city and community some professional escapists. They cannot give, they claim, much as they would like to do so. They are cardiac cases, their heart will not let them perform that elemental duty. How can one help these poor folks? How can one cure them of their sickness? How can one procure vitamins for their moral debility? Our *Torah* offers the cure in a single line: *Naton titen lo vele yere levavkha betitkha*[8] *lo* (give again and again and thy heart will not trouble thee when thou givest to him).

You can acquire the art of giving again and again. Form the habit of being your brother's keeper, either as an offering of gratitude to the Father of all humans for the boon of life, love, success and happiness that He has bestowed upon you; or because of a deliberate pursuit of social obligation; or out of native sympathy for those He favours: the widow, the orphan, the alien. Learn to give generously so that you meet the recipient's need as far as you truly are able to do so! Learn to give fast, especially in emergencies and also in normal situations because you never know which is the moment of crisis in the life of your fellow-man or how long he can bear the affliction of dependence, the bitterness of lonely pain, the frustration of prolonged want or failure. Give graciously, with words gentle and respectful, with a face of warm smile, with a firm and warm handshake, for you would never know which of these attitudes or acts will produce the crowning harvest of your *mitzvah*!

Giving is an art. It requires a vision of beauty, a clear plan, a trained skill. A generous person is his or her own greatest benefactor. Charity results in ever renewed vitality, in never-flagging interest in life, in a pre-vista of happier human relations produced by comrades in the army of the Lord, marching on for a happier period: from civil rights to orphanage, to old age home, to local charitable enterprise, to global abolition of hunger and disease. What wondrous panorama of happiness, from Federation to Rabbonim Aid, from the Passover Relief to the all-embracing miracle of the United Jewish Appeal – all sources of spiritual comfort, emotional satisfaction, of peace and longevity!

IV

There was one Jewish institution serving such educative purpose. No poet so far has done justice to it, its message has not as yet been set to music. It was your mother's and grandmother's humble tin box, the prosaic *Pushke*. Every Friday eve, before kindling the Sabbath lights, her hands, firm in early age, trembling with the weakness of later years, would put a coin into that box – a nickel, a dime, a quarter, or a dollar. She would thus associate the Sabbath with loving kindness, her festive joy with thought for the poor. The beneficiaries were needy scholars in Israel or an array of *Ḥebras* (societies) for the poor, the aged, the sick. Through the *pushke*, charity became a self-evident part of religious life, a normal expression of faith in Him through care for His children. That box brought a proud smile to the family, a glow to the Sabbath table, as it brought food, shelter, healing to 'the brother that is low.'[9]

A large part of the book of *Shemot* (Exodus) deals with the erection of the portable sanctuary in the wilderness, the gifts for which came from every one 'whose heart prompted[10] him.' Men and women offered of what they had, of what they knew, in truth, of what they were. Women serving that sanctuary, wove precious works and let them speak for their reverence. Artists devoted all their perception of beauty, all their cunning control of fabric and tool, eager to give generously, graciously, and with all dispatch so that that symbol of His mercy, the fountain of abiding God-consciousness, may summon them to His service. From the hearts of these artists emanated holiness, which poured into the Tabernacle. From the Tabernacle came flowing the spirit of reverence, righteousness, and compassion to refine the faithful as it blessed them.

V

Thus shall it be forever: The art of giving wiping out the dark places of the community; the fervour of charity conquering resentment, despondency, despair in human hearts. The knowledge, beyond words, of human interdependence will continue building sanctuaries in the world, the nation, in every community, in every heart.

Notes

1. ad Exod. xxv, 2.
2. Prov. x, 2.
3. Mal. iii, 20.
4. *Logotherapy* by Victor Frankl, 1965.
5. E. J. Hertzman, *Mussar Haskel* a.l.
6. Exod. l.c.
7. Exod. xxv, 2.
8. Deut. xv, 10.
9. Lev. xxv, 35.
10. Exod. l.c.

The Anatomy of Freedom

I *Law and Freedom*

The *Talmud* records[1] a division of opinion: 'The world was created in the month of *Nissan*,' said Rabbi Joshua. 'It was in the month of *Tishri*,' said Rabbi Eliezer. These scholars debated more than details of the calendar. What they had in mind was not the physical origin of the world, but its moral beginnings. Human history, according to the former, commences with freedom. Slavery involves space, time, and people, but there is no world to cherish, no record worth preserving. Only free men and women write the chapters of meaningful life.

Rabbi Eliezer, however, avows that freedom, like knowledge, like possession of health or wealth, is but opportunity or promise. Without moral awareness it will be abused, leading to chaos and misery. It is only the Conscience Days of *Tishri* when we make our peace with God and man that lend significance to our life. The world of human beings commences with the authority of conscience. Millennial experience bears out the essential truth of both positions, one complementing the other.

The word 'anatomy' is defined as the science of the structure of an organism or idea and of its composition. What, then, is the anatomy of freedom? Which are its basic ingredients, its vital conditions? Real freedom first of all must be horizontally unlimited to all. 'Proclaim ye liberty to the earth for all its inhabitants,'[2] says the holy *Torah*. Unless every citizen is granted that minimum, nobody's freedom is secure.

To underpin the horizontal realm of freedom, law is essential. Objective, self-evident, lucidly framed law guarantees an indisputable right. The shameful early 1960 battle in Congress about civil liberties, the worse riots in the south, are but oblique testimony to the fear of the power of law, which upholders of evil entertain.

'There shall be one law and one statute for the alien and the home-born,'[3] proclaims the holy *Torah*. For it is the major asset of law that it is universally valid. That is why patriotism for the Jew is not only a civic but a religious obligation. Indeed, only when the state issues its laws as generally valid, does the principle of *Dina de-malkhuta dina* apply: that in all matters that do not interfere with the laws of our religion, the 'law of the country is the Law for us'.[4]

II *The Law and the Negroes*

The best of the U.S.A. Negroes, in their valiant fight for their rights and their dignity, have chosen the lawful way of passive resistance, including sit-ins and boycott, to help implement the Supreme Court's unmistakable decision against segregation.

The coloured people of South Africa, now suffering degradation, violence, every trick of conscience-less politicians, are, through their resistance, helping the cause of liberty everywhere. Their eventual day of vindication will have a profound impact on the nations of the world, even as the *Shofar* has had on Jewish conscience throughout our history; nor will the echo of that message be long lost even outside the synagogue.

But freedom, to prevail, needs also vertical rivets. Law, with all its majesty, can be thwarted by gross abuse of power, though invisible and almost uncatchable, and by ruthless cunning. Law, to be creative and effective, must be anchored deep in the heart of men and women. It is 'education in depth' that will prove the timeless foundation of liberty. To that end, freedom must be trained into the mind of children, made all-persuasive to the adolescent, becoming for mature men and women as obvious an ideal and a way of life as the bread which we eat and the air we breathe. It will be a blessed reality only as long as any attempt to restrict or undermine it would evoke a spontaneous, impassioned opposition from the whole community. There have been and there may be for a long while yet, insidious pressures to which even good people too often yield. The German nation, for the last hundred years, has suffered periodic moral decline and ultimate catastrophe because her men of science, even her clergy, have lacked the strength of conviction, the depth of understanding, to resist the blandishment of national glory, military prowess, commercial supremacy, with which the *Generalstab* (the hierarchy of the Prussian War Lords) and their henchmen, the captains of industry, have lured them.[5] In every case there resulted a diminution of freedom, an increase of tyranny, a revival of arrogance, and as its ultimate harvest, a ruthless, bloody, lost war.

III *Education for Freedom*

Only intensive, consistent, systematic education for freedom can ensure its prevalence. 'I am the Lord your God, Who brought you out of the land of Egypt,'[6] is a daily reminder for worshipping Jews that freedom is a divine principle. 'I am the Lord Who brought thee out of the house of bondage'[7] is the first of the Ten Words (or Commandments) which every school child is taught at home, in the *Talmud Torah*, and to the reading of which we listen three times a year in the synagogue; with its refrain twice a day in the *Shema* and in countless admonitions, encouragements, maxims, and tales throughout rabbinic literature.

Freedom must be conveyed to the mind so that its benefits be adequately and dynamically demonstrated. Through universal freedom mankind derives the harvest of the creative achievement of all our fellow men and women. It must be conveyed to the heart of young and old so that they all unhesitatingly vote for freedom, believe in freedom, promote freedom out of an intimate understanding of both the agony of serfdom and the joy of liberty.

Just as the rule of law would both establish freedom and prevent its degeneration into licence, so would a full scheme of education in freedom bring forth, as promise and challenge, the contribution of every segment of our citizenry towards the realization of the American dream. The Biblical words about freedom, the historical references to freedom, the luminous leaders in the emancipation of humanity, the glorious champions and fighters for freedom, an international, interdenominational Freedom's Hall of Fame, would help to perpetuate its hold upon the people, encourage an ever-enlarging horizon, and promote, together with a more abundant life, a nobler co-operation among all races, creeds, and colours.

IV *No Tariff*

The furrows of humanity need to be ploughed over in every generation, to prevent stagnation and corruption. In every age there are some men, frustrates, victims of moral malnutrition or other environmental defects, who dream of great power, of personal achievement at all costs, and who are attracted to force and deceit as means to their end. Only a well-informed, morally well-trained public opinion can prevent their incipient growth, a social infection, producing the Hitlers and Stalins of every age and clime.

Thus, the anatomy of Freedom discloses that it is a two-dimensional asset, horizontal in its universality, vertical in the deep roots it must strike in the personality of individual and collective man; that the former must be based on legal enactment and the latter is achievable through an all-embracing scheme of training; that freedom is at once a divine principle, an indispensable foundation of social welfare, and a vital condition for human culture. The creative impulses of humanity, liberated by freedom, and restrained by law, hold the greatest promise for a long chapter of human happiness and worthwhileness. 'Freedom,' says the *Talmud*, 'is the privilege of the traveller to move everywhere: and to bring the assets of humanity to all the corners of the world;[8] for freedom means emancipation from the isolation of exile, the fear of death,[9] from the agonies of humanity.[10] A free man affirms life,[11] his own freedom encourages general liberty,[12] his goal will be the proclamation of freedom for all His children everywhere.'[13]

Notes

1. *Rosh Hashana*, 2a.
2. Lev. xxv, 10.
3. Num. xv, 16.
4. See my *Jewish Foundations of the New World Order*, *Jewish Library*, Vol. iv.

5. See F. W. Foerster's *Erlebte Geschichte*, Nuremberg 1953.
6. Num. xv, 40.
7. Exod. xx, 2.
8. *Rosh Hashana* 9b; see also Ibn Ezra on Lev. xxv, 10.
9. *Midrash Shem.* R.32.
10. *Ibid.* 41.
11. *Tanna de be Eliy.*
12. *Kiddushin* 15b.
13. *Sifre, Behaal* 77.

The Challenge of Humanism

I *Potent Arguments*

In the confusion of our days the question has been heard again and again: Does one need religion to live a good life? Do not the extraordinary successes of the human mind justify the proud boast that man can now assume confidently responsibility for his own attitudes and actions without reference to, or dependence on, supernatural powers, i.e. God?

One does not fully answer this argument by pointing to the modern dilemma, between the promise of unheard-of progress and the threat of total annihilation, both fruit of the atomic age.

Indeed, the attack on faith may be strengthened by the lamentable record in human relations of the world's most efficient organized religion. I have heard the Christian dogma of original sin cynically endorsed by reference to wellnigh two millennia of Church persecution, ungodly priests' ranting against helpless outsiders, and by Protestant cruelties from Luther to our own times. From countless pulpits in our days one may still hear ruthless condemnation of the whole Jewish people of today for what according to the Gospels some folks in Jerusalem are reported to have done two thousand years ago. There still are persons guilty of half-hidden incitements to every form of anti-Jewish actions from social discrimination to bloody pogroms. The good that some Christians have performed is overshadowed by the terror of the Inquisition, the hatred of Polish and Croat and Slovak priests during the second World War. Today, Judaism is still the only monotheistic religion which does not condemn outsiders, which, as a matter of law, for the last two thousand years has proclaimed that the righteous among the (other) nations of the world are accepted by God and have a share in the world to come; that they must be granted fair and kindly treatment by Jews, individually and collectively.

Fifteen hundred years ago the Church created the Ghetto, cut off from nature, a habitation of darkness, danger, and utter misery. Early in the nineteenth century the Russian Pale, decreed by cruel illwill, reduced millions of our people to poverty and made them helpless pariahs. Such systematic affliction would have warped the nature of any group, making them bitter, furious in deadly resentment, callous to human suffering.

The testimony of our very persecutors, and the reports of modern sociologists reveal the Ghetto and the *Shtetl* of Europe, as a place of noble moral milieu. 'These accursed Jews,' admits a baffled medieval German, 'never beat their wives, engage in drunkenness or turn the hungry from their door.' It was the fruit of a life in God, unaffected by man's inhumanity to man.

From a Jew there should come no question as to the moral efficacy of his religion. It has been in shining evidence throughout *Galut* and Ghetto.

II *Jewish Humanists*

Nobody is more blind than he who does not want to see; none more intolerant than he who attributes intolerance to our Holy *Torah*. Authentic Jews, nonetheless, may not denounce such unjust assaults as due to sheer hypocrisy. They, rather, indicate a kind of self-deceiving obtuseness. When the Emancipation came, many of our people were overwhelmed by its roseate promise and they rushed out of the synagogue into 'German freedom and brotherhood.' It took one hundred years of Teutonic calculated illwill, culminating in Nazi beastliness, to teach a broken remnant the wisdom of returning to the Jewish way of life. Contemporary Jewish humanists suffer from similar error; hence, long after Wellhausen's own disciples had demolished the citadel of Biblical criticism, it was that Jewish 'intelligentsia' that clung piously to his discredited position. John Dewey was misinformed as to the *Torah*'s point of view by some of the same group; in their iconoclastic zeal they identified the faith of our Fathers with every fundamentalist folly and every un-Jewish narrowness.

There are two types of Jewish assimilationists as yet unredeemed. The first, on their knees before Western culture, looked down upon refugees from behind the iron curtain of Czar or Soviet and aimed at but one hundred percent Germanism or Frenchism, ignoring, belittling, or denying, their Jewishness. The second World War taught them a sobering lesson. There were also Eastern European assimilationists. The corruption of the Czarist Church had afflicted labouring classes who, in their reaction, identified all religion with the cruel hypocrisy of the Russian hierarchy. Israel still suffers from that type of collective psychosis: many of its leaders are still unrid of that irreligious infection from the experiences of their youth or the partisan literature of 'Bund' and other radical movements.

Some American preachers of religious dissent blithely deny the authenticity of Moses and the very existence of God. But they wax furious with anyone daring to cast doubt upon the implied utter finality of their own theories, their sociological insights, their ultimate wisdom! They lack a sense of humour.

The Jewish humanists are our burden, objects of our profound sorrow. It is only by the example of wise, patient, consistent life in accord with the teaching of our traditions that we may hope eventually to restore them to a measure of authentic happy Jewishness: as they re-discover the source of all Israel's nobility, the rock of Jewish history, the classic faith in *Avinu Shebashamayim* – our Father Who is in heaven.

III *The Courage of Faith*

A former inmate of Auschwitz, apropos of a recent attack on religion, told of her experience: 'The ingenuity of our tormentors grew in subtlety and horror from day to day. When matters of camp administration kept them busy, our suffering was normal, heavy but still tolerable. When they were at leisure, their sadism knew no limit. It was under the impact of such dreadful humiliations that some of our fellow-victims threw themselves against the electrically-charged fence for an excruciating but speedy end to their agony.

'But not a single religious woman in the *Lager* resorted to that act of despair! Our faith sustained us in the darkest nights as no system of science or philosophy could have done. We lived and many died without any inner surrender to the evil world around us.'

What this *Torah*-true woman related, has been borne out countless times in the annals of Jewish history. With a wisdom unrelated to logical finesses, the pious folk of Israel have clung to faith in God and His *Torah*, whilst some of their 'more cultured' brethren forsook the ethical sublimity of our tradition for the 'refinement' of their past oppressors. No *Torah*-true Jew or Jewess, even in seemingly hopeless condition, would betray the timeless task of our people: to stay dedicated at all costs to freedom of conscience, to the programme of reverence, righteousness, and *raḥamanut*, the *kedushah* (holiness) of Jewish life.

It was the Jew's faith in *El raḥum ve'ḥannun* (God, merciful and gracious), which had rendered those qualities solid realities of their life. Not for them Nietzsche's sneer of moral ideals being but the sheep's self-deceptions, illusions of the weak, temporary devices for national survival or communal coherence! To our ancestors as to loyal Jews of today, our historical ideals are the very conditions of a human, humane life.

The life of our forefathers was based on the moral postulates of the *Torah*, the revelation of God's creative will. Hence not the darkest valley could dim their light, nor the wiliest despot rob them of their challenge and promise. We know of no humanist generation strong enough to survive its loss of faith. But we do know: *ve-attem hadevekim bashem elokekhem hayyim kulkhem hayom* – (You who cling to the Lord your God, are alive, all of you, to this day) and for the future.

IV *The Double Orientation*

Ne'eman – the Hebrew word for 'faithful', in Rashbam's perceptive interpretation means 'riveted, immovable'. One who reaches that level of utter faithfulness, will, indeed, find in God the immovable Rock of the Ages who grants security, solace, and serenity to him who is a true believer, *ki be-y-ah Hashem tzur olamim.*

We must stay ever aware of the human situation: whilst the 'soul which Thou gavest us is pure' it is subject to temptation. Jews reject the notion of original sin which damns and dooms all unbaptized human beings, from the baby at mother's breast to the noblest of non-Christians. But we do know that happiness and worthwhileness (*yeshuah*) are achievable only through consistent strenuous effort towards realizing the perennial challenge of our faith: that we overcome the *yetzer ha-ra* (the temptation to do evil) through the *yetzer tov*, which means the determination to translate our faith in God into the upright, kindly, humble programme of our life.

No human being is beyond redemption as long as he is conscious, in however tenuous a manner, of the ultimate basis of the good life: the faith in a just, merciful, omniscient Father in heaven. Neither is a human able to build a place of dignity, moral significance, or stability who does not recognize as the objective unchangeable foundation of his life – faith in, allegiance to, and mandate from, a divinely devised and directed moral cosmos. There is no greater evil, said the Psalmist, no deeper source of corruption, than the fool's assertion 'There is no God.' It is that pronouncement which both provokes and explains 'his perverse and abominable ways.' The total tyrannies of our generation offer melancholy commentary to that hoary wisdom. Only on the basis of such actual denial of the divine could the 'Thousand Years' Reich' have persisted during the twelve years of its hellish regime, with its *tum'ah* (moral filth) infecting four continents. Only that ultimate uprooting of humanity through defying the existence of God could have produced the organized lie, the cynicism of Fascist or Soviet ruthlessness.

Humanism, at best, is inspired by a hopeless optimism, empty of an understanding of the double orientation of the human soul and of its position between the heaven of the godly life and the inferno of a presumptuous faith in godless man. Humanism needs the catalyst of common sense to come of age.

V *The Case of the 'Righteous but Irreligious Individual'*

It happened at a public discussion of this topic, engaged in by a teacher of philosophy who was born a Jew and his opponent, a rabbi of *Torah*-true views. The humanist speaker offered his trump argument: 'You know me as a man of rectitude, liberalism, and common decency. I have no prejudice against any human being and am ever ready to help a person of any race, creed, or colour. Yet I accept none of your theistic position. I never put on *Tefillin*, observe no dietary laws and do not go to *Shul*. I am opposed to organized religion claiming monopoly of salvation and I'll have no truck with parsons of any denomination. I for one did not and do not need theistic religion to teach me morality.' (Observe how he lumped together Jewish tolerance with non-Jewish fundamentalism!)

When the self-satisfied professor had sat down, the rabbi countered his argument: 'You suffer from a very narrow view of your own personal history. Being completely sunk in the contemporary scene, you forget that your way of life did not start with yourself. The set of moral principles which you adhere to, are to but a very limited extent the fruit of your own thinking and living. You are the product of many generations of Jews who believed in God and lived in accord with His law. You are actually living on the spiritual capital of your pious ancestors whom faith in God inspired to noble living. They transmitted to you with their physical genes also their spiritual and moral assets. For an assessment of your life – devoid of faith in God and acceptance of His *Torah* – we shall have to wait for your grandchildren, if, indeed, your attitude will be bequeathed to them as a decisive set of principles. By that time the assets of your own ancestors may have suffered sufficient corrosion and therefore the character of your progeny, the grandchildren, may indicate the value of your own way of life. Until then, you are being morally fed from a source which you deny, but whose benefits, consciously or unconsciously, you are enjoying. The *Talmud* urges: 'Do not throw stones into the fountain from whose water you have drunk.'

Let Jewish humanists of every hue remain humbly grateful for the moral nourishment they have drawn, before their 'enlightment' rendered them impervious to the light of the *Torah*.

VI *The Survival of the People*

The Jewish prophets, in accord with the teaching of *Moshe Rabbenu*, foretold and interpreted the destruction of the Jewish state, the burning of the Temple, and the sufferings of the *Galut*, as divine punishment for our ancestors' stiff-necked violation of the laws revealed in God's *Torah*. The same supremely courageous men held out hope for eventual restoration as a reward for national return to God. 'On the day the Temple was destroyed, the Messiah was born.' The rabbis stress that repentance came with the fulfilment of the divine threat and when penitence will be complete, genuine, and universal, the Messiah will initiate the ultimate ingathering for universal peace and happiness. The longing for such consummation has ever inspired the Jewish people. Their prayers have been surging heavenwards in yearning supplication, in contrite plea, in solemn pledge, ever since they were flung out, bruised, naked, helpless from the gates of Zion and the land of our Fathers. In *Galut*, in a hostile world, they found themselves utterly alone. The sun of kindness shone exceedingly rarely upon their misery. Contemptuous hatred rendered their centuries bitter and dark.

What sustained them was faith in God's mercy Whom they knew as *Elokim*, stern Judge, and *av haraḥaman*, compassionate Father. Whilst the world laughed at the Jewish dream of a return, they prayed on undeterred. Religious Jews would brave a thousand perils to wend their way homewards, a thousand years before Herzl, and ever after. When Hellenistic compromisers would rush to fashionable heathen rites, the religious Maccabees won a heroic fight for the ancient faith. The rewards offered for conversion to Christianity and disappearance from the 'poor, storm-tossed nation' were tremendous, but they failed to sway the stubborn faith of our forefathers. Zion and Jerusalem remained living assets, luminous promises, eternal challenges. Based on Judaism, the Jewish masses withstood both periods of levelling universalism and ages of nationalist fervour. His Book of Books gave them root, rock, and direction.

Modern Israel could not have come about without our people's timeless faith in the coming redemption. The very nation that gave us the interregnum of the mandate looked upon Israel's return to Palestine as a biblical promise come true. Israel as people, Israel the republic, owe their origin, history, survival to faith in God.

Jewish humanists may well take that lesson to heart. It may bring them truth, peace, happiness.

VII *The Promise of Israel*

In a remarkable book by Justice Zilberg of Israel's Supreme Court, the author complains about the republic's failure to draw on principles and precedents of Jewish law for the adjudication of civil cases and criminal offences. Some time ago I had occasion to animadvert on the lack of wisdom which keeps civil law in the *Moledet* on 'Turkish crutches and British wheelchairs instead of on the soaring wings of *Shekhinah*,' the oral and written tradition of the *Torah*.

The social ethics of Judaism, preserved in *Torah*, *Talmud*, and Codes, are derived not from Jewish mental brilliance, but from the teachings of the Divine Lawgiver, Creator of the World, and omniscient Father of every human being. The protection of every individual against discrimination and oppression is enjoined in the Holy *Torah*. The fair treatment of the alien and of all underprivileged persons is as basic as the law concerning *Shabbat* and *Kashrut*. Arbitration as the way of justice and peace has been a hoary institution in the annals of Jewish law. Not only the land of Israel is God-promised, but what has inspired judges and statesmen from Moses to Rav Assaf is God-derived.

Humanists, who would fain deprive us of these foundations, would have to go shopping for their new code from court to court, to assemble a motley of laws and legal customs for a *pot-pourri* of their choice.

The very notion of International Law appears first in the *Torah*, in the Seven Noahide principles, the observance of which guaranteed to any non-Jew in the Jewish state citizen rights and privileges without obliging him to join the country's official religion; and this at a time when the foreigner in every other country of the world was a welcome prey of king and commoner, suspect, abused, robbed, killed, without recourse to any court of justice.

Israel's sturdy population of two millions has made great contributions to democratic life, in the fields alike of literature, science, and technical progress. Our people there have literally followed a glorious biblical example: 'building with one arm, defending themselves with the other.'

There has been some indication of a new appreciation of the power, wisdom, and beauty of life according to the *Din Torah*.

Israel may yet teach Jewish humanists (in her own borders as well as *bekhol tefuzot hagolah* – all over the dispersion of the *Galut*) what they truly need: a sense of proportion and an appreciation of the enduring grace of the God-given culture of our people.

VIII *The Goal and the Way*

Devekut (clinging to God) does not mean passive attachment. Judaism does not offer us any soft pillow to rest on, no soothing dogma the acceptance of which would at once bring us peace of mind. The *Talmid Hakham* (scholar of the *Torah*), the only nobleman recognized in our sacred literature, whose standards in theory and practice are very high, is warned that 'no peace awaits him anywhere,' the *Torah* issuing especially to him a challenge to just action and generous attitude throughout his life.

The discipline of the *Torah* insists on theoretical acceptance of its ideals, and on practical conformity to them as equally important. The *Torah* also insists on submission to a programme of study and character-training for the concretization of its ideals and the realization of its ultimate goals.

Both, the goal and the way towards it, are part of the divine mandate. Every individual *Mitzvah* (commandment or good deed) forms an indispensable part of the programme to form habits resulting in a personality strong and good enough for steady progress towards the beckoning goal: living, God-inspired Jewishness. In this training, symbol and ceremony have their role: they help to bring about the turning from evil, the choice of the good in the hundred acts and attitudes of life, the encouragement through repeated decisions of proper tendencies, the weakening and gradual cancellation of wrong urges by repeated avoidance of the factors which encourage them. It is the road of benevolence and public prayer, personal effort, and courageous commitment to law-abiding fealty; of devotion to truth and benign judgment of one's fellow man. The total programme of the *Torah*-true life includes the voluntary acceptance of its discipline in the conviction that submission to its method will promote the perfection of one's ethical personality and as a consequence will result in acceptance by God.

There are basic doctrines the normal Jew accepts and the study of whose meaning is part of the calendar of Jewish duty. But such acceptance and study, if unsubstantiated by the calibre of his life, would remain but intellectual exercise or abstract declaration, bereft of any influence on his moral development. The study of the *Torah*, for its complementation and fulfilment, requires simultaneous living in accord with its laws. Matter and form, letter and spirit, theory and practice, are interdependent. No mere conformity without genuine endeavour to understand, no mere study without the discipline of living, can ever result in full Jewishness!

It is as the fruit of their interpenetration, achieved in the emanation of spirit from moral exercise, in the refinement of pious adherence by a questing devout mind, that *kirvat elokim* (nearness to) God blesses His children all over His world.

IX *The Unknowable*

The man of faith sees the whole world, life, man, as having had their beginning by the creative will of God. That, beyond all philological and homiletical ingenuity, is the meaning of the first verse of the *Torah.* As to what happened or was before then, it is vain to enquire. All knowledge of nature or man deals with the moment of the creation and what followed.

The man of science or philosophy essentially faces the same limitations to his search and insight. The story of the beginning will eternally baffle them. The knowledge of new elements and what gives them essence or causes their disintegration, all the countless discoveries in laboratories, all the working theories emanating from fertile and ingenious minds, leave the question of the when and why of the beginning unanswered and unanswerable. Poor Thomas Huxley's boast that at the end of the road of science ultimate truth beckons, has for almost a hundred years been a vain boast.

The pious thinker sees religion and science as two parallel ways towards ultimate verities converging in the infinity of God and leaving a margin, narrowed in the process, but never totally abolished. The humanist, in rejecting supernaturalism, substitutes human wisdom and self-achieved perfection for the omniscience of God and for His standards of moral values. What distinguishes a religious person, a theist, is his acceptance of bedrock foundations of morality, unchangeable because God-given. His is the conviction that since the ideals rooted in them are realisable, they will eventually be accepted and acted upon by normal persons, with the claim to their fealty as self-evident as the preservation of life or the pursuit of happiness.

The man of faith has his problems. The book of Job, the chapters of *Kohelet,* the discussions in our sacred literature of the problem of evil, of suffering and sorrow, all the animadversions of *Talmud* and *Zohar,* of Baal Shem Tov, the Gaon of Vilna, and Rav Kook, bear eloquent testimony to the believer's ceaseless effort to grasp, within human possibilities, the mind of God in the affairs of man. Leibnitz, Kant, and a few modern thinkers have laboured in the same field.

For the humanist, in his self-imposed darkness, there are few answers besides Bertrand Russell's pessimism or the sterility of agnostics. The humanist has abandoned the hope for discovering the answers which faith offers. He pursues the quest for the true, the good, and the beautiful without assurance of their ultimate meaning or any universal authority to civilize man forward and upward to their realization. With every individual as the single source of his conscience, all humanist principles and ideals hobble along on the crutches of irredeemable relativity.

X *The Panorama of our Religion*

Many Jewish humanists would like to reduce Jewish religiosity to a dark corner in the museum of national antiquities. They claim that *Torah*-true Judaism is interested but in community prayers (which 'modern Jews do not have to attend'), in *kosher* butcher shops (which humanists for the benefit of 'primitive Orthodox' are willing to allow to continue), in indigestible dishes totally unrelated to Judaism (for which, curiously enough, emancipated swallowers of *Tarfut* have incredible craving), and in tearful *Yahrzeit Kaddish* (which, for 'folkway reasons,' the most hard-boiled humanist generally espouses).

But the panorama of Judaism knows of no confinement. There is no aspect of the good life that has not been fostered by the faith of classic Jewry. Every form of philanthropy is a hoary Jewish religious institution. Social responsibility has throughout our history been translated into private conscience and public administration, from the laws of *Vayikra* through the *takanot* (ordinances) of the *Soferim* and the enactments of the Jewish *kehillot*, from ancient Babylonia through medieval and modern Germany, Poland, Italy, and Greece.

Few things are more amusing than the assumption or claim of some Jewish humanists that they have discovered, or first advanced, the cause of righteousness, tolerance, or intelligent study of ancient texts and temporary conditions. The teacher in the *Mishnah* who urged that we immerse ourselves in the ocean of *Torah* knew that there is no facet of human activity that has not been ennobled through faith in God, no problem of good and evil which has not engaged the close and earnest attention of the God-dedicated teachers and disciples of *Torah*. Some Jewish humanists deplore and oppose the fact that rabbis 'play too great a role in Jewish life' (*halevay!*) and urge their replacement in the councils and the executive work of the community by 'enlightened secularists.' They proceed on the quaint assumption that the abandonment of faith in God automatically endows the atheist with deep knowledge, unselfish devotion, and a host of other virtues and skills. It is the most recent version of the superstitious belief that the eating of a ham sandwich bestows upon its consumer some mystic gift of righteousness and mercy denied to the loyal adherent of *Kashrut*.

We would offer this sincere advice to the humanists in our camp: Cultivate a sense of humour and of modesty! A sage of old put it thus: 'Be exceedingly humble, for the hope of a mere mortal (unrelated to God) is but the worm.' *Shalom al Israel.*

XI *The Practical Difference*

What really matters are not philosophical differences, important though they may be. The *Torah* does not pretend to be a text-book of chemistry, though it teaches abiding truth about the Creator of the elements. It eschews offering detailed instructions about every aspect of economics although it states the principles of social welfare in unmistakable terms.

He who accepts 'the yoke of the kingdom of heaven' thereby subscribes to a set of laws, approaches, attitudes which teach the way to peace and the road to worthwhileness; whereas he who will be guided by his own thinking only, will find it more difficult than a religious person to withstand temptation and will be less eager because of consideration of ethical ideas to desert his chance for temporary happiness.

That men normally religious have stumbled is no argument against religion. Their faith was not strong enough, wise enough, to make them follow its teaching through. The conscience of the religious person, rooted in God, will bring him back after a lapse, because it will plague him till he recognizes the error or wrong he committed. The man whose scruples and inner mandates derive from his own thinking, with himself as the ultimate authority, will, under the pressure of his desires, suffer from an inner dichotomy, a veritable schizophrenia. He may, as 'a superman beyond good and evil' view his actions as at least as justified as those of the strict 'slavish' followers of the law of Moses. All of us have been saddened by the contemporary example of atheistic national depravity, proving the truth of this assertion.

True, the profession of religion *per se* does not guarantee ethical conduct. The *Talmud* quotes a great sage who would refuse to accept mere performance of ceremonial duties as proof of righteousness. But faith in God, in Hermann Cohen's pregnant phrase, has the proof for the reality of righteousness, love, loyalty. Because He is the All-wise, All-just,

All-merciful Father, He stands behind them and establishes their reality. Hence a man of faith cannot lose permanently the sense of their vital importance.

Even the cowardly or traitorous soldier may find the way back to his flag. But if it be lowered or changed, he will not find it and his fine impulse may be thwarted or cancelled. This is the worst aspect of humanism: It lowers the moral law from a divine, sublime, hence eternally potent essence to something left to the judgment of man, who is ever subject to change, often rootless and bootless.

We pray and shall be ever eager to work, for the humanists' return to the source of all goodness, truth, peace: the Lord of the world, Father of every human being, Who has given us the glorious, often most painful task of being His ambassador to mankind; to teach His life by the tenor of our acts and the quality of their motivations.

Religion in the Concrete

I *The Personal Programme*

What is religion? A set of mystic ideas? A twilight dream? A palatal habit? A combination of unworldly ideals, a never-never land of fog and superstition? Religion is a system of thought, faith, and action: thought to provide a mental frame, faith to lend it direction, action for challenge and promise. Faith endorses the meaning of the world, of human history, of one's own career. Faith upholds the ultimate core of decency in the normal personality: the possibility (as a minimum) and potentiality (as a development) of human endeavour towards a period of global peace and security.

The root meaning 'religion', derived from the Latin, is a state of being 'tied-up', first with God as Creator, Providence, and Lawgiver. But such relation needs another to make it creatively meaningful. A religious person must be tied up with the problems of his fellowman, with the pre-vision of co-operation and mutual aid, of justice as the basis and compassion as the crown, of social responsibility. 'It is in your mouth (to utter), in your heart (to feel, cherish), in your hands to do it'.[1]

The twentieth chapter of Exodus, dealing with Revelation, is followed immediately by the one prescribing legislation. 'Place the *Sanhedrin* (Supreme Court) next to the altar', is the meaning of this context, say the Rabbis.[2] National and communal justice, constructive interest in the poor, the widow, the orphan, is Religion in the Concrete.

II *Words versus Deeds*

As general principles these behests are attractive, lending themselves to passionate oratory and loud popular approval. But these principles are too precious to entrust to the wholesale care of governments or congresses. They are our intimate, basic, private concerns. Too often, as they interfere with private ambition, with ruthless egotism, they become unpleasant to the individual ear. Conscience at times is as harsh as the voice of the *Shofar*, too loud for the comfort of the heedless pusher towards his own ends, who is undisturbed by decent regard for truth and mercy. Because the voice of conscience cannot be abidingly stilled, its very incessant demand provokes a countervailing emphasis on 'If I am not for myself, who will be for me?'. But he who voices it is unaffected by Hillel's warning: 'But if I am for myself only, who am I?'[3] The crux of the problem lies in public acceptance and private rejection of ethical religion as the sole arbiter of conduct.

The danger to religion in our own days comes not from Moscow or Peking. Both are symptoms of a deeper problem: the gap between profession and practice. What embitters the best of our students is the failure of organized religion to stand up valiantly, uncompromisingly, for the prophetic imperative: 'to do justice, to love mercy, and to walk humbly with thy Creator'.[4] What our young men and women are missing is an 'establishment' whose 'Yes' is 'Yes', whose 'Nay' is 'Nay',[5] whose 'whereas' comes not to camouflage evasion and moral flabbiness, but aims to present both sides of any problem, collective or individual, in clear language and blessed by consistent action. What they resent is the proclamation of high ideals at conventions, in smooth articles, and fervent speeches, whilst private programmes are motivated by sordid considerations of profit, financial or social. What aids communism and atheism are not philosophical or sociological ideas, but the lamentable failure of modern democracies to live up to their poetic or prosaic constitutions. 'If some one sees troubles encompassing him, let him examine his own conduct,'[6] Granted, some longhaired students go beyond what is right and proper in their violent protests, that the raucous messages from Moscow share in equal measure extreme insincerity and the shabby quality of 'double-think'[7] (allowing the same innocuous words to describe polar differences of sentiment and action), the wisest, truest way of dealing with them is less of violent reaction exclusively to their low moral standards and more of re-examination of one's own record. Foaming at the mouth as yet has never produced happier, finer human relations.

III *Of Moral Corrosion*

The single purpose of our history from Abraham to the days of the Messiah is this unerring, unchanging recognition of life as a challenge. 'To be a kingdom of priests and a holy nation'[8] is a goal, not a starting point, for every generation and for every individual Jew. It was as hard and unpopular a task in the age of universal heathenism as it has been ever since and in particular in our own times. In the periods of Israel's loyalty to this programme we were indeed 'the light to the nations'.[9] From the womb of such noble dedication came the two daughter religions and, indeed, also the liberalizing and humanizing movements of the last two centuries. What the unbiassed Gentile knows, the uninformed Jew has as yet not absorbed: the conviction that moral corrosion from within is more deadly to Israel than all the organized illwill from without. Truly, we are not the chosen people unless we choose in every age to stay committed in thought, word, and action to our religion and to the atmosphere which renders its laws real.

We have had the majestic utterances of Isaiah to lend contemporary and timeless emphasis to the *Torah*'s programme of the good life. His statemanship has impressed the noblest leaders of men in many centuries and countries. The sobbing plea of Amos has penetrated the heart of many a king, general, and other sinner since it was first uttered. But it is in particular one of Jeremiah's speeches that has unique meaning in our own days. Throughout his ministry he emphasized the moral élite of his flock as the single purpose of their life. Throughout his life he castigated evasion, no less than reckless pursuit of selfish conduct, as treason both against God and against the decent aspirations of the common folk. He had spoken out in unmistakable terms aginst the stupidity, cruelty, and corruption of heathenism. None had castigated more bitterly the unclean superstitions of neighbouring kings, priests, and potentates who kept their people in dark fear of demons, devils, and witches, who deadened their sense of justice and mercy and drove them into ever more gruesome roads of perversity and abasement. But Jeremiah knew with even clarity that whilst one may acknowledge the misery of idolatry, the accent of a true prophet must remain on the tragedy of the unbridged gap between ideal and real, between profession and practice, among those that belonged to what is now called the 'Establishment'.

IV *Samaria versus Jerusalem*

In three timeless verses does he offer his message: 'I have seen unseemliness among the prophets of Samaria',[10] but that was neither unexpected nor fatal in their environment. The kings, queens, and soothsayers of Samaria were a reprehensible, morally low group. From them one could expect nothing else. To them Jeremiah's messages had been delivered, but since they openly opposed the Lord and his ethical imperatives, one could continue preaching to them whilst staying aware of the deplorable level they maintained. But it was different with Jerusalem. There, the Establishment protested its loyalty to God. There, so-called prophets proclaimed in fervent words their fealty to the *Torah* of Moses. There stood the Temple in all its glory, the sacrifices never stopped, the priests offered their service and pronounced their blessings. But their voices were not the voices of holiness, their messages were falsifications. What they gave the populace was fake religion. What they lived was shameless defiance of divine rules: 'In the prophets of Jerusalem I have seen the horror of venality':[11] principles for sale, convictions changed in accord with the highest bidder, every moral principle subject to sordid bargaining. It is not from heathen Samaria but 'From the prophets of Jerusalem hypocrisy has gone forth into all the land'.[12]

V *Jeremiah in Mid-Century*

This is the message of Jeremiah for mid-century American Jewry: in the synagogue, as in the place of business, in the privacy of the family, and above all in the sanctuary of our conscience, we must stay ever committed to the *Torah*'s moral imperatives. True, atheists and their confrères, communists, and fascists, are a thorn in the civic body and a perpetual source of trouble. True, 'the moral élite' repudiate their lying propaganda and condemn their outrageous conduct. But they themselves, too often, by their conduct, are denying the Source of all goodness, truth, and beauty and openly worship the idols of irresponsible powers, some thinly disguised racial mythology, made to order to befog heedless followers. Theirs is not merely what Jeremiah calls *Tiflah* (unseemliness).

The real danger to Jews and Judaism, as to any worshipping group, comes not so much from theological theories as from the profound gap between words and deeds of the 'established' laity and ministry. What Jeremiah says is: Few among you are guilty of the major vice, hypocrisy. Few of you cheat in business or in your professional work. But the impact of even a few evil personalities on the many who observe their conduct or hear about it, is deleterious indeed. Half-truths uttered by 'orthodox' Jews are infectious. They create derision, scoffing, and eventually, hypocrisy. The merely smart rabbi, the prevaricating teacher, the popular leader with his ear to the ground and his eyes playing heavenwards to mislead the unwary: the man whose word may never be taken at full value: the layman or minister whose cleverness lets him 'get away with evasions' when truth proves unprofitable – all of them are sources of *Shaarura*, scandalous venality, odious disease. Such phony rabbinic statements about Justice, Truth, and Mercy become evil in the light of their own performance. Theirs is a pernicious cheapness of conduct which poisons the mind and heart of youth. In one of his wise plays, Ludwig Fulda has his hero say: 'I do not believe in principles, having seen so many having holes through which a man and his family are slipping to profitable violation of what they are meant to uphold'.

VI *Careless Conformists*

Such violation starts from apparently petty offences. One is the disregard for the sanctity of the House of God. Unfortunately that has, for generations of American Jewry, been almost the hallmark of orthodox services. The offenders, deplorably, are not the ignorant alone, but some whose knowledge ought to prevent the bad behaviour because of which Orthodoxy had, for decades, been a bad joke in the consciousness of American Jews. The *Shulḥan Arukh*, our code of law, in many a chapter, urges respectful prayer and complete silence during services. The men who know the code and often successfully and unselfishly lead communal enterprises, seem smitten by intellectual blindness, hence they enter the *shul* with cheap cocksureness, wave, improperly but energetically, to friends and relatives, later on to bestow upon neighbours right and left the benefit of the latest anecdote or the profound wisdom of their animadversions on men and affairs. It is selfish lack of self-discipline which interferes with the dignity of the worship and, too often, robs their unfortunate fellow-worshippers of a chance to commune with God, to meditate, to concentrate on the sacred text.

But the effect on the character of the offenders is more injurious. They learn to consult only their convenience, hence lack consideration for others as they ignore decent standards of behaviour in the synagogue. Their own personalities eventually show the mark of such low indulgence and what they offer to their children is an inferior image of Jewishness. From synagogue such attitude enters the home, the office, and the counting house.

VII *The Ultimate Evil*

Our problem is not faith versus science. Great scientists, from Einstein to Compton, have declared that, all academic achievement notwithstanding, science can neither explain the origin of the world nor, on the basis of its own categories, offer guidance for the good life. Scientists have become more modest since old Huxley. Religionists, on the other hand, have learned to distinguish between fealty to the law of their denomination, and freedom of interpretation in metaphysical matters. What the Establishment has failed in, is the promotion of justice, mercy, and security in our days and in the creation of a finer image of ecclesiastical teachers and leaders. 'The only vice that cannot be forgiven is hypocrisy', said William Hazlitt.[13] What we need to regain our youth, to achieve moral and emotional stability, is integrity, consistency, and unselfish love for all our fellowmen.

What Jeremiah castigated, his disciples, the Rabbis, in *Talmud* and *Midrash* have made the perennial object of their discourses and warnings. 'A hypocrite will never see the face of God',[14] his falseness is the Iron curtain barring him from vision of His perfection. 'Since the fist of hypocrisy became strong, justice was perverted and conduct became corrupt'.[15] The world's misery in no small degree is due to the hypocrites who pretend knowledge[16] of the *Torah* (wrapping themselves in the *Tallit*, donning *Tefillin*, aping the manners of the scholars) but living unaffected by, or in clear contrast to, its principles. 'One should publicly denounce hypocrites, for they cause the desecration of His name.'[17]

The worst harm comes not from self-confessed evildoers, but from sanctimonious men and women who take His name in vain and render it shabby and religion despicable by the abyss that separates their words from their deeds, the motive in their heart from the words of their lips.

The higher a man's position, the greater his responsibility. The more chosen a nation, the more horrendous its deviation from His path.

Jeremiah's voice sounds to all of us, with ever greater potency, today.

Notes:

1. Deut. XXX, 14.
2. *Yer Makkot* II, 6.
3. *Abot* I, 14.
4. Mic. VI, 8.
5. *Baba Metzia* 49a.
6. *Ber.* 5a.
7. In George Orwell's prophetic *1984*.
8. Exod. XIX, 6.
9. Isa. XLII, 6.
10. XXIII, 13.
11. *Ibid.* 14.
12. *Ibid.* 15.
13. In *Characteristics*.
14. *Sotah* 41b.
15. *Ibidem*
16. *Midr. Koh. Rabbah* IV, 1.
17. *Yoma* 86b.

Zechariah's Realism

'And on that day the Lord will be One and His Name One.'[1] Zechariah was a realist, as can be seen from the fourteenth chapter, which describes the horror of war before the advent of peace, all the cruel passion begotten by man's undisciplined urges. How could he foretell the day on which 'He will be One and His name One', or, still more optimistically, that such a day will ever arrive? We, children of an age removed from his generation by millennia, feel more despondent about its probability.

For that day is not to be one of mere formal declarations, or even unanimous United Nations resolutions. It means the advent of a time when individuals and groups will act on the acceptance of God's law in their relations to fellow men. The One God implies the one human family, every one of them granted a minimum of equality and fair play, of justice and kindness; human interdependence, recognized not only as a postulate of religion, but as the self-evident basis of national and international relations.

I

Succot serves as challenge, promise, and symbol of such equality for it stresses co-operation as vital to harvest: prosperity, security, and peace. To the celebration of that festival, to the acceptance of its guiding ideas, the rest of mankind are summoned by the prophet, in the name of God, to Jerusalem, city of peace and cradle of liberty.

Of that acceptance Zechariah is sure beyond any doubt. Of the fulfilment of the *Succot* ideal he is as confident as he is of the rebuilding of the Holy City and the return to its homeland of the people banished in Assyria or lost beyond the ken of history.

But he has gruesome affliction to report about the nations that 'go up against Jerusalem' instead of joining her in psalm, with *Etrog*, *Lulab*, *Hadassah*, and *Arabah* (the cluster of the *Succot* service). What could he mean by pronouncing that 'This shall be the plague wherewith the Lord will smite all the peoples that have warred against Jerusalem . . . that go not up to keep the Feast of Tabernacles: their flesh will consume away while they stand upon their feet; and their eyes shall consume away in their sockets, and their tongue shall consume away in their mouth.'[2] In his 'images the prophet is taught to see a Divine message, which he conveys to his people'[3] . . . The visions are of the nature of parables.

II

Our own days offer startling illustration of what the prophet may have meant to present: The British Empire, a few years ago, appeared still powerful, standing on its lion's feet. But its oppression of the Indians and its betrayal of Israel, were a denial of God's Oneness. His rule of justice was ignored for the sake of maintaining the hold on colony and mandated territory. The punishment was not long delayed. The Empire's flesh 'was consuming away', until the leaders of the nation saw the error of their ways, broke the bonds of oppression, gave India her freedom and changed the character of its inter-continental rule to a commonwealth of nations. Some nations are achieving independence, others are in the process of emancipation, or are retaining willingly their old association. The new Federation has been based on the recognition of the One God's law of equality for all the nations. And now the flesh of the empire is no more consuming away and a better knit and more secure brotherhood augurs a happier chapter of Great Britain's history. Empires from hoary ages have been found incompatible with the Ten Commandments. They have challenged God's rule of right and as they have defied Him, they inevitably have prepared their own ruin. From Rome through the Medieval Church, to Czar and modern dictators, they have dug their own grave by their ruthlessness. But the process had an almost monotonous sameness: First the initially unobservable 'consuming away of the flesh,' of the substance of power, 'while standing on their feet,' apparently as strong as ever. Then the inevitable self-deception, a false vision of abiding security. As they plan to maintain rule by ruthlessness, they become utterly blind to the approaching destruction: their eyes consuming away in their sockets. 'They have eyes, but they will not see.'

III

The worst tragedy associated with Little Rock does not touch our coloured fellow-citizens. Freedom and equality will be theirs today or tomorrow. But whatever culture the South represented, whatever grace organized religion could have spelt in those states of the Union, whatever noble contribution to the nation had been made below the Mason-Dixon line, it was 'consuming away' whilst the states 'were still on their feet.' Governor Faubus, in days to come, will be condemned not alone as an unrighteous leader, but as a real enemy of the South, who for the applause of the mob, had battered away the infinite potentialities of Arkansas and her neighbours in the realization of the American dream. The White Councils of his entourage will be despised as the recruiting force of subversion in the country and the source of enormous Communist power in the world. So blind does the sinner become, blind to his own interest, unaware of the pit he is digging for himself in his very march towards the goal his benighted followers hail in unending cacophony!

IV

The rule of the One God is the foundation of the American dream. Equality under the law is its smallest promise. The greater harvest is the enrichment of the nation through the creative work of the immigrant. There was a time in our country when, at best, in parochial blindness or, at worst, as a mask of privilege,[4] powerful parties in the U.S.A. wanted to keep foreigners out or, if for economic reasons they grudgingly admitted them, emphasized a determined policy of indoctrination, once they were admitted to this country. To the would-be immigrants they would say: 'You are coming to a new, wonderful country, a new land blessed by an utterly unique asset, called Americanism. So that you might enter upon this priceless possession, forget whatever you knew before! Throw into the deepest part of the ocean your national attitudes, language, way of life, political views. Bring a fresh, blank mind to this country and it will offer you uncounted values.' Many people accepted that cribbed view of America, even some Jews. Thus, a lifeless imitation-creed developed in the place of living, loyal faith. But about the turn of the century, great minds like John Dewey, Nicholas M. Butler, President Wilson, brought a totally different message. They knew that America was an ongoing civilization and that, for wholesome development, she depended on the moral, spiritual, and esthetic contributions of the newcomers; that the old, intolerant way meant, 'a consuming away of the national life whilst still on its feet', an increasing and perilous myopia. These new leaders of thought appealed to the men and women about to embark at Hamburg, Cherbourg, Genoa, or London: 'For the sake of Heaven and of your own happiness, no less than for the good of America, do not cast into the ocean what you cherished from the past, what upheld you in the present throughout the troubles, and what made you look upon the United States as the land of your future. Whatever you consider precious, your sense of order, your passion for freedom, your arts and crafts, your love of nature, hold it tight to your heart, bring it over to the new country, develop it, perfect it, and then offer it up as the first fruits of your gratitude upon the altar of America... For America is blessed by its newcomers. In the give and take of American life there has been the exchange of cultural assets, of skills and insights, of devotion to ideals, a riot of colour, a plethora of the good, true, and beautiful that has made the American dream the proud possession of her citizenry on its highest level.'

It is this increasing recognition of the One God whose law protects all His children, black and white, Christian and Jew, Moslem and Hindu, poor and rich, employer and employee, that has made America strong and full of meaning to herself and the nations of the world.

May the Eternal Father guard us from the ranting patrioteers who create and obey mobs. Were they in control of national affairs even for a small fraction of time, they would dissipate the glory of our country, its power would be consumed. They would blind both leaders and rank and file. America would have no message for its own folks, 'their tongue would consume away in their own mouth', they would have 'a mouth' uttering platitudes, speaking self-deceit, but no words of nobility to win the youth, no comfort for the oppressed, no voice for the submerged peoples of the world.

V

The prophet knew with a knowledge past words that the day will come when the Lord will be One and His name One. His words convinced his people, and for three millennia we stubborn Jews have proclaimed that promise and lived and died a thousand times to uphold its glory. For its sake we have endured untold agonies and watched through lightless nights, assured in our hearts of the coming of the dawn. In our own days it is the only message which can unite mankind and uphold its dignity and its hope.

Notes

1. Zech. XIV, 9.
2. *Ibid.* 12.
3. Soncino edition, p. 268.
4. In Carey MacWilliams' formula.

The Wilderness and the Faith

I

'For seven days shall ye dwell in booths so that your future generations will know that I made you dwell in booths when I took you out of the land of Egypt.'[1] The sweet saint, Rabbi Israel Meir Hakohen of Radin, universally beloved as the author of the volume *Ḥafetz Ḥayyim* emphasized that *Succot* should have been celebrated in the spring, because that was the time of the Exodus. But, at that time, all go out of their home into the quiet beauty of the garden so that *Succot* in the time of the year would not have expressed our gratitude to Him for breaking the chains of our bondage. In the fall, most humans return to their home and we Jews move out into the hut, to recall and relive the protection His clouds of Glory gave us in the wilderness between Egypt and the Holy Land.[2]

A modern archaeologist ascribes to the desert an abiding major influence on the faith of the Hebrews.[3] But the poet of old has said: 'two men look out of prison bars, The one saw mud, the other – stars.' The neighbours of the Hebrews saw only the harshness of the desert, its cruel storms, its ravaging heats, its hopeless sterility. Their 'religion' hence reflected but fear and force and dreadful superstition. Their gods demanded human sacrifice, sex orgies, relentless oppression of the weak. But the Hebrews saw the starred sky, rejoiced in the wide open spaces, revered His sun, and from the orderly sequence of the day and night, summer and winter, knew about the power of God, His care, and His mercy.

II

The crucial word for our faith is *Bittaḥon*. The Hebrew language is unique in beauty as in power of expression. It is radical in that a study of the root meaning of its words opens up undreamt-of vistas of thought and sentiment. But biblical Hebrew is not rich enough to offer all the charming, challenging matter of word origins and cognate information. Among its sister languages it is rich Arabic that reveals much of the hidden store. In arabic *bataha* means 'to lean against an immovable rock,' hence to feel absolutely secure.[4] That is what *betaḥ*[5] in our Bible conveys, a bedrock feeling of protection.

Nine times in the Sidrah of *Ha'azinu*, the song which is Moshe Rabbenu's bequest to the Jewish people of all ages and climes, does the term '*Tzur*' (rock) occur. He is the Rock of the ages. In our *Siddur* we pray so often about *Y-ah Hashem, Tzur Olamim*,[6] and whilst the words give us much comfort, it is only after reflection on their true meaning, that we derive the full benefit they are meant to convey: Our faith (*bittaḥon*) is in God, in the Rock of the Ages, the only immovable, ever-present, ever-potent Creator of both the universe and the human race. The emphasis in our liturgy is first on the creation of the latter, for only through His creation of man has the world meaning and value.

The clouds of glory which protected us in the wilderness were the fruit of that absolute faith in His mercy. The word *Tzur* is of such vital importance because without *bittaḥon* in that rock we could not have persisted, prevailed, survived in the three wildernesses which have encompassed us – individuals and people – from the moment of the exodus. In the saddest moment of our life, at the fresh grave of a most beloved person, we recite 'The *Tzur* of perfect work.'[7] Beyond argument, oblivious of the suggestions of anguished reason, we have been asserting our faith. Countless heartbroken children, parents, husbands or wives, brothers or sisters, have been insisting that the unbearable affliction, in some manner not yet appreciable, comes from the just, merciful Rock of our life.

In the bitterest periods of our *Galut*, the abysmal pain of which the *seliḥot* of *Ellul* and *Tishri* speak, when we were despised, robbed, tortured, driven into ghastly deserts of inhumanity, we found courage to go on, restoration of our spirit through a fore-feeling of dawn in deepest night, because of our *bittaḥon* in the immovable Rock of our people and of human history.

III

Today in the tense decades of this century, we hasten to the frail *Succah* and feel secure in its thin walls and grateful for the beauty of the flowers which adorn it. The tallest skyscraper with its most luxurious gadgets has kept man fidgety, insecure, worried about tomorrow. But in the humble *Succah*, in the circle of family and friends, we welcome the guests (*ushpizin*) of the past, feeling deeply anchored in our people's history and proudly riveted to the memory of Abraham, Moses, David, to the heroes, singers, prophets, and the nameless millions of our past. They have shouldered every burden, suffered every pain, marched foot-sore and with undaunted hearts from continent to continent and from century to century because they had never thought of surrender, because they had always known how to lean against the immovable rock, the *Tzur* of their *bittaḥon*. *Teshvu ke'en taduru*:[8] they found spiritual comforts in the lightless ghettos as if they inhabited comfortable cities.

IV

Rosh ha-Shanah brings us the voice of conscience. *Yom Kippur* enjoins our re-atonement with God through our moral rehabilitation. *Succot* teaches us the wisdom of undoubting faith. In all the howling wildernesses of our historical migrations we heard His voice: 'I shall bless you in whatsoever you will do.' *Succot* warns us that throughout the year we remember that faith in Him, to be crowned by co-operation with fellow-Jews, with fellow-men. The cluster of the four plants vividly impresses upon the thinking worshipper in the synagogue that such co-operation must not know any discrimination or artificial divisions. Jews are of various types and true service is an orchestration, the harmony to be achieved by the joint effort of brain and brawn, of teacher and student, of management and labour, of craftsmen and professionals.

Thus *Succot* is the crown of *Tishri*. *Bittaḥon* becomes concrete and blissful in joint enterprize. Only when we have united all types of man in common labour, can we feel assured of the meaning of individual life joined to universal effort, can we achieve for ourselves and convey to our fellowman a sense of that utter peace and security which comes from *bittaḥon* in the *Tzur* – the trust in the Rock of all men in all ages of human history.

Notes

1. Lev. XXIII, 42–3.
2. *Orah Ḥayyim* DXXV, 1.
3. N. Gluck, *Rivers in the Desert.*
4. J. Barth, *Etymol. Studien.*
5. Deut. XII, 10
6. *Shaḥarit.*
7. Funeral Service.
8. *B. Succah* 27a, 28b.

Of Civil Courage

A characteristic of our tradition has been its consistent interpretation of both history and law as sources of moral principles. To the Greeks as well as to some modern philosophers, history presented itself as but a meaningless series of cycles: one people after the other, rising from the soil of humanity, gaining strength by favourable circumstances or special ability, reaching its peak, and then inevitably going down to disappear from the concert of the nations. From Aristotle to Spengler, the 'Decline of the West' has the same monotonous ring.

It is our *Torah*, our Prophets, our Sages, who see the fate, alike of individual and group, as conveying one basic lesson: those who lived a righteous life, co-operating, within their frame, with the divine plan for the human race, survive. They may face a thousand problems, undergo countless privations. They may stumble and fall, but they rise again, upheld by their vision of ultimate peace and security as the fruit of the good life.

I

Some half a century ago, Freiburg's Professor Krauss, a medical luminary, taught that no person had merely a bad leg, or foot or intestine. It was a sick person whose affliction called for a cure. In the last decades, the term 'psychosomatic' has become popular beyond medical conventions. It emphasizes the double aspect, body and soul, of the individual and the interdependence of physical and psychic health. But, long ago, our Sages had found that perception through the study of God's *Torah*. To them leprosy was no accidental physical malaise, but a normal consequence of evil act and attitude that, in order to prevent a spread of the disease, required segregation.

In the *sidrot* of *Tazria-Metzora* three symptoms of leprosy are mentioned: *se'et*, *sapahat*, and *baheret*, 'rising,' 'accretion', and 'bright spot',[1] suggesting a 'bloating of the ego, accumulation of goods, and conspicuousness.' Indeed, without violence to the original text, one may find in these chapters of the Holy Writ a pre-vision of three modern unpleasant types: the financial snob, the social snob, and the intellectual one, each of whom spells pain to the sensitive, a darkening of the fairest day, and invasion of social peace by uncouthness.

The financial snob represents a case of mental immaturity. Unaccustomed to his money, he sees himself on the supreme heights of monetary exclusiveness and in his boorish arrogance looks down upon those whom he suspects of possessing less than himself of stock and bonds or first mortgages on fashionable apartment houses. He has not begun to perceive that a man's worth depends not on what he has, but on what he is. The less dignity a person possesses, the more does he crave for dignities; the poorer in honour he is, the more does he crave honours.

No more winsome is the social snob, who has forced or cajoled his way into what he considers the élite, from Café Society to millionaires' country club. He talks with imitation-superciliousness of the 'common folk' and revels in the shadow of the 'elect' who have just admitted him to their magic circle. Both types, the financial and the social snob, present sorry examples of humanity. Both are victims of early complexes, of frustrations, real or imaginary, which prevent them from seeing themselves or others in their true light.

Still less bearable is the intellectual snob. That phenomenon has its high school foundation. Adolescents, deprived of proper guidance, look upon themselves as possessed of all the wisdom of mankind and upon all parents and their coevals as old fogies in the thrall of ancient ignorance or superstition. But that folly increases with age and moves into academic quarters. I remember a revered teacher at Cambridge contrasting two essays by two scholars on the same difficult problem. The first spoke of 'conclusive evidence' in favour of his theory, the other opined: 'It may therefore not be too hazardous to suggest' or 'the assumption therefore may have some basis'. Old Epictetus used to say: '*Prolepsis prolepsei ouk machetai*[2] – one opinion does not fight another,' i.e., they are both only working theories requiring the test of experiment or research to establish their truth. Some instructors hurt their innocent students by witless finalities, proclaimed as absolute truth, which they offer with more emphasis than justice. Einstein, Whitehead, Planck, have admitted the mere relativity of all knowledge, the distance between assumption and verification, between search and its goal. That perception is the hallmark of genuine scientific attitude. But the self-deceived snob magnifies the detail of his knowledge into a mighty principle, a very fortress of the intellect. He substitutes loud assertion for the result, patiently, painstakingly, and systematically achieved, of true effort. What this exemplifies is not only an emotional and mental defect, but beyond both, moral immaturity.

II

To protect the community against the ravages of leprosy, the *Torah* imposes segregation. If the modern snob were to feel, in unmistakable harshness, the condemnation of cultured people – the sorry smile he evokes in the responsible rich, the contempt he provokes among the real leaders of the country, the abysmal chasm separating the loudmouthed scoffer from the giants of the scientific world – there is a reasonable chance that the *ayfer parah adumah* ('ashes of the red heifer'), an awareness of the transient vanity of mere wealth, of social climbing, and pseudo-knowledge, may cleanse him of his rudeness, roughness, and ludicrousness. A single Biblical verse offers opportunity for deeper appreciation of the point involved. The householder, observing some mouldiness on the walls of his house, is to report: 'Something like an affliction appeareth to me in the house'.[3] *Rashi* quotes the comment of the *Sifra*, an early *halakhic Midrash*: 'Even if the householder be a learned man and knew for sure that it is a plague, he shall not offer the statement as a certainty, saying 'an affliction has shown itself to me', but 'something like a plague has shown itself to me'. The Sages in the *Talmud* advise:[4] 'Do teach your tongue to say 'I do not know'!" Such cautious modesty will immunize one against the plague of cocksureness, of intellectual snobbishness.

III

It is not easy, as it is not agreeable, to fight snobs. Segregation has occasionally some chance of reducing, if not curing, that affliction. But since snobs have a built-in lack of a sense of humour, normal social disciplines do not affect them. One of the more hopeful methods is based on civil courage. The soldier has military regulations, group spirit, the prospect of rewards, verbal or practical, to inspire brave action. Civil courage requires different motivations, above all a thorough commitment to an ideal, a disregard of social or financial danger, or of public denunciation. Rarely, except in countries of tyranny or in states of ruthless oppression, does civil courage land one in mortal danger. Civil courage has luminous examples to inspire the good citizen, from the prophet Nathan to Gandhi, from the Maccabees to Garrison.

Courage must be rooted in high principle to render it fruitful, but even then it is beset by handicaps and temptations. The democracies of the world, for years, were unwilling to face the moral leprosy of Fascism and Nazism. In the thirties, in our country, Henry Stimson stood almost alone in his condemnation of the Japanese rape of Nanking. The big industrialists and their satellites in France, England, and America, who chose to ignore the obvious signs of contemporary European tyranny, to no small degree had succumbed to the tempting illusion that the methods of Mussolini and Hitler might prevent the rising power of Labour. Pope Pius missed the greatest opportunity for presenting the organized power of the Church as a force for universal social good. Not only as Jews, but as citizens of the world, as believers in the Supreme Father of all humans, we should have rejoiced, had there come from Rome, or from Protestant fortresses of their faith, an unmistakable, uncompromising, powerful denunciation of the moral monsters of the Third Reich. Consideration of expediency, doubly deplorable when evidenced from the peaks of clerical authority, proved the stumbling block and prevented the spiritual enhancement of Religion in our century. Political leaders, too, tied to special interests, were blinded to the very dangers to themselves, bound to come from the conscienceless leadership of dictators. All of them transgressed the *Torah*'s prohibition: 'Do not stand idly at your brother's blood being shed!'[5]

IV

This Sabbath is called 'The Great Sabbath', because, with its message to the faithful, it crowns the earlier ones of its four predecessors which are meant to prepare us for a full understanding of freedom – its glory as well as its problems, its blessing as well as an awareness of what prevents its flowering. It is fine to do one's bit for the common good (as the first lesson demands), otherwise those who do more, in turn demand higher privileges which gradually destroy the liberty of the average citizen. It is essential, as the second Sabbath teaches, for freedom's devotees to eliminate from public and private conduct the very memory of Amalek, the prototype of oppressors, who 'pounce upon the helpless in the rear'.[6] It is wise, as the third Sabbath urges, to shun cocksureness in suggestion, in research as in working theory and to recognize, humbly, the mystery of the cosmos and of human personality. It requires thought and discipline to study and live Judaism, as the fourth Sabbath urges, so that the Faith of our Fathers remains fresh and precious as the autonomous selfcommitment of the Jew. But all these qualities must be crowned by courage, tested in the battlefield of human thought, proclaimed and defended in a hundred climes and ages. For us *Komemiyut le-artzenu*,[7] to enter the blessed homeland, not as desperate refugees from man's inhumanity, but as pioneers of the divine message, private and public courage are indispensable.

The vacillating attitude of Pope Paul has brought dismay to millions of believers in the Father of all men. Hochhuth's documented charge of Papal lack of courage in Hitler's time seems tragically re-endorsed by the present Pope's repetition of the millennial slander. The very 1964 pronouncement by the Church authorities of a tentative repudiation of Christian unrighteousness, the very denial by Catholic leaders of Jewish guilt as falsely represented in the New Testament, as fostered by countless fathers and priests and honourless preachers of hatred, all these bright promises are robbed of their moral power by the Pope's latest sermon. The millions of innocent Jewish victims of Christian defamation seem re-murdered, re-slandered at the moment, when men of all creeds, with bated breath and in prayerful expectation, were awaiting the confirmation of the new spirit of truth and justice heralded from Rome.

V

As incorrigible optimists, all our horrible historical experience notwithstanding, we hope for an early rectification of that moral error. Such correction would bring to the awakening consciousness of Africa and Asia a wholesome note of Religion on the march towards God. To the sensitive conscience of numberless Christians it would offer some consolation, some relaxation of an inner anxiety which has been plaguing their noblest meditative hours. To us Jews, after the inevitably slow percolation from the throne of the Pope to the pulpit of the priest and the programme of bishops and monsignors, it would eventually sound like a manifestation of the harvest of timeless Jewish teaching in the fields of universal religious endeavour.

Against this blessed consummation militate organizational, political, practical considerations. Moral courage has achieved its greatest victories in the past as men and women clung to true ideals undeterred by fear of mundane consequences of their devotion.

Let us hope that this message of the Great Sabbath will penetrate heart and mind of the leaders of men and achieve the rise to a nobler height of faith and action of His children everywhere.

Notes

1. Lev. XIII: see *Ritva* on *Erubin* 13b.
2. Discourses I.
3. Lev. XIV, 35.
4. B. *Berakhot* 4a.
5. Lev. XIX, 16.
6. Deut. XXV, 18.
7. Grace after Meals.

From Afar . . .

As a loving and stern father, Moshe Rabbenu had criticized his people. In language both sternly terse and yet full of affection, he had described their fickleness and their ingratitude, warning them that lack of stability would bring suffering as its inevitable consequence, and prayerfully predicting ultimate moral rehabilitation as the prelude to their salvation. As *Rashbam*[1] indicates, the *Shir Ha'azinu* is not a song, but a didactic poem. At its end, however, it is Moshe who is reprimanded. He who had taught Pharaoh to recognize God's power and the warrior kings Sihon and Og to bow to Him, had failed in the task of *Kiddush Hashem* within the Jewish camp. *Venikdashti betokh bene Yisrael* ('I am to be sanctified among the children of Israel')[2] had been the divine command and for his failure to achieve that goal, Moshe was told 'You will see the Holy Land from afar, but you will not enter it.'[3]

For the failure of leaders is treated more severely than that of the common people. Theirs must be a higher level of conduct, they are 'being judged for even a hairbreadth deviation from the divine path' (*sevivoh nisarah me'od . . . afilu kehut hasa'arah*).[4]

I

To see the blessed land only from afar, to be unable to enter it, has been the fate of many a man and woman, almost the human situation as a rule.

How many of us dream of such blessed fulfilment and then must adjust from afar to the reality we face. The young man and woman pledging their mutual love and devotion under the *ḥuppah*, envisaging a *Gan Eden* of undisturbed bliss, awake one day to the shattering or depressing recognition of a chasm separating their married life from the image that had inspired their wedding day. How many a physician, dedicated to the conquest of disease, entering upon his research 'with a boat of a thousand sails,' finds himself denied real progress in his quest and is tense with the sense of failure![5] Abraham Lincoln, a hundred years ago, issued his emancipation declaration. Today, in our own beloved United States, the blessed land of universal equality is still unreached: the dismaying delay a source of tension to all devotees of the American dream. Self-respecting, God-conscious congregations in some synagogues exist too often only in the Rabbi's fervid imagination. The meaningless prattle of men and women during the hours of worship (*Tefillah betzibbur*) too often form an iron curtain, preventing *Kirvat elokim*, the very view of the authentic synagogue filled with Jews and Jewesses wise enough for their undisturbed and undisturbing reverence to bless them as they leave the house of God, spiritually happy, morally ennobled. How many an artist, a social worker, a communal leader does reach the goal, to which he has committed all his faculties, all the time and energies with which he was endowed?

II

Indeed, *en adam met vehatzi ta'avato beyado* (no man dies with half of his desire accomplished')[6] Pope John XXIII had the courage, benignity, and vision, of his church emancipated from millennial prejudice and cruelty, of the world's largest organized religion serving God by a platform and programme, by proclamation and practice of love and justice. All mankind, conscious of ugly past attitude, was inspired by his declaration, breathing sincerity and wisdom in rare coalescence. The blessed land of his prayerful hope is still far away and even if the Ecumenical Council proved strong and noble enough to follow his path, it will take many years, if not decades, for Christian moral rehabilitation to bless its adherents and to initiate a happier chapter of human history.

Some people, frustrated by what, in spite of genuine pursuit of their goals, has happened to their dreams and visions, have become despondent cynics: 'What is the use to fight against unconquerable forces of evil, against callousness and apathy, against the timeless folly of selfishness?' *Carpe Diem* – said the Latin proverb: 'Pluck the joys of the day'! Let tomorrow take care of itself. Don't fret because of the hundred road-blocks! Men are as they are and you are wasting your life trying to improve them. If pursuit of an ideal is bound to end in disappointment, stop pursuing it. If your set of values proves insufficient, replace them with others that will bring you satisfaction, granting you success and happiness!'

To them the *Mishnah* replied:[7] 'It is not upon thee to complete the task, nor may you give it up.' Men and women, who follow the cynics' advice, are neither happy nor worthwhile. We all have met those whose foolish wishes are punished by being granted, who believe possessions or sense indulgence to be ends in themselves. We know too many who have everything to live with and nothing to live for. Their pleasures become stale, they lose vibrancy, vitality, becoming old in middle age.

III

Perchance the rabbis' statement may be interpreted to mean also: 'No man is dead, when only half of his desires are achieved.' For the major benefit of good work, of unselfish effort, of wise planning, may lie not so much in the eventual complete accomplishment, a rare occurrence, as in the vitalizing effect on their personalities engaged in noble pursuits. Said the Lord to King David who dreamt of building the Temple, 'Thou didst well that it was in thine heart.'[8] Practical idealists – with their common sense, and wise use of means to their fine ends may experience tensions, may occasionally become impatient, may know momentary despondency. But the, as yet unachieved, other half of their desires also keeps them eager, stimulates their mind, keeps them young for years beyond the aging processes of the benighted cynics. The work for God and human destiny is its own reward. The *Midrash* has Moses pleading for the supreme joy of entering the Holy Land and the Lord saying to him: 'Yours is not a superficial aim. What you are in truth craving is the full life in the spirit of My *Torah*, which you had achieved, what you laboured for. Your whole life was a saga of dedication. You took the horde of slaves out of Egypt. You suffered their backsliding, their murmurs, their ever-changing sentiments, their descent from the heights of Mount Sinai to the depths of the Golden Calf. You carried upon your shoulders burdens which would have crushed another man. You have entered the Holy Land by merit, though with your physical eyes you may behold it only from afar.'

IV

An aristocrat asks: 'What is my duty? I cannot be at ease until I have fulfilled it.' The Sages plead: *Mitzvah ha-baah leyadkha al tahmitzenah* ('don't allow a good deed which you have a chance to perform, become sour by delay'). The only impatience which is noble is that which prompts a good person to act forthwith when the call comes.

A vulgar person insists: 'What are my rights? I want to use them at once and fully. As to my duties, they can wait! One of these days I'll attend to them.' Hence, here in the richest land of the world there is a great deal of human misery. Hence, for years, the slums that cry to be re-built. Even the Holy Land knew *Ma'abarot*, now blessedly almost a matter of the past, unpleasant interim quarters for refugees from Hitler's hell and Moslem hatred, because in the American Jewish community there were too many who had to have their costly fling first before considering their brethren's plight. Luxury as a prestige symbol reveals both folly and meanness in even proportion.

All these people, mobs of excitement-hunters, awaiting their heaven at the entrance to nightclubs, racing and gambling place, present a sorry, unaesthetic example of humans in the grip of their urges and removed from a vision of the blessed land: the golden vista of generous co-operation for our brothers and sisters, their parents, and children, whose keepers by God's law we are appointed to be and remain.

But the Jews, whose faith in God is deep enough, are also fully committed to His practical programme for man-achieved care, health, and sustenance for all. They will not give up the work because of the shabby example of the pleasure-seekers at all costs. They will not be guilty of the self-deception of the slaves of their riches, which keep them in deadly bondage and prevent them from doing their share in making His world better for the lame and the blind, the poor, the sick, and all others who are handicapped.

Even though they can see only from afar the consummation of their dreams of universal benign brotherhood, good Jews will not relax their effort, nor slacken their hand, nor diminish the power of their eager spirit, until the dark night of suffering due to indifference is over, until our neighbour's problems become so much our own that the dawn of a happier society reveals to all of His children the beauty, the power, the sheer indescribable happiness of a blessed land of peace and security, extending all over the six continents, for years without end.

Notes

1. Deut. XXXI, 30
2. Lev. XXII, 32.
3. Deut. III, 27.
4. *B. Yebamot* 121b.
5. *Koh R* I, 34.
6. *Iggerot G'r'a.*
7. *Pirke Abot* II, 21.
8. I Kings VIII, 18.

The Wages of Repentance

Three verses from the potential *Haftorot* for this day offer thought for our reflection, but the prophetic message of this *Shabbat* is a composite of the words of Hosea and Joel. The three verses read:[1] 'Return O Israel close unto the Lord thy God, for thou hast stumbled in thine iniquity whenever thou hast transgressed His Law.' Whatever momentary profit such transgression may have brought, it brings failure in its train.[2] 'Seek the Lord, for He can always be found. Call on Him, for He is always near.' One needs no intermediary for His prayers, any man or woman or child, truly anxious to commune with Him, will find the gate of heaven open. 'Sound the *Shofar* in Zion,'[3] the voice of individual and national conscience, is the ever-valid source of moral recovery.

I

The word 'sin' occurs most frequently in the *Maḥzor* for the High Holy Days. It is rarely found in our secular literature, from newspaper to essay, to novel. One hears of social 'sin', which means failure to follow the fashion of the day. Men, no less than women in abject surrender, will wear hats, suits, the form, breadth, length and other aspects of which some arbitrary tyrant in Paris or New York has decreed.

But what is 'sin' in the realm of Judaism? Its meaning is crystal clear: 'Sin' is action or attitude against law or principle which our God revealed in His *Torah*. It includes transgression (*Pesha* or *averah*), sins of commission, as when we do something we should not have done, like lying, stealing, defiling ourselves with *trefah* food, abusing someone dependent on us, violating the Sabbath or any other holy day. *Ḥet* is a sin of omission, not doing things we ought to have done, like failure to don *Tefillin*, to take care of the poor, to eat *Matzah* on *Pesaḥ*, failure to help build up the homeland, Israel.

As to awareness of sins committed, there are degrees of ethical sensitiveness, from almost moral apathy of the smug enjoyer of thoughtless indulgence, to the sublime level of the ancient bio-chemist Baba bar Butta,[4] who, of his own free will, brought a suspensive guilt-offering every day except only the day after the Day of Atonement. It was the 'Guilt-offering of the Pious', not due to any consciousness of sin committed, but in order to appease an easily troubled conscience.[5]

II

But what are the 'wages of sin' for the average person? How do they affect him or her? They are of three types: One is the corrosion of personality. In our sacred books it is viewed as a stain on the soul, which we beseech God to wipe away (*kapper*)[6] by His divine power. No human being can do that for us. Repentance and restitution may achieve escape of punishment, even a fellow-man's forgiveness as the offender begs his pardon. But the effect of carelessness, cruelty, selfishness on our character remains; indeed, it increases with repeated wrongdoing.

A second result of wrong conduct is the narrowing of one's horizon. The egoist sees only his desire and in indulging it he ignores his mate, his neighbour, a whole set of ethical principles and social considerations. The shocking recent mistrial in the southern town which freed a killer, is due to such constriction of vision, shutting out the whole world in exclusive pursuit of local fears or goals. Another penalty of all wrongdoing is the inevitable recoiling on oneself, due also to the fear of facing moral issues, the resentment against any outside voice of criticism or warning. Nobody is more alone than the evildoer! He hates the neighbour who may be a living protest against his own action which the voice of the sinner's suppressed conscience would endorse and – what he is unconsciously afraid of – thus add to the incipient unhappy inner reaction to his wrongdoing.

In every human, conscience is never completely dead. In his heart there is an abiding conflict between the *Yetzer hara* (the evil impulse) and the *Yetzer tov* (the good one). Because of the fact that with the average person both tendencies are alternately or simultaneously present, one of the consequences of sin is the creation of a vacillating, confused personality: honest on Sunday, Tuesday, and Thursday, less scrupulous on other days of the week; arrogant in the morning, affable in the afternoon, timid beyond words when the shadows of the evening grow longer. That feeble person becomes an object of commiseration or contempt to his neighbours, ultimately to himself. In the happy years of adolescence, we see all humanity in two colours: white and black. The bleaker wisdom of maturity recognizes a spectrum from darkest black to whitest white, with the majority of men and women in varying degrees of greyness. The total wages of sin, then, are: corrosion of one's personality, narrowing of one's view, and becoming a playball of conflicting emotions – all leading to eventual worthlessness and unhappiness.

III

But, says the prophet Ezekiel, it is never too late to mend: In the name of God he proclaims: 'I do not desire the death of the man (who will be destroyed by his own sins), but, (rather) that he turn from his (wrong) way and live.'[7] Nobody is too old or too wicked to seek such return to Him; the way is clearly defined: through a return to decency, justice, and kindness. *Teshuvah* (repentance) is a mighty source, never failing him or her who truly seek it.

Our Sages offered the formula for the good life in a one-line counsel[8]: *Lo nitnu hamitzvot ella letzaref bahen et haberiyot.* The crucial word is *tzaref*. It has three meanings in Hebrew: to refine, to strengthen, to unite.[9]

The translation of that counsel then reads: The total purposes of all the *Mitzvot* (divine commandments) is to refine human beings, to purify them of base desires, to inspire them with a sense of decency, righteousness, and mercy. Their second goal is to strengthen their character through habituation (the steady performance of His laws) and in consequence through intellectual sympathy with goodness, truth, and beauty. The ultimate purpose is to make them aware of each person's infinite significance in the concert of mankind, of his opportunity to bring light, hope, sustenance, and peace not only to the domestic hearth, but to the community, the nation, to all the families of the human race: to unite man under the wings of the *Shekhinah*.

That is why *Teshuvah* is both privilege and duty. That is why repentance of last year's evil is essential for a better year of conduct for harmony and security. Against the threefold bane of the wrong life, there is the threefold harvest of the good one: 'In thy mouth, thy hand, thy heart, to achieve it.'[10]

The words of the Sages elaborated the Biblical plea: As a human you have two ways before you, good and evil. Good is blessing, evil is curse. Good is life, evil is death. 'Choose Life!'[11]

Notes

1. Hos. XIV, 2.
2. Isa. LV, 6.
3. Joel II, 1.
4. *B. Gittin* 58a.
5. *B. Kerit.* 25a.
6. *Rashi* a.l.
7. Ezek. XVIII, 23.
8. *Midr. Vay.* R. XIII, 50.
9. *B. Yoma* 72b; *Yer. Yoma* XVI, 15; *Baba Kama* III, 13, *Makhshirin* V, 7; *Kiddushin* 40a, *Nezikim* 34b.
10. Deut. XXX, 14.
11. Deut. XXX, 19. Also the title of a noble book by the late Erich Gutkind.

Children and Parents

Adam le-amal yulad ('man is born for toil'). Our Sages suggest that this verse applies in particular to parents: *lilmod al menat lalammed* ('they must ever learn, to be able to teach, by word of mouth, by training, and by example').

This is the difference between animal breeding and human parentage. This is also the difference between the cub's instinctive attachment to its mother and a human child's filial loyalty. What is involved in human relations is a set of principles and attitudes, of emotions and ideas. The first feeling towards one's parents ought to be gratitude. It is only when we have children of our own that we can begin to appreciate the infinite devotion, patience, and loving effort involved in the training given to us by father and mother. Because gratitude, of late, has become a lost art, it is essential that we recall that basic obligation. It should be as natural as the breath which we draw and the bread which we eat.

But gratitude is not enough. On the way from childhood towards adolescence, there ought to be added to it a feeling of respect and sympathy – respect for the parents' undeviating tenderness, and sympathy for the problems with which every generation finds itself faced. From prehistoric ages to our own days, and probably to the end of time, every generation had and has problems of its own with which to deal. Every adolescent boy or girl, on the way from high school to college, is convinced of the fullness of his or her own wisdom and of the relative obsolescence of the parental point of view. Incipient maturity becomes aware of this universal, timeless experience. When one of our Sages was asked why our prayer speaks of 'the God of Abraham and the God of Isaac and the God of Jacob' when the statement would have been clear enough had it read 'the God of Abraham, Isaac, and Jacob', he answered: 'Because the father's concept of God differed from that by his son, and was considerably modified by that of his grandson.' All of us achieve clarity, emotional steadfastness, and consistency of action only slowly and not without pain. Children ought to have respect for their parents' struggle towards maturity, as they should have for the labour to reach, rung after rung on the ladder, their own goal.

You all have heard of the Fifth Commandment, 'Honour thy father and thy mother so that your days may be lengthened on the earth which the Lord thy God has given to you.' It seems strange that a reward should be promised for what ought to be a self-evident obligation, cheerfully and enthusiatistically shouldered. But the Fifth Commandment does not so much offer a reward as it does sage counsel. The *Torah* does not command us to love father and mother. That sentiment towards normal parents by normal children is taken for granted. Honouring father and mother means paying attention to their advice, considering in spite of all the perfect understanding and wisdom of youth, that the parents, in the course of their own development have undergone trial and error, have reaped disappointment no less than fulfilment, and in the process have acquired intuition and awareness, a capacity to see beyond the moment and not to be dazzled by appearances. It is the young people who often are swept off their feet before they have learned to cultivate the art of suspended judgment. When son and daughter are willing to consider their parents' advice, objection, and encouragement, they may save themselves many a disillusionment, many a tension, and many a heartache. They will stay happy and healthy longer. That is what the Fifth Commandment, is its simple prose, may be conveying to us.

Children can be a source of abiding blessing, in a way the continuation of parental record, the comfort of their declining years, the source of their undiminished vitality. Children may also be a source of unmitigated evil, causing endless frustration, the gradual burying of the father's and mother's hopes. To stay conscious of both potentialities means to have reached decent, benign, wise maturity.

You may have heard of the ancient story of a man who had grown rich and hopelessly self-centred, who saw only his own ambition and grew full of hatred to every even imaginary competitor. His personality deteriorated as his riches increased. Whilst boasting of his possessions to friend and foe, he allowed his old father to live in a miserable hovel. One day, the story reads, in winter time, this soulless person said to his only son: 'Your grandfather has been complaining about the cold. Take a blanket, bring it to him in his basement, and tell him not to trouble me so much; every day he asks for something else.' The young boy took a long while and when he returned, his father upbraided him: 'You could have taken that blanket to your grandfather and returned much faster.' The boy answered: 'Yes, I could; I was cutting the blanket in two halves. I gave him one part and the other part I am keeping for you, father, when you will be old and sick as he is.'

Every parental compromise with decency produces ten deviations from right conduct on the part of the children. Parents in more than one sense could be the luminous examples for their progeny to follow. Parents in more than one sense may cause a lower attitude, a corroding of the children's ethical personality. Any form of inconsistency with regard to the way the Lord wants us to go – in Jewish life, in general life, at home, in the counting house, with regard to our social responsibilities, results in a lowering of our children's standards, in a weakening of the spiritual heirlooms we plan to leave them, in a gradual failure as Jews, as citizens of the world, and as human beings. Parenthood implies responsibility – alert, consistent, practical, from the child's birth to its self-sufficient maturity.

The Peak of Self

The *Torah* proclaims and offers approaches. Its message comes in behest of simple prose, in between lines suggestion, in hint for the alert (all the way from *Peshat*[1] to *Remez*).

Just before the account of Revelation,[2] the story of Amalek's heartless treachery is recorded. Oppression leads to more oppression or to a cynical despair in human nature. Fascism and communism, brothers under the skin, flourish in such troubled areas or ages. Amalek is as attractive to ruthless egoists as it is destructive to the unprotected. The law may solve some problems. Fear of its severity may deter the aggressor. Knowledge of its power will reassure the weak. Yet the law is not an end, but a major means to the end of a happy humane society.

The *Midrash* describes in poetic form the revelation on Mt Sinai: *Tzippor lo aphah . . . aryeh lo sha'ag*[3] ('No bird was flying, no lion roaring'), there was a profound stillness in nature as the Lord revealed Himself to the Children of Israel, as Moses conveyed the divine message to them and to all humanity. It was the greatest event in history because it banished forever the superstitions, the fears, and the cruelties of heathenism as it proclaimed the God of the Universe, the merciful Lawgiver, the Rock of the ages.

But what does it mean to our own days, to the confused generation which commutes to Europe, which in a short while is to spend weekends at the moon, which trembles between the danger of atomic annihilation and the unimaginable peace and prosperity that science and technology have been promising? What is the road for a lost generation to be guided back to harmony and security?

'I shall be the Lord your God'[4] means 'Abandon the idols of the market place, and move towards a happier future!' All the unwholesome rash of today, from beatle-ism to twist, from marital adventures to marihuana, the new kind of assimilation along the path of alcoholism, with young people impudent Sunday, Tuesday, and Thursday and too timid for words for the rest of the week, can be overcome by three principles, holding challenge and promise. They are self-acceptance, self-discipline, and self-realization.

I

What is self-acceptance? It means the overcoming of the modern malaise of alienation and rootlessness, hence the prevailing of insecurity, hence indulgence in every kind of drug, from canned pleasures to rumbles, from extremist clubs to sheer noise as an expression of unhappiness and of the revolt against the *status quo*.

The Ten Commandments today offer the way to self-acceptance: 'I shall be the Lord your God' conveys the assurance that there is a controlling power in the cosmos, that human life and destiny are not victims of accident. The Lord allowed man wide margins which he abuses to his own detriment and to the hurt of his fellow-man, but mankind as such is safe. There will be no other flood to engulf them!

For self-acceptance one must get rid of all the heathenism, ancient and modern, from power to race, from money as an end to the delusion of belonging to an exclusive élite safe from doom and having the monopoly of salvation. The acceptance of God must not be taken lightly: 'His Name must not be taken in vain.'[5] The security which comes from faith in a benevolent, just, merciful Master of the cosmos becomes concrete through the Sabbath of the Jewish home, twenty-four hours every week, which are free from the tensions and frustrations of the work-a-day world. *Mishpaḥah*, the Hebrew word for 'family', suggests *sappeah* ('belonging, unity'). If parents are wise and consistent, the seventh day Sabbath will be a period not of prohibitions but of an ingenious programme of the enjoyment of family unity: father, mother, and children blessed by a feeling of belonging, by peace based on affection and mutual devotion.

Christopher Hibbert, in his seminal work *Roots of Evil,* acknowledges the very low percentage of Jewish antisocial or criminal persons as due to the traditions of the family – a place of harmony and devotion. Its *Ḥinnukh* (moral and spiritual training) etymologically refers to 'palatableness.' At an ancient Semitic initiation ceremony, the adults smeared the *Ḥekh* (palate) of the youth with honey or fig juice. Education must be both goal-conscious and pleasant. Self-acceptance is the fruit of faith in a benevolent Deity and of a benevolent parental training.

II

But this self-acceptance might end in snobbishness, in a smug assumption of excellence. It is but a basis of a good life. Self-acceptance needs self-discipline for the harvest of such promise.

Self-discipline, the fruit of parental guidance and of eventual ever-increasing adolescent awareness of moral and spiritual values, creates personalities and atmospheres which are likely to produce a happier society. I recall an incident in the decades old programme of spiritual hospitality, which The Jewish Center used to extend to many Gentiles – students, teachers, nurses – who annually came to the synagogue to hear the rabbi expound 'abiding God-consciousness as the basis of Jewish life.' A long time ago, it was a large number of New Jersey Sunday school superintendents who listened earnestly to the lecture, after which their leader put this question: 'Could you help us with regard to a problem that has upset many of us? Our children are very ungrateful. The more we do for them, the more they demand. What do you Jews do about this lost art of gratitude?' I answered: 'We do have a method. When the child of three asks mother for an apple or a piece of cake, she would say: 'Yes, my dear, you can have it but before you eat it, we shall pronounce this prayer: 'Blessed art Thou our God, King of the Universe, who hast created the fruit of the tree.' A similar prayer of gratitude precedes every enjoyment. A young girl getting her dress will thank the Lord 'who covers the naked.' In this manner enjoyment is always linked to expression of gratitude and not only to the Divine Giver, but also to father and mother and uncle and aunt and any friend. Thus gratitude becomes a matter self-evident, natural.'

More significant is another method of self-discipline. The Jewish high school boy or girl who learns how to control his desire for food if no *kosher* victuals are available is thereby taught to ignore a present desire for a higher principle. If the parents are wise and consistent, this habit, too, will spread in the consciousness of the child over all the fields of religion and when later on the opportunity arises for gain or profit in a manner not honourable, the youth will understand that such pleasure too would be *trefah*, that such benefit would have been achieved by violating God's law. Such self-discipline, developed out of self-acceptance, holds a great promise of a fine character emerging.

III

What is meant by self-realization? There has been for decades a tendency of some psychiatrists and educators to stress self-expression as the major moral obligation and as the major asset of youthful growth. Misquoting Sigmund Freud, they oppose the control of any impulse as somehow hurtful to the development of free and happy folk, and they grow eloquent on the vital prerogative of self-expression. But, in truth, adolescents do not yet have a self that needs or deserves to be expressed. When a full plate of ice cream, the enjoyment of a movie, or the banter of teenagers are viewed as supreme joys, that empty way of life does not bestow any benefit through conveying its message. In England and in our country another voice has been increasingly heard: what a child needs is a maximum chance of self-fulfilment, of gradual concretization of the native abilities and powers he or she possess. If parents are wise and consistent, at once comradely guides and luminous examples of right conduct, they will foster an increasing manifestation of kindness, fair play, and an earnest pursuit of fine goals. Self-acceptance and self-discipline are the basis and the walls of this human structure, the crown of which is self-realization achieved through the right attitude towards one's fellowman.

IV

This is what the two tables of the Law proclaim: Through faith in God, taught and trained in the spirit of self-acceptance, through consistent self-discipline, the self of boy or girl is shaped towards a good character operating at home, in the community, in the life of the nation and ultimately in the arena of the world.

A scholar found in the Ten Commandments this challenge and promise: Accept Me as the Lord thy God, have done with all the folly and fear of heathenism, be blessed by the peace of the Sabbath, by fine parents-children relationship and you will not steal; you will not murder; you will not in any manner abuse your neighbour; you will not desire that which doesn't belong to you.

That is why the Ten Commandments commence with 'I shall be the Lord thy God' and end with 'all that belongs to your neighbour.'[6]

Notes

1. Israel Frankel, *Peshat*, Toronto 1956.
2. Exod. xx.
3. *ad locum.*
4. Exod. xv, 2.
5. Exod. xx, 7.
6. Exod. xx, 17.

Programme and Destiny

I

The second book of Moses commences with the story of the Children of Israel and their experiences in Pharaonic Egypt. Throughout the *Torah*, there are frequent references to that country. The initial chapters of Exodus have it on every page. *Mitzrayim* is mentioned in later ones, and throughout the Pentateuch, in connection with the warning to be heedful of the stranger and not to oppress him,[1] with the story of the golden calf;[2] in the text about the holy days, as well as in the account of the building of the *mishkan* (temporary sanctuary of the wilderness).[3] The affirmation of the *Shema*, repeated twice daily, ends with 'I am the Lord your God Who took you out of the land of Egypt'[4] and the *Kiddush* of the Sabbath emphasizes its holiness as a memorial of the exodus from Egypt. Yet we are bidden 'not to abhor the Egyptian . . . because thou wert a stranger in his land.'[5] Why this extraordinary preoccupation with an empire long lost in the dusts of history, with a dynasty which today is of interest only to archaeologists and a few specialists among historians?

The answer is that 'what happened to our forefathers in Egypt,'[6] has been a recurrent experience throughout the millennia of our history, recording both our suffering and our reaction to these grievous wrongs. But they also served as the matrix which shaped our programme, individual and collective, in a perennial linkage of idea and ideal, of dream and fulfilment, of destiny and its consummation. Our historical programme and our destiny have their roots in Egypt.

II *The Recurrent Theme*

In Egypt we were termed aliens.[7] As aliens we were enslaved and afflicted, as aliens we were outside the law and had no recourse to any court of justice or forum of fair dealing. As aliens we entered the Roman empire and as private individuals we were ruthlessly destroyed in our sovereign land. The godless medieval church called us aliens in the Christian collectivity and enslaved us, locking us up in lightless, airless ghettos, denying us access to field and vineyard, and afflicting us with cruel tax, humiliating garb, and the fury of incited mobs.[8] As aliens we were enslaved by Czarist and Soviet Russia. Dubbed alternately capitalists and proletarians, accused of imaginary crimes, our people were driven out of pleasant habitations, forced into the Pale, and subjected to the pogroms of drunk *mujiks*, the *nagaykas* of barbarous Cossacks.[9] As *volksfremd* (alien to the native population) we were deprived of our possessions, our civic rights, our jobs, and horribly, of our very lives, in Hitler's empire. As aliens we were herded by his hellhounds into concentration camps, men, women, and children, and exterminated with devilish cunning and with the scientific accuracy of Prussia gone mad.[10]

Thus Egypt has lived in our history, in a hundred forms and disguises, penetrating centuries and continents far removed from the ancient empire and its Mideastern tyranny.

Our tragic years in the country of the Nile had historical significance far beyond its contemporary horror. They created in our hearts, together with passionate yearning for freedom, a passionate hatred of oppression; together with contempt for cruel nationalism, they aroused a native devotion to universal tolerance; together with profound revulsion against any affliction of alien or stranger, they helped the burgeoning of a perennial love of *raḥamanut* (compassion, pity, mother love). So that the essence Egypt, in the alchemy of Judaism, changed from the base metal of *ḥamass* (violence)[11] into the golden flow of human sympathy which the *Torah* formulated, encouraged, preached, and little by little achieved as the normal expression of Jewishness.

III *The Method*

But what was the method that changed the spirit of frustration, prevented abiding compulsive passion for revenge, the agony of unrelieved suffering, the bitterness of prolonged degradation? What changed the spirit into a collective and individual attitude of human sympathy, into eagerness to help every child of God, into dynamic Jewish co-operation in any scheme or planned activity to aid the underprivileged anywhere, to take care of the widow, the orphan, the aged, and the helpless, 'as our normal, self-evident duty'?

It was the inbred, habitual association of God with these principles which the *Torah* has been stressing. He, Who took us into Egypt, where we learned of the helpless shame of the unprotected stranger, brought us out of that land of bondage. He broke the power of the Pharaoh and then and there proclaimed for all time the stupid futility of oppression and the basic right to freedom of every one of His children. The God Who defeated the wicked will of the Pharaoh is the God of the *Torah*.[12] The God Who sent the plagues to subdue his ruthless rule is the God Who gave us His commandments. In our prayers, our thanksgiving, in the ceremonies of home and *Shul*, we remember God every day, to remain conscious of His care, His goodness, and of the obligation He has imposed upon us. The God Whom the *Shema* recalls is the God Who bade us judge the cause of the poor. The God Who gave us the Sabbath is the Lord Who made us remember Egypt as we lift up the cup of salvation in welcoming it through the *Kiddush*. Through eternal God-consciousness we tread the path towards goodness, truth, and beauty. Through a life in which every occasion postulates gratitude, recognition of His care and guidance, we keep Him through every *Berakhah* ('continually before us').[13]

Every *kosher* meal reaffirms our fealty to the God Who led us out from under the burdens of Egypt. Food helps to keep alive the human personality. *Kashrut* teaches that every aspect of life is sacred and God-directed. Every Sabbath observance keeps us *en rapport* with the Father in heaven Who took us from the ugly pyramids to the beauty of Zion. Every home based on unselfish kindness, every love cognizant of the

God-commanded respect and affection for our mate, buttresses at once our loyalty to Him and our constant awareness of the task to promote His plan of universal justice, mercy, and peace to be achieved by man.

IV *Character as Destiny*

If our principles, our songs, our destiny were limited to the people of Israel, we would be one nation among many others, of only local significance, and doomed to be swept away by the dustmen of history even as the oppressive dynasties, kingdoms, dukedoms, tribal monarchies in all continents. If we had no aim beyond the satisfactions of our national ambition, we should long ago have been lost. Sunk in the contemporary scene, in narrow vista, we would neither have deserved to survive as a self-willed minority, nor indeed would we have had the fortune of looking back upon a four-thousand-year-old culture, a many-coloured, many-vistaed, many-faceted record, to account for our existence and to bring a message to a disturbed and inwardly insecure human family.

But the children of Israel, from their very inception, were given a different set of commands, a unique marching route. On the one hand the bold, inspiring, and ennobling task, 'In thee all the families of the earth shall be blessed,'[14] on the other, a detailed scheme of life which has aroused the sneer of the cynical self-seekers of every age. The prophet Isaiah has held fast for us the unchanging type of those 'heroes' of the rowdy voice and the ready blow, drunk with power and luxury, devoted to debauchery and drink. They would roar their raucous contempt: 'Whom shall one teach knowledge? Them that are weaned from the milk? Them that are removed from the mother's breast? For it is precept by precept, precept by precept, line by line, line by line, here a little command, here a little ordinance.'[15]

Every *Mitzvah* we form is a link in the chain. Every symbol we serve is a page in the book of the good life. Every conquest of spiritual flabbiness, every moral discipline we espouse, keeps us attuned to the melody of the hope in a better epoch of human effort. There is nothing accidental or planless in the totality of Jewish life and lore, in the classic patterns of conduct which loyalty to the *Torah* has been weaving for so many centuries. Serving the spirit, we had illumination, compassion, and sweet hope throughout the bitter *Galut* nights of darkness, cruelty, and corruption. The God who took us out of Egypt is the God Who promised the

Eternal land and Whose prophets envisioned, described, and prepared the ultimate harvest for which the life in the *Torah* is at once training, preparation, and promise.

V *There are no Outsiders*

The *Seder* nights in the Jewish calendar offer annual emphases of ancient plight, present duty, and future accomplishment. They end with a prayer in which we beseech our Heavenly Father to grant us His aid so that we might move *me-avdut le-ḥerut, miyagon le-simḥah, mi-shibud li-geulah, me-afelah le-orah,* ('from bondage to freedom, from grief to joy, from enslavement to redemption, from darkness to light'). But lest we forget the Father of the universe in the passion of national exclusiveness, in the joy of our expected deliverance, our *Torah* (from the message of Abraham, the prophets in the calls of Micah and Isaiah, our noble thinkers and sweet singers, the masters of ethical instruction and the teachers of mystic lore) has insisted that freedom must be for all men, black or white, lowly or noble of birth; that joy must come to His children in every age or clime; that if darkness is to be conquered permanently and thoroughly, light must bless all.

That is why we recall Egypt every day in our prayer; that is why we mention it in the *Kiddush* heralding our Sabbath or *Yomtov*. That is why it is included in every echo of the past; that is why its sombre message vibrates in the heart and mind of every Jew or Jewess who understands our faith and the meaning of our history.

With the second book of Moses starts the record of the Jewish people and the account of its suffering in Egypt, in slavery and affliction. In the achievement of the latter days, the tragedy of the Pharaohs will have been vanquished in a world which is aware of the interdependence of human welfare, justice, and brotherhood, with none denied his basic right and no tyrant, collective or single, to darken his sun, steal his possessions, or make him afraid.

Notes

1. Exod. XXII, 21.
2. Exod. XXXII, 4.
3. Exod. XXIX, 46.
4. Num. XV, 41.
5. Deut. XXIII, 8.
6. *M. Tan, Lekh.* 9; *ibid Vayig* 10.

7. Exod. XVIII, 3, cp. S. R. Hirsch's comments a.l.
8. J. R. Marcus, *The Jew in the Mediaeval World.*
9. S. Dubnow, *History of the Jews in Russia and Poland.*
10. Wells, *The Janowska Road*; Kaplan, *Agony.*
11. Throughout our Bible, an equivalent of ruining corruption.
12. See Note (4).
13. Ps. XVI, 8.
14. Gen. XII, 3.
15. Isa. XXVIII, 10.

Freedom and Responsibility

I

The business man in his counting house, the craftsman in his shop, the professional in his office or study, the youth upon the field of sport, must each look upon his physical prowess, mental strength, upon knowledge or skill, not only as a gift from on high, but as a boon involving the obligation to use it morally and wisely, justly and benignly. To represent Judaism properly means to use the community's power and institutions in accord with the principles of the *Torah*. The synagogue, the *Kosher* restaurant, the Hebrew school, the *Mikvah* – all must bear the mark of the communal commitment *hitnaeh lefanav bemitzvot* – to express Jewishness in a manner satisfactory both morally and aesthetically.

The *Sidrah* we are reading today contains but forty verses, one of the last addresses of Moshe Rabbenu to his flock. His message is couched in words of utter simplicity, from the shepherd to his flock, expressed now in ruthless censure, now in accents of a father's loving concern for the life, happiness, and future of his children. Every word is chosen, not by philological finesse, but by the wisdom and tenderness of our immortal teacher. The words, which commence and name the portion of the week, invite reflection. *Attem nitzavim lifne Hashem Elokekhem* is usually translated

'You are standing before the Lord your God,' but the normal Hebrew for that would be *Attem Omdim*. You know the inscription over the Holy Ark in the synagogue *Da lifne mi attah omed* – 'Know before Whom thou art standing.' *Nitzavim* suggests something else.

Moshe Rabbenu's addresses to his people in his last days derive their timelessness not only from their quality, but from a tense awareness of the passing nature of individual life. He told his flock: 'I am over, passing from earthly life to the great beyond, even as every man or woman is bound to do, but you, as a people, the *Kehilat Yaakov*, the *Am Yisrael*, will be *nitzavim*, enduring, as a monument of God's wisdom and mercy. I have known you in your stubbornness as in your devotion, I have dealt with the idiosyncracies of countless individuals, but I have never lost sight of the character of the whole people. You are going to be the abiding entity – *matzevah* – in the concert of the nations, at once the proof for the existence of God and a living symbol of challenge of occasional defeat and ultimate victory.[1] So, before the sun of my life sets, let me speak to you. Today and every day of the infinite future you will be standing – *Koolkhem* – before God.'

The word '*kol*' in Hebrew has two meanings: One, 'all,' the other, 'the whole.' All the Jewish people, its heroes and villains, its leaders, the *neviim* (God's spokesmen), its teachers, craftsmen, and men of business, an interdependent group – all always are facing Him. *Rashekhem shivtekhem* ('your heads, your tribes'). S. R. Hirsch pointed out that the expected text would read: *Rashekhem le shitvekhem* ('the heads of your tribes'). But this is not what Moshe had in mind. His urgent teaching was: Your leadership will be responsible for the character of the folk under its care: 'Your leaders, that is your tribes,' an identity of character and quality. 'Your leaders, even as your officers,' and all of the pattern-creators together who shape every personality in Israel. If all kings, judges, elders, men in authority, were always conscious of their tremendous opportunity and as its corollary, of their infinite responsibility, Jewish and general history would have been made and written in brighter colour. But it is not only officialdom that is both warned and encouraged. The ultimate foundation of society is the family. In the economy of modern life, the father plays less and less of a crucial role in the moral and spiritual development of the child. That task has fallen upon the mother. Every freedom implies commitment to use it fairly, every asset spells responsibility: physical strength, intellectual power, material possessions, they are both opportunities and tests to protect home, community, nation, the human race. We need the brawn and courage of men, the teacher's wisdom and devotion, the working man's fair labour, the rich man's moral awareness. *Tapkhem Neshekhem* 'Your children' said Moshe Rabbenu, 'That means, your women.' Theirs is the abiding influence, theirs the chance, to train the infant from its earliest days, in reverence for God and man, in right habits and attitudes. If women realized their vital role in the destiny of their people, they would be blessed by happy self-assurance, by domestic peace, more harmonious lives from adolescence through maturity. Woman's intuition, motherliness, her maximum chance to organize her daily agenda, her common sense no less than her tenderness, are utterly indispensable factors in the life of the community.

Ve-gerkha asher bish-arekha ('Even thy stranger that is in thy gates, in the midst of thy camp') belongs to its moral climate. How he has been treated does in definite manner shape the history of the whole group. We in our beloved United States, of late, have learned that lesson. Recent Negro violence, unpleasant, reprehensible, disturbing as it has been, is yet to no small extent due to the underprivileged in their own ranks or in the unhappy ghettoes of minorities. The stranger, fortunate enough to have enjoyed genuine hospitality, equality before the law, and communal care, will be inspired to similar attitudes and thereby to advance the Jewish ideal of faith in God translated into consistent justice and mercy to man.

II

But it is not only all of us whose happiness, moral worth, security, are interdependent. Moshe Rabbenu has another message, surprisingly modern. In a recent publication of the American Medical Association two articles appeared, one by the world-famous William C. Menninger, the other by the noted theologian, Prof. A. J. Heschel, both stressing an insufficiently understood fact: The patient is a person, a total personality and only one who views him as such can hope to cure him. There is no sick leg, or head, or chest, there is only a sick person. Only the physician who is concerned with the whole man: 'All he has ever been, all that he is and all that he hopes to be . . . his genes, his chromosomes, his original and his current family, his hopes and his aspirations, his psychology and his sociology,'[2] will know how to treat him. Medicine and religion must combine in the endeavour to restore him, body and soul, his total personality. How can one accomplish the ancient ideal and the counsel of modern psychiatry? How can one bring about the flowering of humaneness, consistency, kindness – the total programme of religion which Moshe Rabbenu again and again stressed – *Koolkhem*: The whole of you, of every man and woman in our Camp?

Our religion does not offer an ocean of fog, in which intelligence is drowned, with uncontrolled emotion rising sky-high. 'It is not above in heaven, nor beyond the sea,' said Moses.[3] But it needs the affirmation, the inner commitment, the concrete work of the whole of your personality: 'The charge I bring you in the name of God does not call for a hermit's meditation in his lonely hut on a mountain top.' Nor is isolation from fellowmen advocated for the task the Lord has imposed upon you. 'It is in your mouth, and in your heart to do it.'[4] First of all: in your mouth. Acknowledge it with your speech, as an expression of your view of life. Affirmation is an essential duty. Acknowledgment of God's law as the standard of human values is mandatory for the good life. It requires both thought and courage. We are still impressed by Jonah's declaration: 'I am a Hebrew and I revere the Lord of the heavens Who made the sea and the dry land.'[5] Such fearless acknowledgment has been ever vital in the record of any minority and in particular of the Jewish people, not only in mature life but in youth as well. Many problems faced by college students are solved as they state their religious affiliation and take for granted the right to be different as the essence of democracy. The worthwhile professor, later on the industrialist, regards such declaration as evidence of a good character and accepts it as a personal asset, bound to enhance the benefit of the young man's affiliation with his academy or business. But whilst such declaration may be impressive, it has no significance unless it is the expression of a definite commitment, of a sentiment solid enough to influence his attitude and action. Said Moshe Rabbenu: 'It is in your mouth,' but it must also be 'in your heart.' Nothing is easier than the pronouncement of identity, or of noble ideals. It may be superficial, fabricated for gain, fraudulent. In his pithy speech, that leader of our people completed his lesson: 'To do it.'[6] What is necessary is the clear word, the inward thought, and action based on both. This is how Jews ought to live. This is how they ought to build their homes. Declaration of love for the mate is natural and precious, but that speech must be based on depth and permanence of sentiment and made concrete in the fabric of the average day. Conduct as the harvest of word and feeling is the only right goal of pedagogy. Let the child hear that you love him! Let him feel your attachment by your attitude. Let him see it in the hundred big and little actions of parental life!

That is how your neighbour should experience it: The friendly word, the sincere sentiment which prompts it, the solid social conduct which promotes harmony and hence security. A Jew living in accord with this teaching will retain his intellectual awareness, his emotional balance, his pervading optimism. The programme of his life will remain flexible in manner and method, but changeless in principle. He will promote the welfare of the people and stay blessed by an inner assurance of the value of individual and collective life. He will not be the victim of conflicting emotions, panicky at any display of Gentile hostility, or in trying for majority approval, escape into soulless conformity. He will say with Moshe Rabbenu: 'The unknowable future, *hanistarot* – the hidden things, still in the womb of history belong to the Lord our God. In His hand rests the ultimate chapters of Jewish history. But for us and our children, for generations without end, they are *haniglot*, the revealed directions of life, the *Torah* with its principles and practices, ideals and attitudes, commandments and promises.[7]

'Not above in heaven, nor beyond the sea.' This faith requires no superhuman exertion, no life-escaping mysteries. The way to its goal and its marching song are contained in three orders for every day, interdependent and complementary. *Befikha, bilevavekha, la'assoto:* 'Speak it with your mouth, feel it in your heart, do it!'

Notes

1. See S. R. Hirsch's comments on this verse.
2. *The Patient as a Person.*
3. Deut. xxx 12, 13.
4. Deut. xxx, 14.
5. Jonah I, 9.
6. Deut. xxx, 14.
7. Deut. xxix, 28.

Thanksgiving and the Family

I *No Favourites*

'*Leolam lo yeshaneh beno habbanim* (Let no man favour one son above the others)', for, because for the weight of two *shekalim* worth of silk which Jacob spent on Joseph alone, his brothers became envious and matters developed so that all the family went into exile to Egypt.'[1] Our Rabbis' advice applies equally to the family, the country, and to mankind. Wise, patient, devoted parents, will avoid above all making arbitrary distinction between one child and the other. They will thus keep the family at a minimum of tension and at a maximum of harmony.

Wise, devoted statesmanship will allow no discrimination against any citizen and thus will promote peace and happiness among all. The United Nations will succeed globally only if that principle and attitude is preserved.

This weekend, all over the country, the pulpit is dedicated to thought and sentiment of Thanksgiving. Out of the chaos of Europe's cruelty, bigotry, and violence grew America – the greatest power for democracy. We Jews in particular share with joy, the pride and promise of the United States: Freedom under the law, a constitutional guarantee of fair play to any citizen, the gradual solidification of the rights of every inhabitant, white or coloured, Christian, Jew, Mohammedan, or Hindu. They make of this country the hope of a happier chapter of human affairs everywhere.

From Rome comes a message of the Catholic Church having finally collected enough courage and wisdom to undo two millennia of slander and horrid persecution. On many occasions I have pointed out that Anti-Semitism, whilst it afflicts the Jew, essentially is a Gentile problem. Many noble Christians must have been heavily burdened by the knowledge of their Church's guilt in Jewish suffering. Malcolm Hay,[2] Travers Herford,[3] George Foot Moore,[4] and other righteous people among the Gentiles, who now have a share in the World to Come, as well as many others, whose life is guided by conscience and intelligence, will rejoice in the meantime tentative proclamation. For us it is not of fundamental importance, although it brought us welcome news. It is the beginning of what may well develop into a new period of Jewish-Gentile relations. We ought to rejoice in the fact that organized Christian religion, in one branch at least, has emancipated itself from the moral shackles of the past.

II *The Jewish Family*

We should give thanks to our Father in Heaven for the foundation, in His Holy *Torah*, of the Jewish Family, the ultimate haven of a good life, potentially of greatest blessing: the Jewish home, as its harvest of happy, fine children, its music, its serenity, its promise of the realization of the parents' dream of raising a group of Jewish personalities, reverent, upright, merciful and upheld by pervading serenity.

We have good and ample reasons for humble thanks to our Father in Heaven. But every opportunity implies responsibility; every promise imposes devotion.

All positive elements in today's global situation have not appeared for the first time in Jewish history. Did not the rabbis say: '*Mah she'ira le'yaakov ira levanav.*'[5] The family is the foundation of Jewish life and a single hope of our national survival. The family is a laboratory of Jewish ethics with unselfish parents guided by consistent wisdom and wise care; the family can become a miniature sanctuary from whose portals can emerge the fine personalities of sons and daughters. But a family uninformed by Jewish principles, ignorant of the methods of Judaism, can deteriorate through selfishness and disintegrate for the lack of both proper parental guidance and children's co-operation.

America is the second chance offered to the victims of European folly and cruelty, but America needs not only wise statemanship, but a citizenry ever aware of the principles of the Constitution, the rights of every individual and the interdependence of local, national, and global interests. To the Jew, America is more than an opportunity to reach success in business or profession. Unless our country's programme remains a challenge, the average American might develop into a soft weakling whose moral fibre evaporates for lack of ideals. It is only when every citizen is aware of America as a developing civilization and emergent culture, of the fact that we still have a long way to go to realize the ideals of the Founding Fathers, that we shall be willing to forgo private ambition for the public good.

III *The American Dream*

Not only the Roman Catholics, but many Protestants have joined in manifestations of a new attitude towards our people. That does indicate a justification of some hope for a happier period even though it may take a long time until the new voice of Roman conscience reaches every parish priest, and until the declaration of Protestant world leaders causes the average minister to change the millennial hostility to our people in both matter and manner of his sermons, especially before Christmas and Passover. But unless we Jews remain disciplined in our position of dignity and courage, the new movement may undermine our loyalty in a vain hope that the time of the Messiah has already arrived.

There are two popular philosophies – pessimism, which sees no good in human affairs or in the history of the universe – and optimism, which accepts this world as the best of all possible ones and which looks at human history through roseate spectacles. Neither of these two philosophies is that of our faith. Judaism is not pessimistic because it has never given up hope in the eventual humanization of humanity nor surrendered its faith in the providence of our moral and merciful God. Judaism is not optimistic because it is only too much aware of human frailty, carelessness and selfishness.

IV *Meliorism*

The philosophy of Judaism is meliorism which means the assumption that the world is neither good nor bad, but that the world must become *melior* (which means better) by human effort to walk the way of the Lord through righteousness and mercy to achieve ultimate peace and happiness.

Thankgsgiving, this year, came three days before *Ḥanukkah*, and that festival emphasized that nothing abidingly good can be achieved without *Ḥanukkah* or dedication. The spirit of dedication depends upon *Ḥinnukh* which means training, self-discipline. The home, the school, the Synagogue, the national councils, organized religion, the United Nations may all achieve their purpose through the iron-clad principle: 'Let none favour one son over the other, one citizen over the other, one race over the other.' For that way lies inescapable trouble, sore exile, death. But we Jews have been trained to believe that the programme of *Ḥanukkah* is not a vacation dream, but a solid goal for every Jew as for every child of God everywhere.

Notes

1. *Shabb.* 10b.
2. Author of *Foot of Pride.*
3. Author of *Talmud and Apocrypha* and *Pharisaism.*
4. Author of a 3 vol. book on *Judaism.*
5. *M. Tanhuma, Vayigash* 10.

The Human Situation

I

'This is the history of Isaac: Abraham was his father.' The luminous example of the pioneer, his rectitude and benignity, his loving kindness and obedience to the God he proclaimed, trained the son to walk in his ways.

But the second chapter of Isaac's history was not as simple in its background. He married Rebeccah, the daughter of Bethuel, the sister of Laban. If you study chapter xxiv of *Genesis*, you will discover that the spokesman of Bethuel's family was not the inconspicuous father, nor the almost anonymous mother, but the crafty Laban. It was Laban, who, 'When he saw the ring and the bracelets upon his sister's hands',[1] went to the man and said: 'Come in, thou beloved of the Lord.' It was her brother and her mother who said: 'Let the damsel abide with us a few days.'[2]

It was Laban who sought to trick Jacob out of his hire and thus evoked his reaction. It was Laban who proclaimed his hypocritical interest in the daughters, Jacob's wives, and who, on his gentle son-in-law, inflicted a gratuitous sermon on the obligation not to afflict them. The second generation of Isaac's family would not be able altogether to escape Laban's influence. Do not the rabbis suggest that the sons resemble, physically and morally, the mother's brothers?[3]

The *Torah* reports that 'when the children struggled together within her,' Rebeccah proclaimed (in anguish): 'If it be so, wherefore do I live?'[4]

It seems difficult to assume that hers was the first case of twins in the country or that the discomfort involved would drive her to depair. Rebeccah was distinguished by a keen mind and considerable presence of mind. What caused her fear was rather an awareness of the conflict between what she had learned to know about Abraham and what she knew Laban stood for. She foresaw the collision of these polar attitudes in her unborn children. So she went to inquire of the prophet (according to Rashbam's interpretation)[5] who gave her the Lord's answer that the two children would, in their personalities, represent the conflict between the tradition of Abraham and the way of life of Laban, but that ultimately the better, younger son would prevail. Her anxiety was overcome, as she accepted the situation.

II *A Universal Experience*

In truth, it was not a unique problem. It is a universal experience. Every human being, every child born into this world, presents this problem. It is the primeval struggle between what a modern philosopher calls the will for unity and the will for dispute, known in the Jewish tradition, as the war between the *yetzer tov* (the good impulse) and *yetzer ha-ra* (the impulse for evil).[6] None of us is perfectly white or angelic, none hopelessly black. This is the human situation: that we are exposed to a double orientation. The *Torah* does not want us to lose our balance in futile worry about it. We must face it as the human problem and then set about solving it. Facing it, we have taken the first step towards overcoming it.

Esau did not start out utterly evil. He had his occasional good intention and fine emotion. When under the impact of his appetites, he became blind and deaf to any other consideration. When he saw those red lentils, he demanded them fiercely, almost stammering his plea: 'Let me fast swallow some of this red, red pottage.' He suddenly finds that 'I am at the point to die and what profit will the birthright do to me.'[7] His parents had warned him against the low daughters of his heathen neighbours, but, when his passion was aroused, he took to wife the very Hittite women because of whom his mother was weary of her life.[8]

Yet the same Esau, when he saw that 'the daughters of Canaan pleased not Isaac his father, went to Ishmael and took his daughter Mahalat to be his wife.[9] When he went to meet Jacob, his brother, he took four hundred men with him, not to hurt Jacob (a smaller number could have done that), but as Rashbam rightly explains, as a matter of ceremonial honour. Indeed, the *Torah* reports: 'Esau ran to meet him, and embraced him and fell on his neck and they wept.'[10] He was capable of affection and did not hesitate to show it.

III *Esau and Edom*

Esau lacked emotional stability, self-restraint, and self-discipline. Thus he gradually deteriorated. Edom, his clan, developed into the hereditary treacherous enemy of Israel, his image etched in eternal contempt by Obadia: 'For the violence done to thy brother Jacob, shame shall cover thee and thou shalt be cut off forever. In the day that thou didst stand aloof when strangers carried away his substance, even thou wast as one of them . . . Thou shouldst not have stood in the crossway to cut off those of his who escape.'[11]

Esau, victim of his appetites, became our people's bitterest enemy. Heartless Rome and the persecuting Church were given his name as a symbol of cruelty, of the murderous, looting, exiling, slandering priests, kings, and governors who for fifteen hundred years brought unimaginable misery to our people, and whose descendants only of late have shown promise of a more humane conduct towards the nation that ended the kingdom of heathen arrogance by proclaiming the One God of justice and mercy.

Every child, Jewish or non-Jewish, is born to that human situation. Every son may become an Esau or a Jacob, moving from unconscious infancy, through the pangs of adolescence, towards disciplined maturity; or growing only physically, beset by increasing desires and becoming their slave.

Every Jewish mother, guardian of home and children, from their early age, must reckon with this double-edged potentiality, must plan her strategy: to encourage every good trait, to discourage every evil one – by good example, by a judicious scheme to reward and punishment, by granting wise wishes and denying wrong ones. Every *mitzvah* offers such pedagogic opportunity.

The Hebrew word for education (*ḥinnukh*) is derived from a root meaning 'sweetening the palate', making good habits pleasant, evil ones unpleasant, in careful training. That parental task is grave but not too exacting; father and mother must stay conscious of it: (*ashmurah shlishit: tinok yonek mishde immo veisha messaperet im ba-alah*) 'when the baby is still at mother's breast, husband and wife shall discuss the goal and methods of its future education.'[12]

Where such consciousness is ever present, the *ḥinnukh* becomes a source of steady delight, an increasingly successful venture. Children look upon wise, firm, benign parents as their closest friends, and the pattern of their conduct becomes the ideal of their own life. To be like father is the boy's normal wish, to imitate mother's word, gesture, action is the girl's happy ambition.

IV *Personality*

Early in life, the personality of the children receives its decisive form. Parental politeness begets the youngster's courtesy. Father's reverence inspires the child's attitude.

The adult must be conscious of the inescapable consequence of attitude, speech, action. The child's mind absorbs them resourcefully, critically, eagerly. That the parents must maintain a united front before their offspring, goes without saying. That there must be perfect harmony between principle avowed and one's own conduct, is a trite truism. But the logical acceptance thereof is deplorably in advance of its translation into the hundred acts of daily life. The *Yetzer hara*, at times, hides behind polysyllabic argument, the 'need to be realistic,' 'overwork and consequent strained nerves' or 'sad forgetfulness.' Upon the youthful mind, every rawness, carelessness, little or big hypocrisy, is etched in enduring emphasis.

The kindness, chivalry, rectitude of father and mother stimulate the child's heart and mind in amazing fashion. Every *Mitzvah* offers fine opportunity for encouraging good habits and discouraging evil ones. Every social lie uttered by the parent corrodes the personality of the adolescent. To teach children *Kashrut* and Sabbath observance means to bring home to them the thought that present enjoyment must occasionally be ignored because of greater issue or later consequences. The high school child, ready in a momentary emergency to go with little or no food in order to stay loyal to the *Din Torah*, will easily be led to forgo, later on, attractive unrighteous profit for the sake of the ideal of honesty. Devoting time to study the *Torah* will prepare the adolescent for the need to consult higher considerations than love of pleasure.

Every mother occasionally may feel like Rebeccah, as her children's character is unfolding. Every father, from time to time, should ask himself: 'If that be so, wherefore do I live?' To seek the answer of God, to search for the goal and way in the sacred texts of our *Torah*, means to retrace individually the path our people have trodden in a thousand confused areas and times.

The solution of the problem will come in unmistakable terms: Teach your child self-discipline! Use the *Torah*'s method of habituation by example, by consistent teaching, by feeding mind and heart! In infancy, it is benignity and firmness, in adolescence generous attention to the son's or daughter's problems, *Weltschmerz*, the need to be accepted, to be encouraged, to be respected. From a home of parental wisdom and goodness, out of a parental capacity for self-restraint, out of the milieu of *yirat hashem*, *ḥen*, and *ḥessed*, will eventually emerge children of moral stature, transmitters of our heritage, to justify our life, bring comfort to our old age, and destined to stay *Yissrael*, fighters and workers for the good world, into which the Lord set us *leavdah uleshamrah* – to work develop, beautify, and guard it.

Notes

1. Gen. XXIV, 30.
2. Gen. XXIV, 55.
3. *Midrash Rabbah a.l.*
4. Gen. XXV, 22.
5. Gen. XXV, 22.
6. Paul Haeberlin, *Das Gute*.
7. Gen. XXV, 30.
8. Gen. XXVI, 35.
9. Gen. XXVIII, 9.
10. Gen. XXXIII, 3, 4.
11. *Obad.* 10, 11.
12. *Tosephta Berakhot* 1.

Hayom Ḥarat Olam (Our Inner World may be ever Renewed)

I

Consciousness distinguishes man from animal. Self-consciousness marks a higher level. God-consciousness in one form or another has blessed and challenged man from time immemorial. But it is spiritual awareness and ethical sensitiveness which distinguish a religious person.

II

The technical revolution has given us increasing control over matter and has steadily weakened our depth of security. Expansion has spelt horizontal progress and vertical regression, hence a 'generation of the wilderness,' hence frantic atheism and frantic revivalism, hence too often a youth without faith, middle age without dignity, old age without grace.

III

To them all speaks the Wisdom of the Ages, the timeless tradition of our people: 'Nothing is younger than the hope of faith, nothing more old-fashioned than the negations of *apikorsut* (irreverance).' Families are reared on reverence for *ha-kaddosh barukh hu* ('The Holy One blessed be He'); men and women become rootless when they abandon faith in Him. The *Shofar* and all of *Tishri* teach that He shall be the Lord our God, source of our standards, at once Creator, Father, Lawgiver. Through *Halakhah* we move Godwards, peacewards, towards outer security and inner serenity.

IV

All that is not a mere gift from on high, but the fruit of self-criticism, recognition of our failures of yesterday. Through such re-orientation we can, may, should, always rebuild our life: *Hayom Ḥarat Olam*.

To all my Center family, to all Israel, to all His children everywhere: A happy, peaceful, blessed year!

At-one-ment for Atonement (A Radio Address in critical times)

Within a very few hours American Israel, from home and store, from office and apartment, will be gathered in the synagogue to spend twenty-four hours in fasting and self-examination. Jews will enter the House of God knowing that unless each of them, by earnest effort, has endeavoured to right every wrong, unless he has sincerely asked his neighbour's pardon for any offence committed against him, his prayers and his fasting will be in vain. It is only after his re-at-one-ment by genuine penitence before the great day that *Yom Kippur* will bring forgiveness to him.

This year's *Yom Kippur* is fraught with graver significance than any we have faced. The whole world around us is in great peril. Not only our beloved country, but everything else that has been sacred to us, is assailed with frightful violence. The things we count on from without, the things we live by from within, alike the basis of our body politic, and the foundations of every soul – God, Faith, Love, Justice, Mercy – are being denied the right to live, in order that *Lebensraum* may be provided for the most hellish combination of cruelty, coldness, and corruption.

Unless we are determined, past cavil and compromise, to serve with all our heart, to promote regardless of sacrifice, the cause of democracy in its meaning for war and peace, our pilgrimage to the House of God will be vanity of vanities and futility of futilities. Against Hitler's purpose of total destruction nothing will avail except total dedication to truth and justice.

A great rabbi was preparing his flock for the Day of Atonement, and to render its message vibrant and efficacious for the rest of the year, he said to them: 'The holiest day of the Year is the Day of Atonement. The holiest place in the world is Jerusalem. Holiest in Jerusalem is the Temple, the most sacred part thereof is the Holy of Holies. The holiest man is the High Priest beseeching on that holiest day in that holiest city the forgiveness of the holy God for His people.'

'In truth, my children,' the Rabbi continued, 'this moment is not restricted to an annual occurrence. Every day may be *Yom Kippur*, every city Jerusalem, every home a holy of holies, every man or woman a high priest, even *every* soul praying for God's mercy upon His Children everywhere.'

The message of *Yom Kippur* is beyond the synagogue and timeless. Its tocsin sounds not to Israel alone. We all, Jew and Gentile, white and coloured, need this at-one-ment. At-one-ment with each other and atonement with God. At times faith in the Divine Father of us all will bring us a sense of blessed one-ness with our fellowmen everywhere. At other times, the precious sense of unity with every human conveys to us a new understanding and a new one-ness with God. But, whether it comes from man to God, or from God to man – the one unity lacks significance without the other.

If any war were to be fought for America, or for England, or for the democracies alone, we would not be able to marshal the enthusiasm, to collect the stupendous energies vital to its successful conclusion. As long as we keep our faith limited to family, group, or nation, we shall be handicapped by our tepid spirit against the unlimited fervour of the enemies. We shall lack the power of persuasion, the divine spirit of dedication that alone can make this nation rise like one man, conquering all smallness and selfishness, in the great battle to reclaim God and humanity for the dark horizon of the present.

But, if any war be fought as the great re-at-one-ment for all His children, in a united humanity anxious to bring light, comfort, peace, and security to every man, woman, and child on earth, then the sweep of our righteous imagination, wedded to the deathless impulse of His battalions, will lend us power and irresistible marching strength, which will overwhelm the citadels of evil and lead us up the glorious hill to victory.

Yom Kippur demands of us that wisdom of the heart, that strength of soul, which comes from the resolve to build a better world for our children and our neighbour's children, to wipe tears off every face and to lend a helping hand to every brother and sister. The prophet appeals to this inward one-ness when he proclaims: And on that day the great *Shofar* of freedom will be sounded, a banner to the peoples of the world, and there will come the banished from Babylon and the scattered from Egypt – all the world's victims, all the forlorn, forgotten, lifeless, lustreless, hopeless, the exiles from peace and comfort, the endless army of the bruised by violence, and the crippled by coldness and the crushed by corruption – streaming towards the field of At-one-ment, in the blessed hour when we have found our peace and happiness in an unconfined brotherhood of man.

This is the goal. The way thereto lies over many a fertile field, over many a yawning abyss, over enchanting sunsets, over dried bones in deep valleys, over strikes and lockouts, over revolutions and world wars.

May we be blessed to live to see its dawn, an era of peace and security for all man. May we be blessed to enter the House of God tonight and tomorrow, informed by this vision and true to its calling, from one end of the world to the other.

'It is Easy to be *Froommer*'

I

The message of last week emphasized three times about Abraham and Isaac: 'The two of them went together.' This week's *sidrah* speaks of the life of Sarah and of her demise. Into the vacuum between the two portions of the *Torah*, the wisdom of our sages put a most significant statement: *Meah p'eyot pe'atah Sarah immenu*, which means: 'Mother Sarah sobbed a hundred sobs, groaned a hundred groans at the time of the *akedah*,' as she feared that Isaac's life might be over and the heritage of Abraham lost forever. But before she died, she knew that the Lord did not desire his life, but only his father's readiness to stand the supreme test of offering his choicest hope, his greatest asset, if He desired it.

This assembly is a wonderful instance of the undying spirit of Abraham. Early in the '20s, I delivered my first address to the Convention of the Union of Orthodox Jewish Congregations of America. And today, I have the privilege of making the fourth or fifth. Between these two dates, there came the indescribable catastrophe that befell our people and the incredible restoration of the Homeland: *Athalta diathalta digeulah*, the beginning of the emergent Redemption.

What inspired the difference has been the spirit of Abraham, the timeless dedication of Israel which dispersed the beasts of prey, the croaking ravens predicting disaster to loyal Jews in our country. Indeed, we have moved from grief to joy, from darkness to light. The Union's farsighted leadership, noble rabbinic influence, and faithful rank and file have been blessed, in particular, also, by its Women's Branch, whose rank and file combine charm with efficiency and intuition with dedicated labour. Of great significance in the renaissance of classic Judaism in the United States has been the vital and wondrously effective *Torah Umesorah* movement mainly responsible for the almost four hundred Jewish Day Schools in the United States which help to raise a new Jewish laity – one which learned to know and love Judaism as creed and life. You have seen today a preponderance of fresh, dynamic spirit, an effective representation of our academic youth, and the appearance on your platform of men distinguished alike as scholars of the *Torah*, as scientists, and as teachers in American universities. The Union's work is reaching from one end of the North American continent to another and its influence reaches far beyond these frontiers.

II

Our times have been described as falling in the century of the youth. The Biblical verse: 'And the two of them walked together' (interpreted as a command: 'And the two of them, young and old, parents and children, shall walk together'), early in this century, was given undue emphasis on the rights of youth. Progressive education by now has barely recovered from its excessive methods of favouring the younger generation at all costs. Leaders of pedagogy have recognized that self-expression of the youth as a major cult suffers from the fact that there may not be a self to express. The accent today is on the self-realization of our children. We *Torah*-true Jews dare not gamble with this vital task. *Ḥinnukh* (religious training), to be fruitful, must be based on the combination of the Jewish tradition with the assured results of modern pedagogy. We do need all sympathy; we do have all affection for our children. We do recognize the paramount importance of devotion. But it must all be combined with *emunat Avraham* (the faith of Abraham). The integration is achievable only through the consistent loyalty to our Holy *Torah*. Our people's immortality rests not on Jewish nationalism alone, nor on matchless philanthropic enterprise, but on *ruaḥ Elokim* (the spirit of God).

The world today is beset by the primeval contrasts of *gashmiyut* and *ruḥniyut*, i.e., the quest, above all, for comfort, physical ease, material possession, as opposed by the realm of spiritual values, social ideals, the faith, thought, and life of Judaism.

The very first chapter of the Holy Torah describes *ruaḥ Elokim* (the spirit of God) resting upon the incipient world. Our sages offer the remarkable comment that it was *ruḥo shel Mashiaḥ* (the spirit of Messiah). They declared that the Lord created the world with the purpose of a classless, warless, humane society brought about, in the latter days, by the son of David, the Messiah. In order to struggle against *gashmiyut* (the impulse and power of today's mankind) we pray that our Heavenly Father bestow upon us the boon of His *ruaḥ*. We implore Him to be *mashiv haruaḥ umorid hagashem* – to allow His Spirit to float, to hover over human affairs so that He may lower the *geshem* of materialism to its proper level. As his partners in the ever-emergent creation, we must ever wait with bated breath for the manifestation of His Spirit and allow it to guide us in our private, communal, and national affairs.

We have always been the smallest of the nations. The *Torah* never promised us military prowess or political dominance over others. Tonight you will be reciting the precious verse containing promise and hope for our people: *u-mashalta be-goyim rabbim u-vekha lo yimsholu*. We translate it as: 'You will rule over many nations, but they will not rule over you.' My sainted father saw a different meaning in this verse. He compared *malakh al* (which means 'rule over one' as a king used to rule over his subject or the master over his slave) with *mashal be*, which means ruling *in* one. One can rule in a person through a set of principles and ideas which one has inspired in him. The Jewish people was never meant to rule over others. It was their being granted the blessing of the Divine Spirit which would enable them to rule *in* the nations of the world by making them aware and appreciative of the ideals or righteousness and mercy for which Israel has been called into being, by reason of acceptance of which Israel has become God's ambassador, and in the pursuit of which Israel will bring peace and happiness to all God's children everywhere.

III. '*Pray, do not take Thy Holy Spirit from us!*'

Without God's Spirit, our 4,000 year-old ethical, spiritual tradition would be, gradually, in danger. Without His Spirit, our laity would become afflicted with deadly sluggishness, our religion reduced to a palatal habit and to emotional excessiveness on sad or happy occasions. Without the Spirit of God, our rabbis would lack the courage of leadership, the fulfilment of their task thwarted by *paḥad hahoraah* (fear of rendering decisions). *Halakhah* needs *ruaḥ Elokim*. The two are interdependent. *Halakhah* without the spirit might become, God forbid, conformity without dedication, completely spiritless and lifeless. Jewish spirit without *halakhah* would end in confusion, debility, and chaos.

The study of the *Torah* is of vital importance. Pride in the national accomplishment of Israel is legitimate. Charitable interest is the solid expression of Jewish social responsibility. The U.J.A. is a sacred cause. But all these things are but the fruits of a life in accord with the *Din Torah* (Jewish Law). It must remain the abiding major purpose of our Union to encourage, promote, organize, and assure nation-wide, collective as well as individual, loyalty to the *Din Torah*.

With Eliezer, the servant of Abraham, we must say to them: 'Pray do not delay me. The Lord has prospered my way. Let me depart so that I may go to my Master.' Some folks would involve the Union in side issues which would tax its time, energy and means, and thereby diminish its power of concentration for the single goal to be achieved. For we Jews have but one single task: to summon all creative human power and to dedicate it exclusively to the realization of our religious ideals. That means, as a matter of course, labour for the betterment of our fellow man. That means, as a matter of course, to live with the Gentile in constant co-operation, in constant exchange of thought and action. That means, normally and self-evidently, all that is good in local patriotism. But it means, above it and yet with it labour for the general improvement of humanity at large.

In a critical moment of our history, an arch enemy Haman, described us as a people '*mefuzar u'meforad*' (scattered and divided). Our rabbis in the *Talmud* interpreted *meforad* to suggest *kehada fredah she'enah molidah* (like a mule that cannot give birth). Rabbis, deprived of the divine spirit, would sink into hopeless sterility, creating subdivision after subdivision, each of them kept up by the delusion that their splinter group alone has the key to *Gan Eden*. 'It is easy to be *froommer*. It is much harder to be *froomm*, *Torah*-true, in theory and practice.'

IV

The Union, in collaboration with the Rabbinical Council, inspired by the Yeshiva University and the other *Yeshivot*, has concentrated on positive, unifying issues. We may humbly and gratefully offer the timeless blessing of *Sheheḥiyanu*. But our task is far from complete. The scope of our work, the dimensions of our understanding have deepened and widened. But, *makom hinihu lanu avotenu lehitgadder bo*, our ancestors have left us some points to excel in, some fundamental imperatives to be followed for our work to succeed.

The first is clarity. We must understand, plan our programme, and act on our conviction that only a life in accord with the din *Torah* will enable us to transmit the heritage of Abraham to the next generation. *Be'en ḥazon* – without vision, we have no future.

We need *ne'emanut*, (usually translated as 'faithfulness'). But Rashbam (Rabbi Shlomoh ben Meier – Rashi's grandson), in his comment on *avdi Moshe bekhol beti ne'eman hu* (my servant Moshe . . . he is faithful [trusted] in all my house) interprets *ne'eman* to mean *kevua bemassmerim lo yimot* (firm as something riveted by nails that cannot be moved). It recalls the 15th Psalm . . . 'Who can dwell in Thy tent? Who may abide in Thy Holy Mountain? Who is a *Torah*-true Jew?' The heading of this psalm could well read: 'God's Gentleman.' The answer is: 'One who walketh blamelessly, and worketh righteousness, and speaketh truth in his heart.' It is so easy to speak truth with one's lips; but to speak truth in our heart means to translate its words into the motivation of our action. Such a man, the psalmist says: *lo yimot* (he will never be moved). That type of *Torah*-true Jew will strengthen our cause and enhance our pride and joy.

We need a pervasive sense of aesthetic awareness, Samson Raphael Hirsch's modern version of the ancient formula: *Torah im derekh eretz*. But this awareness of system and order is by no means as a concession to non-Jews, as a compromise of Jewish attitude in order that we may feel at home in the world of today. It is authentic Jewish teaching: *hitnaeh lefanav bemitzvot* (to express our conformity to His command in beautiful manner, pleasing to mind and heart). Aesthetic awareness is not *ḥukat hagoy*, (a Gentile asset and tradition) but the spelling out in consistent charm of *hidur mitzvah* (graceful, harmonious performance of Divine commands).

A most important condition is what *Ḥassidim* call *shiflut* (humility).

We must enter our synagogue in a spirit not of cocksure smugness. There are too many among the younger generation in particular, who belong to the group which the prophets have denounced as *sha'anaanim* (careless worshippers). I regret the need to introduce a word of criticism into this happy assembly, but I am pained to confess that in too many synagogues Divine service represents three hours of conversation, occasionally interrupted by prayer. This is nothing to smile about. It is painful and harmful to the cause which unites us.

Shiflut is the attitude of humility which the creature feels before the Creator, grateful for the possibility of *Kirvat Elokim* (closeness to God). Instead of such a sense of awe before the wonder of His world and the sublimity of His moral law, some young men enter the House of God with their hands, as it were, in their pockets, magnanimously ready, in between careless socializing, to bestow a few laudatory remarks on the Lord of the universe, then to go on blithely with their conversation; they feel too much at ease in Zion; they offer to their neighbour their wisdom and wit during the reading of the *Torah*; selfishly engrossed in their animadversions on things and affairs, they have a good time whilst the Prophet's message is recited. These people without discipline commit the enormous blunder of looking upon themselves as the élite of the people. A healthy possession of *shiflut* would add to their Jewishness and enhance the moral tenor of the congregation.

V

By all means, the Union must extend its work. There are too many un-synagogued Jews and too many sons and daughters of our people formally in the synagogue but far removed from its thought and practice. The Union must act on Isaiah's plan – *Ha'arikhi metorayikh* (lengthen your cords,), widen your curtains, invite more and more children of our people into Jewish life, but *yesedotayikh ḥazeki* (make your foundations firm!). Our slogan must not be the commercial 'bigger and better,' but the prophetic 'deeper and nobler'! How up-to-date Hosea's complaint sounds: 'Israel forsook His Maker, and built temples!' We must emancipate ourselves from million dollar buildings as the alpha and omega of Judaism. We must realize that the foundation stone is laid and our problem begins to challenge us only *veḥotzi ha-even roshah* after the great edifice is completed and the mortgage is paid!

VI

Finally, the universally recognized head of the *Torah* in our years – the sainted *Hazon Ish* – has laid it down as a matter of *halakhah* that since we do not know the wise art of proper reproof – *lehokhiaḥ* – we should read nobody out of the synagogue. We should treat with infinite patience and great love even *mumrum lehak'hess* – those who deliberately and provocatively transgress Jewish law as *tinokot shenishbu* (children, captives of foreigners) who lacked the chance to hear *Torah*, live *Torah*, and become wholesome types of Jewish men and women.

The Union has gone far in approaching the realization of its goal. The Union must offer to our people and to our beloved America the timeless spirit of Israel as a harvest of the Spirit of God. We must call in, persuade, encourage those still outside of our fold. We must raise their Jewish stature. We must lower their assimilationist impulses. Ours is the duty to raise the average Jew to the high level of living Judaism, to put down by firm rejection the ruthless careerists, manipulators of ideals, movements, and principles, and bring the uninformed and the merely formal Jew closer to the task of the chosen nation. We must spread the light of the *Torah*, the warmth of our faith, until the whole of the *golah* of America becomes a flame of living inspiration.

So let us determine to work together in order that the eternal religion of Abraham may become the abiding possession of his people, and that its light may send forth rays of righteousness and mercy, based on faith in God, to all the corners of the world.

The Lost Art

I *The Problem*

The Romans distinguish between expressing gratitude, feeling it, and acting upon it. One of the most dismaying aspects of modern life has been a wellnigh universal malaise of ingratitude. In the days of Carlyle, it was still a phenomenon rare enough as to earn his celebrated caustic definition as the main difference between a man and a dog. In our own time, gratitude has been described as a lost art and ingratitude generally has been taken for granted. In all spheres of human activity, both Jewish and non-Jewish, ruthless careerism has taken the place of decent awareness of kindness received and of acknowledgment, in thought and deed, truly due. Many men have been put up in business by generous souls; students in their years of struggle have been aided by friends or strangers; professionals have been granted promising and lucrative opportunities – all of which to be promptly forgotten in a heedless pursuit of more profit or advancement, without a single thought of indebtedness to the benefactors. A modern *Anthology of Great Quotations*, which includes such items as ambition and cross-breeding, bigotry and cybernetics, has no reference at all to gratitude or what has increasingly taken its place: ingratitude!

What is the cause of this phenomenon, as deplorable as unpleasant? Some teachers condemn it outright as due to sheer wickedness. An ingrate (*kefuy tovah*), in our sacred literature, from the Book of Psalms through

Talmud and *Midrash*, is considered a contemptible person. Some psychologists find its roots in a person's dislike of being (consciously or unconsciously) reminded of the time, when, in the throes of material or intellectual poverty, he depended on someone's aid. Thus, early traumas or complexes are offered by experienced psychiatrists as sufficient grounds for that sad attitude.

But, no matter what the ultimate cause may be, ingratitude is aesthetically, no less than morally, repulsive. The *Midrash* quotes this view: 'In the time to come, all offerings will be abolished, but the thank-offering will never be abolished.' The *Talmud* of Jerusalem likens an ingrate to one who denies the Lord of the Universe.

But how does the *Torah* combat that tendency or seek to prevent its growth? Beyond its teaching about the origin of the world and the role of man in the universe, beyond what are called symbols and ceremonies, principles and ideals, our Holy *Torah* is the programme for a good life. What then are its method, theory, and practice, for creating the quality of gratitude and for combating the opposite tendency among those who accept its guidance?

II *Individual and Society*

In its innocuous form, nationalism means devotion to the people's welfare. Brutal, conscienceless nationalism is the 19th century disease. It ignores moral principles and makes the goals of the group ends in themselves. The horrors of Nazidom present a modern example of its devilish potentialities. The last decades have taught the most obtuse of man that human security, prosperity, peace are interdependent.

The individual cannot thank the many people involved in the production of the food he eats, the dress she wears, the car he drives. American statesmanship has become increasingly aware of the fact that its own welfare, especially in the United Nations, depends upon the good will and co-operation of newly emerged African and Asian states. Individual traits, well developed, gradually penetrate the consciousness of ever larger groups and become national characteristics. National ingratitude is as hard to bear as individual ingratitude. National awareness of human interdependence has unlimited possibilities for collective prosperity and security. To make gratitude an effective asset in the life of the Jewish people, the *Torah* records this law: 'When thou art come in unto the land which the Lord thy God give thee for an inheritance, thou shalt take the first of all the fruit of the ground, and say "I have brought the first of the fruit of the land which thou O Lord has given me. I have put away the hallowed things and have given them to the stranger, the fatherless and the widow according to all the commandments Thou hast commanded me."' Gratitude to the Divine Giver is spontaneously associated with generosity to all in need. This obligation upon every citizen makes gratitude a national law and asset! Even as the child, so is the adult continually trained in thanksgiving and the consequent generous spirit towards all men.

Thus, the blessing the young child utters and the declaration of the adult householder are based on the same principle, devoted to the same purpose and have proved a successful method of achieving fine individual and collective personality. But that achievement was not self-evident, nor natural, nor inevitable. The tendency to forget past favours is as strong if not stronger than the impulse to feel, express, and act upon, gratitude. An ingenious *peshat* (interpretation of Biblical verse or Rabbinic law) may supply a demonstration of this fact.

III *An Ingenious Comment*

Two verses in our Holy Bible seem to contradict each other: 'The heavens are the heavens of the Lord, but the earth hath He given to the children of man' sings the Psalmist. But another line in the same book reads: 'The earth is the Lord's and the fulness thereof,' which denies man's ownership of his little globe. The Rabbis explain this contradiction by saying: 'The earth does belong to the Lord with the fulness thereof' refers *ka'an kodem berakhah* to the time before man expresses his thanks; *ka'an aḥar berakhah*, after having acknowledged God's bounty, the enjoyment of fruit and boon belong to him.

A 19th century commentator found a keen lesson about human nature in that *setirah* (contradiction). He referred to man's liability to forget the Giver of all and his interpretation runs thus: *Ka'an kodem berakhah* – before the *berakhah* (blessing) of prosperity, man explains his poverty or lack of success by the fact that 'The earth belongs to the Lord' and hence his own human effort may fail and hence his own failure is vindicated. But *aḥar berakhah*, when success has crowned his efforts, he would strut his independence by quoting: 'The heavens belong to God, but the earth

He hath given to the sons of man,' and 'My power and the might of my hand hath gotten me this wealth.' It is therefore that whenever we enjoy food, garment, or happy events, *berakhot* are mandatory to proclaim the Lord as the source of all good and the obligation to share what He gave us with all His children everywhere. It is for that reason that *bikkurim* (the first fruit of every harvest) are to be offered as sacrifice of gratitude with a declaration of that obligation made in clear language and with full acknowledgment of the social responsibility flowing from that recognition.

Whenever Jews remain loyal to the programme of Jewish life, the lost art of gratitude is recovered. The twin qualities of thankfulness and generosity add lustre and grace to family, community, and nation. Eventually, we trust, all mankind will accept and translate into human relations the principles and ideals of the *Torah's* programme, with its goal – universal welfare, peace, and security.

Three Aspects of *Shavuot*

The lost art of gratitude is one of the saddest aspects of modern life, although it was not entirely unknown in earlier ages. *Hakkarat todah kimeat ruaḥ she-enah metzuyah.* The depersonalization of the last decades, fruit of the inroads of technological invasion of private life, the 'alienation' which has almost become the academic plaint, have too often resulted in men and women taking favours for granted, accepting kindness as automatic occurrences of luck or mechanical accidents and hence giving little thought to the moral obligation of thankfulness. Harvest without a thought of Him Who granted it is the basis of such sad attitude, which in interhuman relations relegates gratitude to useless sentiment. Too many rush from the enjoyment of one benignity to the next goal, without a kind thought or a warm word to friend or neighbour. Well said the rabbis that when all other sacrifices will be abolished the *Korban todah* (that of thanksgiving) will still be mandatory.

The first aspect of *Shavuot* is 'harvest day', when the loyal Hebrew offered his gratitude on the altar of the sanctuary.

Harvest spells success, privilege, the serenity of security. Harvest spells freedom from worry and opportunity for enjoyment. But freedom too often degenerates into licence, enjoyment into excessive indulgence. Freedom needs the moral law to prevent oppression of weaker people. Wealth needs conscience to prevent callous neglect of the poor, the sick, the friendless. Faith needs guidance lest it deteriorate into heathenish superstition or corruptive cynicism.

Revelation is the second aspect of *Shavuot*. The world has never been the same since the Ten Commandments were pronounced on Mount Sinai, as the divine constitution for Israel and all man. To live again the hour of that Revelation, of God as Father of every human, from slave to master, from Jew to non-Jew, of God as Creator and Lawgiver and merciful judge of human conduct, is to receive a priceless message to illumine the rest of the year, to guide the conduct of the worshipper in the paths of justice and compassion.

The third aspect of *Shavuot* is little known. The *Agadah* of the *Talmud* records it and a modern giant of the *Torah* – the sainted Rav Amiel – has left it as his heirloom for our people to ponder and to transmit to future generations. '*Shavuot* is the birthday of the Messiah,' the timeless champion of Israel's redemption and mankind's humanization. Before the ultimate redemption, the story runs, the Messiah, son of Joseph, will appear and after his death, the Messiah, son of David, the true ultimate redeemer. Joseph lived, worked, reached the pinnacle of achievement in Egypt. But his place of rest was the land of his fathers, Palestine. There have been minor Josephs in the history of our people, offering their wisdom, devotion to Pharaohs and caliphs, emperors, nations, and communities all over the world. They did much good, introducing not only efficiency but generosity, not only clever method but unconfined kindness into the sphere of their activity. But their influence was limited. Vested interests, from church to commerce, pursued their wonted purposes and blocked the 'subversive' effect of unconfined justice and mercy. From Rathenau to Brandeis in our own days one recalls not only the honest appreciation of the few, but the raucous criticism of those whose private ambition felt menaced by the former's genuine dedication to the Fatherland and the latter's underpinning of the American ideal. The majorities in the countries of our dispersion again and again fought and defeated the 'Jewish influence' of method and appeal for the benefit of all man. It is only 'the Messiah, son of David' whose message will come from the cradle of all religion, the City of Peace, Jerusalem, from the people of Moses, Hillel, Rambam, and Kook, who will eventually conquer the obtuseness, the folly, the cruelty, of unregenerate man and by the power of his God-inspired personality will bring peace and security to all His children.

Thus, gratitude, the moral power of the Law and the Messianic time are linked in indivisible unity in the message, the three aspects, of *Shavuot*.

I

'Why was the *Torah* given just in the month of *Sivan*, why not in the other months?' asked the sages. This is explained allegorically, as follows:

Because the symbol in the Zodiac of *Nissan* is a lamb, and the symbol of *Iyyar* is an ox, God gave the *Torah* in *Sivan*. The symbol of *Sivan* is the 'twins'; and 'twins – that means man.'

The *Torah* was not given in *Nissan*, for the symbol of *Nissan* is the lamb. Sheer sheepish piety, an unintelligent creed, never could teach God to man. The messengers of the Lord must be a people of courage, of truth, of wisdom stronger than temptation, above the allurements which sweep away those of the street.

The *Torah* was not given in *Iyyar*; for, the symbol of *Iyyar* is the ox, representing brute force, primitive instincts, unrelieved by culture; senseless strength, spent for senseless ends.

'The *Torah* was given in *Sivan*' because the symbol of *Sivan* is 'twins' and that is man. Twin forces are within us, twin natures, twin worlds. The one is primitive desire – lust and passion, greed for money, greed for power; it is a blind force that would destroy everything in its uncurbed quest. It would drag us down to the level of the beast. It starts with the desecration of the law of God and of humanity, in one's little sphere. Wickedness infects neighbours and friends. Like an epidemic it spreads, poisoning the atmosphere. It depraves literature. It degrades statecraft. It starts in the brain of a single individual. But it ends in a world catastrophe which buries millions under its ruins and makes out of God's beautiful world a desert.

And the other force, the innate desire for good – the gentle flame in the heart of the infant: the steady fire in the adult; the voice of sweetness, and the thunder of truth. It is the Godliness in man which seeks brother and sister as comrades in the great struggle of truth against falsehood; of good against evil; of beauty against ugliness. It is the happy faith of the child and the deep conviction of man; the holiness of individual life and the rectitude of communal activity. It is patience which softens pain, gladdens sorrowful hearts, and, by its wise strength, disciplines the mind of the unruly. It is that faith in the Almighty Creator as the All-merciful Father which lights the lamp of love in the family, promotes brotherhood in a nation and good-will among the people of the world. This is the other world in us.

Two powers are within us. And because we can raise ourselves to the high argument of idealism, by our own free will; and, by our own free will, lower ourselves to deepest hell, we have strength for good and strength for evil.

Shavuot is the birthday of Israel as a nation. Even though *Pesach* freed Jewish bodies from the master's whip, it still left us slaves. But on *Shavuot*, with the giving of Ten Commandments to Israel – and, through Israel, to all the world – came spiritual freedom. The Ten Commandments were not given to us as a document of national pride, but as a standard of conduct by which to live. The Jews were chosen to be the banner-bearers of God's ideal. Neither by passionate speeches about Jewish self-consciousness and Jewish pride were they chosen for that mission; nor for the spreading of sanctimonious literature meant to propagate ideals impossible to realize. But they were chosen to battle the forces of evil and darkness, both within the narrow sphere of the individual, and in the market-places of nations. The Jew was to be God's messenger among the nations, proclaiming Him through the honesty of his life.

On *Shavuot* we were given the Law. On *Shavuot* we were given the opportunity to raise ourselves to the heights, or to go down to the depths. Because man is 'twins' and because the symbol of *Sivan* is 'twins,' therefore was the *Torah* given in *Sivan*. On *Shavuot* we were made a chosen people, and on every *Shavuot* we ought to reinterpret to ourselves the meaning of this selection: that it is not for the sake of our merits that God has selected us, but He has called us His chosen people that we may discharge our embassy among men, in a manner neither unintelligent like the lamb, nor merely strong like the ox, but with an idealism, manfully expressed: Judaism lived truthfully – *Shabbat* and *Kashrut*, and *Ḥinukh* and *Taharat ha-Mishpaḥah*, observed faithfully: *Shabbat*, that we consult with our own heart in its holy place, that we may meet with God; *Kashrut*, that we may prepare our body for the higher life; *Ḥinukh* (Jewish Education), that we may raise a generation trained in character, rooted in our tradition, deeply imbued with the spirit of our literature and our history. And

Taharat ha-Mishpaḥah (Jewish Marriage Law), that we may intensify the basis of all – the purity of the Jewish home, the holiness of womanhood, and the sanctity of motherhood.

Through these four agencies we perform our task – spiritually clear, morally lofty, and intellectually sound.

Medico-moral Problems in the Hospital Ministry*

The root meaning of the Hebrew word for healing – *rafa* – is 'to patch up, to repair, to sew together.' This indicates that surgery constituted an early, if not a major, part of the medical art in Jewish antiquity.

From times immemorial, people have appreciated and welcomed the skill of the doctor who could restore a mangled limb or a feverish body to its pristine integrity.

I *The Role of the Physician*

But there was also a wrong view which looked upon the physician's endeavour as opposition to the Lord Who had inflicted disease on the patient. Jewish law rejected that view. It endorses the doctor's effort as in accord with the will of God, emphasizes it as both obligation and privilege, and holds that mental as well as physical illness are the proper concern of the medical profession.[1] From the time of the Bible, through *Talmud* and *Midrash*, in a period of more than three thousand years, there has been consistent severest criticism of, and punishment for, every kind of magic, sorcery, and witchcraft. The pious king Hezekiah caused a book of incantations and charms to be burned because he knew it to be a source

* Address at the U.S. Veterans' Administration Workshop in Atlanta, Georgia.

at best of heathen error or, at worst, of cruel deception.[2] But there is plentiful evidence of medicines, both in popular and professional usage, like balm, spices, honey, and all sorts of herbs containing healing ingredients.

Like the study of Jewish law or lore, medicine appears very often not as a profession but as an avocation. From the third century on, through the middle ages, there are many rabbis, teachers, scholars, philosophers, and poets, who studied and practised medicine as a religious and moral obligation. Jewish achievements in the modern art of healing have been recognized by a remarkable number of Nobel Prize Awards. It is interesting to report a statement of one scholar in the *Talmud* who was doubtful as to the value of medical services offered without recompense, emphasizing the value of interested as above charitable service, for the latter may have a negative influence on the physician's sense of responsibility: 'A physician who serves for nothing is worth nothing.'[3]

Yet the obligation of the community to provide medical aid tot he poor Jew and non-Jew is taken for granted.[4] However, before medical aid becomes necessary, self-protection through precaution is urged. No man should take careless risks,[5] for the *Torah* warns: 'Take care of your life.'[6] Indeed, what is forbidden as a hazard to one's health, is considered a graver offence than violation of a ritual law.[7] It is wrong, say the rabbis, carelessly to court danger and then to rely on miracles.[8]

Cosmetic surgery is frowned upon unless it is due to deformity which may result in one of three evils: psychopathic trouble; or in prevention of a boy or girl from getting married; or as a source of domestic unhappiness.[9]

II *The Value of Every Individual*

The *Mishnah*, the first Jewish Code, composed in the second century of the common era, contains this thought: 'Whosoever preserves a single soul, has thereby preserved almost a whole world. Whosoever destroys a single soul, thereby has almost destroyed a whole world.' This is a basic teaching of our faith, and it indicates the limitless significance of every individual, in the frame of Jewish religious thought. Personal interest in medicine is a religious obligation. In the *Talmud*[10] Rabbi Huna asked his son, 'Why were you absent from the keen lectures of Rabbi Hisda?' he answered: 'He treats merely of matters of health.' Replied the father: 'Health matters are not secular discourses. By all means, go to listen to him.' Rabbi Eliezer said:[11] 'Let every man look upon himself as if God resided within him. The body, as a receptacle of the holy soul, is holy,' and deserves consistent wise care.

'Why do some scholars die young?' asked a sage of old.[12] 'It is not that they are indulging in lawlessness, physical or moral, rather is it due to the fact that they treat their health with contempt,' this is a pregnant statement of too frequent a sin of omission or commission.

Where there is possible danger to one's health the severe laws of the Sabbath rest must be ignored. *Yom Kippur* (the Day of Atonement) is the most solemn Sabbath of fasting, when for twenty-four hours not a drop of water or the smallest morsel of food may be taken by the loyal Jew. Yet when a reliable physician or a responsible patient feels the need for food, to avoid serious danger to one's health, breaking the fast is not only permitted but obligatory. In accord with the degree of danger, smaller or larger meals, even normally forbidden foods, are perfectly in order.[13]

III *The Sanctity of the Body*

There are three who own every person: (1) God, the Creator; (2) parents, or the rest of the family; (3) and last but not least, the individual himself. When someone has been called to his eternal reward, Jewish law insists on speedy burial in the ground. As the *Torah* put it: 'Out of the ground was thou taken. For dust thou art and to dust shall thou return.'[14] This is a fundamental law to be obeyed under normal circumstances. But there is another one, equally basic: 'Neither shalt thou stand idly by the blood of thy neighbour,'[15] you must help him in his trouble. Here is a case of conflicting loyalties due to two apparently conflicting rules of conduct. It addresses itself as a challenge to both, the man thinking of the end of his days, and the relative of a deceased person. If no relative is present or available, it is a challenge to the community in which the corpse is found. What shall decide the issue of autopsy?: The sanctity of his body or the saving of a fellow man's health or of his very life?

IV *Autopsy and Transplantation*

The problem of autopsy has for several hundred years engaged the attention of the rabbinic authorities. May a man, by his own free will, instruct his physician or the hospital to subject his dead body to the normal mutilation of post-mortem investigation, if that examination may help the cure or survival of a neighbour? Is it lawful for him to will his eye to an eye bank or any other part of his body to a similar institution, in order to restore health to a sick person or sight to a blind man whom the sympathetic Jewish lore considers as almost dead? Shall the family permit the body of a revered parent to be subjected to the ravages of that experiment and, for the benefit of a friend or stranger, ignore their own ravaged emotions? There have been many decisions reconciling both principles mentioned above.[16] Essentially they state that autopsy as well as transplantation of parts of the body are lawful under the following conditions: (1) That the deceased while still alive, or the family, after his death, permitted it; (2) that the autopsy or transplantation may be definitely assumed to be a source of the preservation of some other patient's life of whose illness we have definite detailed knowledge; (3) that the rest of the body will be treated with utmost respect and that every part of it will, under the supervision of the holy society (*Ḥebrah Kaddisha*) the religious body charged with interment, be brought to proper burial.

The Supreme Rabbinic court of Israel, to assure complete fulfilment of spirit and matter of these conditions, urged that in addition to the hospital authorities, the private physician of the deceased join an *ad hoc* committee to examine every aspect of the case: from the facts of another patient's disease which may be cured as a result of the autopsy to the definite provision assuring conformity with the laws of interment.

Autopsy may be permitted where the laws of the country demand it; where the cause of the death could not otherwise be established; where, in case of hereditary disease, the autopsy might offer guidance to the family.

Transplantation of part of the body[17] is also permitted when the above conditions are fulfilled. 'Most authorities have endorsed the now classic argument by the present Chief Rabbi of Israel that any tissue from the dead grafted to a living patient, by being literally restored to life, loses its forbidden character as part removed from the dead and may therefore be utilized.'[18] Conflicting concerns create the following problems: The examination of a woman in her pregnancy reveals to the examining physician some abnormalities which may endanger her life when the embryo is about to be born. Two lives are competing for vital attention: the unborn child versus the living mother. The decision reads: Only in case the mother's life is endangered is artificial abortion permitted. Otherwise it is unlawful. However, to save the life of the mother it is not only permissible but an obligation of which the physician, the husband, and all concerned must remain aware.[19]

V *The Handicaps of Moralism*

Truth is universally recognized as a great human value. It is not only a divine command but also essential to human fellowship. If we cannot trust our neighbour's statement, we cannot deal or live with him. Hostility and chaos result. Indeed, Kant and Fichte assert that deviation from truth under all circumstances is an abominable offence, and that they would not tell a lie even if thereby the whole world could be saved. This is the point of view of moralism. The opposing school has a long name: teleological. It stresses the *teleos* (purpose) of a statement or act, and finds some deviation from truth justified when human peace or life itself are involved. Maimonides, great teacher of the law and physician, states:[20] 'If someone was stung by a scorpion or bitten by a snake it is permissible to whisper a magic formula over the affected place. Although the whispering is of no avail, it is permitted to prevent the patient from despair or losing his mind.' Jewish law, in case of dangerously sick persons, permits some such deviation because the saving of a human life is a higher value than rigid conformity to technical truth. What is involved is not an outright lie but a statement which will encourage the patient whilst not in full accord with the facts of the situation. My own experience in hospital work has shown me good results. My conscience was not pricking me when encouraging words helped the despondent patient to regain hope, which proved of considerable therapeutic value.

VI *The Clergyman and the Patient*

An ecumenically alert and empathic clergyman, in the absence of the colleague serving the patient's denomination, can be of vital service to him. All he has to do is to curb the normal, impulsive zeal for his own creed, that means to avoid any missionary effort and stay in full awareness of the special spiritual need of the person he is to serve. I remember an incident partly amusing, partly stirring, during my work at a Pentagon-arranged trip to the Far East. The General whose hospitality for one evening I had enjoyed (his gracious lady provided me with the fruit salad and similar items which my dietary laws allowed) telephoned me late in the evening at the Imperial Hotel in Tokyo about a New York soldier whose mother was dangerously ill and who fervently urged my praying with him for her recovery. As he came in I asked him whether he had a *Siddur* (Hebrew Prayer book). He had never heard the word. In astonishment I said: 'Are you not Jewish?' He answered: 'No, I am Catholic.' For some reason his padre had not been available. After a few minutes, I devised an impromptu service, the soldier repeating every word of my English rendering of the prayer, beseeching the Merciful Father of all humanity to grant relief and cure to his mother. The boy could not thank me enough and I went to bed happy. In a Louisiana hospital a Jewish Wac lieutenant reported to me a deeply moving incident of a Gentile chaplain who brought comfort to a Jewish boy and even knew a Hebrew Prayer.

Summing up this occasionally delicate business, I would say that *any* chaplain could be of profound and enduring benefit to any patient if he treated him with combined sympathy and empathy, with the ethical universalism which translates religious principle into concrete benefaction. The saving of a person's life or the prolongation of someone's opportunity to serve God and man is one of the greatest *mitzvot* (that means commandments or good deeds). Life, in the vocabulary of all religion, is no more nor less than this sacred opportunity. It is easy to find texts in all Holy Writ which emphasize this simple truth. Thus reads a verse in the *Torah* (the Pentateuch): 'These are the commandments which a man should fulfil in order that he may live in accordance with them.' Please note: The accent is on deed not thought; on life, not letters; on this world, not the world to come – although the latter is of great significance too.

VII *Longevity*

Long life has been viewed in the Hebrew Bible as one of the fine goals of human beings. The rabbis advise on the following methods for achieving it: (1) Create an atmosphere of friendship and goodness, of sympathy and empathy; (2) shun anything that causes envy or malice; (3) give the neighbour the benefit of the doubt; (4) pursue worthwhile moral goals and remain aware of the need of self-acceptance! Above all, base your life on faith in God, the Father of all humanity. The Hebrew word for trust in God – *bittaḥon* – means in Arabic, its sister language, 'leaning against an immovable rock,' His eternal mercy.

VIII *Contraception – The prevention of a new life*

The Jewish husband is never permitted to use contraceptive means. Among modern methods, permissible to the wife, is the contraceptive pill, provided it is found to be medically safe. Of enduring benefit are the principles and laws of Family Purity. Alone among modern schools of thought, Judaism assures the wife, as of law, control of her body and personality. The age of consent in international law protects the young woman against the seductive wiles of reckless men. For, if too young a woman is persuaded to yield her body to a man, he is considered as having committed statutory rape and faces many years of imprisonment. But the conjugal rights of a husband, in all civilized countries, include the privilege of approaching his wife carnally at will. The only exception is Jewish law which imposes upon him the consistent obligation to woo her in order to obtain her consent to physical approach. The twelve-day period, every month, of sexual abstinence, not only prevents married relations from becoming cheap, drab, routine which destroys her self-respect and the grace of love, but, by encouraging other basic facets (like a sense of belonging, of mutual consideration, of the interdependence of the mates' happiness) this principle also promotes an abiding high level of married harmony.

There has been comparatively very small incidence of cancer of the cervix among Jewish women, which some physicians ascribed to the prevention of the abuse by too impulsive husbands. Modern medical research views her protection as due also to the absence of infection, which results from his circumcision on the eighth day after birth. In the life of both, the law of the Sabbath, with its emancipation from the tensions of the work-a-day week, creates a home of relaxation, peace, and mutual dedication.

To bring home to the veteran the profound interest in his or her good health and happy spirit, is one of the major privileges of the chaplain. The task of attuning our work to the various shadings of modern life, of conveying to the patient a view of wider horizons, and of combining that endeavour with common sense and the priceless boon of abiding good humour, offers both challenge and promise to everyone of us.

A saintly sage suggests the highest quality of love for one's neighbour. He wrote: 'I learned more from a man in his cups at a wayside inn than from many a heavy tome. As I entered, I saw him, his head buried in his arms, his sobs shaking his whole frame. I approached him and asked: "What ails you brother?" He raised his head slowly and groped for a reply, and then in mingled sorrow and confusion he thrust this question to me: "Do you call yourself my brother and do not know what ails me?"'

To know what ails a patient, to put oneself into his place, to labour oneself towards a full appreciation of the condition of his mind and heart, very often means to have at least half of the answer, half of the solution of his problem, half of the cure he and we hope and pray for.

Notes

1. *B. Kama*, 85a, *Tos.*, s. v. *Shenitnah.*
2. *Pes.* 56a.
3. *Ibidem.*
4. *Gittin* 61a.
5. *Ber.* 50a.
6. Deut. IV, 15.
7. *Ḥullin* 9b.
8. *Shab.* 32.
9. See I. Jakobovits *Journal of a Rabbi*, pp. 160 and 193ff.
10. *Shabb.* 82a.
11. *Taanit*, 11a.
12. *Abot d'R. Nathan I.*
13. *Shulḥan Arukh, Orah Ḥayim* MCXVIII.
14. Gen. III, 19.
15. Lev. XIX, 16.
16. *Noam* III.
17. *Noam* IV.
18. Immanuel Jakobovits, *Journal of a Rabbi*, p. 159.
19. *Noam* VII.
20. *Hilkh. Akum.* XI, II.

'The Invasion of the Cloud'

Introduction

The Holy book *Zohar* is the Bible of Jewish mysticism. It contains a great deal of fascinating material; some of simplicity and profundity like *B'rikh Shemeh*, others requiring prolonged immersion in cognate parlance. A celebrated *Zohar* passage in the *Sidrah Behaalotekha*[1] emphasizes the Bible's inexhaustible source of spiritual, moral, and intellectual teaching. There is the classic *ṖaṘḊeṠ* (*Pshat*, *Remez*, *Derash*, and *Sod*) for the student of the Holy law to stay aware of. Some of the interpretations of Biblical verses come from the midnight reflection of sage or saint, others are revealed by reflection on Jewish history.

We remain aware of both as we study 'The Invasion of the Cloud.' The divine cloud, first over the Sanctuary[2] and then over the Ark of the Covenant, symbolizes both the glory of God, His protection of His people, and the beauty of the good life in accord with the *Torah*. From such loyalty came the new meaning of the *Ner Tamid*, the Eternal Light, even as God's cloud stood for the blessing of His providence; their interdependence is at once the basis and the assurance of Jewish survival.

The Holy text reads: 'Command Aaron and his sons saying: this is the law of the burnt offering: The burnt offering shall be on its firewood upon the altar all night unto the morning and the fire of the altar shall be kept burning thereon.'[3] And again: 'The fire upon the altar shall be kept burning thereon, it shall not go out'[4] and finally: 'Fire shall be kept burning upon the altar continually, it shall not go out.'[5] This perpetual fire, like the *Ner Tamid*, was to serve as a witness of Israel's loyalty to God. Rashbam emphasizes: 'By day as by night must the light burn,'[6] in days of prosperity and peace, even as in times of darkness and trouble. And Rashi comments: 'One who causes the flame on the altar to go out violates two prohibitions,'[7] – he robs himself and future Israelites of the light of the faith.

There are two influences working against that Eternal Light. One is the anaemic Jew – *Neḥshal* – weakened in his knowledge and faith. The other is the perpetual animosity of Amalek. In two passages does the Bible refer to the latter. In Exodus:[8] 'And the Lord said to Moses: Write this for a memorial in the book and rehearse it in the ears of Joshua: That I will utterly blot out the remembrance of Amalek from under the heaven. In Deuteronomy[9] there is the divine command: 'When the Lord thy God hath given thee rest from all thine enemies round about, in the land which the Lord thy God giveth thee for an inheritance to possess it, thou shalt blot out the remembrance of Amalek from under heaven; thou shalt not forget.' The *Midrash Sekhel Tov* reports: 'Amalek was entering near the rays of the cloud to steal souls from Israel. There were among the people cocksure, proud persons, unfit to stay under the protection of the cloud. It was these souls that Amalek lured away and stole.' The *Mekhilta* of Rabbi Shimeon Ben Yohai and the *Midrash Hagadol* cite similar traditions. They refer to the cloud of glory as a protection against wild animals and idolaters.

From ancient Rome through the medieval church, down to our own days, the spiritual heirs of Amalek have pursued their nefarious policies. The Romans came close to the cloud of glory endeavouring to invade it: 'Give up your funny religion, your belief in an invisible God. Give up the many burdens in the Jewish law. Join the freedom of the Roman citizen and we shall offer you all its benefits.' When the Jews refused to depart from the cloud of glory, from the whole atmosphere of Jewish life, the Roman Amaleks seized upon all 'who were feeble in the rear' endeavouring to absorb them in the colourless conformity of the empire. I am sorry to say that the record of the Christian church has been similar in ruthless method and tragic achievement. For millennia their priests and preachers have been using every method to persuade our hard-pressed people to leave the cloud of glory, the protection our faith has given us. Like Amalek they have invaded the cloud, assaulted 'all those in our rear who were weak,' seeking to undermine their allegiance to God, Sinai, and *Torah* and eventually to absorb them into the majority religion.

When four hundred and fifty years ago Martin Luther attached his famous thesis to his church in Wittenberg, he too invaded the Jewish camp, the cloud of glory and he too endeavoured to lure our people from its protection. Hence, in an earlier book he emphasized that the Christian saviour and all his apostles were Jews, and he had scathing words about the Catholic Church's treatment of our people. He hoped thereby to convert the stiffnecked loyalists to his sect. But when the Jews rejected his invitation, he assailed them in most obscene manner in his scurrilous defamation, called *The Jews and Their Lies*. Ever after, he remained our ruthless enemy.

Fortified by his spirit, murderous gangs attacked Jews all over Germany. He received his historical punishment, for the message of his book was quoted extensively by the beastly Nazis. It has become their very Bible. The quotations from Luther's writing in Malcolm Hay's *Foot of Pride* represent a monument of infamy to that much-praised father of Protestantism!

The original Amalek is described in our literature as an ingrate, as a cruel enemy, as a professional robber and murderer. The first quality shines significantly in the utterances and in the conduct of later Amaleks, from the Roman Empire, the medieval Church, through modern creeds and lands, filthy with slander and pogroms, the classic forms of Jew-hatred. Yet our people throughout history, generously and consistently, have lent their minds and hearts to the enlightenment of their heathen neighbours, ancient and contemporary. Jews have introduced and promoted physical, mental, and spiritual health in all the countries which they inhabited. Jewish physicians, teachers, diplomats, and artists, have written their names in golden letters into the records of their hosts. But almost as a rule, these boons and services were forgotten by governments, clerics, and their incited mobs.

On the altar of our people the fire never burned out. The flame of our faith lighted up sunless, airless ghettos. But the great world in which we lived as a maligned minority, knew many centuries of darkness, cruelty, and corruption. A few years ago, a Harvard dean met a confused Jewish student. Instead of guiding him to a Rabbi, he succeeded in getting him out of the protective glory of Judaism by luring him to an Episcopalian minister who cunningly embraced the opportunity to rob him of his ancestral faith and convert him to his own sect. That boy, by now a man, serves somewhere in the American Army and presides over a Christian home.

The spirit of Amalek is not dead. It threatens our people and especially those among us who are afflicted by ignorance of Judaism and its consequence, emotional insecurity. A few weeks ago in Paraguay the only local synagogue was destroyed by fire. A gang of unredeemed Nazis and their followers stood out there scoffing and reviling the unhappy congregation. Nearer home, in Wayne Township, New Jersey, two Jewish candidates to a local school board were defeated in a place which, during the 1930's was a centre of the German–American Bund. Five years ago a swastika was painted on the local high school. Last year Wayne was revealed to be a stronghold of the notorious 'Rat Fink' wing of the New Jersey Republican party. More recently a state court decision disclosed the existence of a screening committee in Wayne that restricted all prospective buyers of homes in the $25,000 to $100,000 class to white Christians with northern European backgrounds.'[10]

We must stay alertly concerned, rather than worried, about such conditions, such Amalek spirit, in odd corners of our country and all over the world.

It is our eternal obligation as a people 'to wipe the memory of Amalek from under the heaven.' We must do so by the quality of our attitude and conduct. Every cruelty recalls Amalek. Every ingratitude continues Amalek's spirit. Every abuse of the poor and the weak keeps Amalek alive. To conform to the teaching of the *Torah* means to cultivate individually and collectively, justice, compassion, and gratitude. This challenge is addressed to every individual Jew as well as to the whole nation. As we meet it, we become God's ambassadors to mankind. Our prophets have promised that the *Torah*'s principles and practices will eventually bring all people closer to the cloud of glory, to the house of God and that as a reward to our uncompromising, steadfast loyalty, we shall live to see the fulfilment of God's promise: 'I shall wipe the memory of Amalek' – of oppression, robbery, and murder – 'from under the heavens.'

No Jew may ever forget that task and that promise. The first involves our obligation to promote Jewish education and to perfect the private and public patterns of Jewish life. Thus we shall not be cursed by disappointed, cynical youth, by 'feeble ones' in remote places or anywhere else in the Jewish community.

The best among the nations of the world have recognized that purifying quality of Jewishness. From Maxim Gorky to Travers Herford and George Foote Moore, they have felt their impact. Our deathless optimism will stay based on faith in the Lord and trust in our people. We shall be working, living, and waiting for the hour when the memory of Amalek will be wiped out under God's heaven from the councils, the homes, and the hearts of every one of his children.

Notes

1. See Preface to P. Biberfeld's *King David.*
2. Rashbam on Exodus. XL, 35.
3. Lev. VI, 2.
4. Lev. VI, 5.
5. Lev. VI, 6.
6. a.l.
7. a.l.
8. Exod. XVII, 14.
9. Deut. XXV, 19.
10. Report in Jewish Congress Bi-Weekly, March, 1967.

The Enemy Within

The *Shulḥan Arukh* explains why the Sabbath preceding *Pesaḥ* is called 'The Great Sabbath.'[1] It is due to an event of unusual quality, a miracle performed not by God, but by human beings, not by military heroes nor any other élite, but by a folk, for centuries degraded, enslaved, whipped, and suddenly afire with the message of redemption: our forefathers in Egypt, faced their oppressors and in bold answer to their question, told them that the lambs which the Egyptians worshipped, would be offered up, in accord with His commandment, to God, the Creator, and Redeemer.

I

Courage has been defined as the triumph of will over fear, and the Great Sabbath presents the memory of a moment in the history of the human conscience which has inspired countless men and women to imitate its spirit.

That triumph of will has three encounters which test its strength. It must face fear, weakness, and evil, each within its time and place, each challenging character and personality.

'They have surrounded me, they have surely surrounded me. In the name of the Lord shall I face them.' chants the Psalmist.[2] The instinct for self-preservation, which man shares with some higher animals, the resentment, fierce and dynamic, against beast or human who threatens one's existence, does arouse a determination to face the enemy as he is about to assail us, to attack him, to put him to flight, even to kill him. The history of war, man's greatest folly and worst affliction, knows many heroes of wondrous strength, ingenuity, and endurance, who have written their names in golden letters into local, national, or global records.

The triumph of will overcomes also weakness. Whenever Israel was 'in Rephidim,'[3] sunk into despondency, lassitude, and self-abasement, it encouraged contemporary Amaleks, desert gangs, lying in wait for defenceless groups or individuals, to pounce upon them, rob or kill them, to race home laden with booty and glorying in their gory victory. To be a Jew means to remain alert to the ruthlessness of folks who are ever ready to attack single humans or any minority. Jewishness has been simultaneously a source of pride and of an abiding sense of social responsibility. The whole history of our people has been a process of elimination. Weaklings have fallen by the way. Men and women, unable to face majorities, have sunk from the plateau of Jewishness into low colourless anonymity, succumbing to the lure of the comforts and other promises of conformity, swelling the numbers of the host country and, in worst punishment, in too many instances, eventually becoming members of the howling mob which attacked the helpless humanity locked up in the Ghettoes.[4]

The survival of the morally fittest is impressively documented by *attem ha-devekim*,[5] the Jews who are alive today, because they adhered stubbornly, unhesitatingly, courageously, to the way of life and to the group that clung to God and His *Torah*.

II

The Triumph of Will faces its greatest obstacle not when confronted by savage beasts or humans. Weakness, too, may be overcome by painful awareness of great danger, by the menace of immediate destruction. There is another enemy, less obvious, because it is covered by rationalization and hence not immediately visible in all its fierce potency.

Of the two primeval impulses which prompt our action the will for unity and the will for dispute, the latter, doubtlessly, is first to press its claim. The will for dispute, buttressed by specious argument or without it, would garner for oneself all the goods of this world, would refuse to consider a fellowman's rights, would include in one's plan of success only oneself and at best one's family or close associates. Most of human misery, from the agony of slaves in the long ago, to the fury of American negroes in our own days, all the wars, from antiquity through the holocaust of the last generation, most of the strikes and lockouts, of discrimination and boycotts, are but the fruit of the uncontrolled will for dispute which knows neither justice nor mercy nor the wisdom of toleration and fair play.

The other impulse is that of unity, inspired by a sense of brotherhood, that would share skill and possessions with all others, cherishing every happy face and hurt by all pain. These two impulses are in constant rivalry over the soul of man, they create social problems as the fruit of his inner conflicts. The *Talmud* warns: *Leolam yargiz adam et yetzer tov al yetzer ha'ra*: 'A man should always stir up his good inclination against his evil one,'[6] until the will for dispute is overcome and one extends unselfish care to one's brother. 'A courageous man,' says the *Mishnah*,[7] 'is he who subdues his passion.' 'A hero is one who can control his wrath,'[8] avers the *Midrash*. The working of the evil inclination has many aspects and subtleties. Some pursue their goals by ruthless attack on rivals, actual or only suspected. Others, by underhand methods: the cunning insinuation, the hypocritical remark, the half-truth. It requires courage to face the 'enemy within.' Righteous self-criticism is a quality or achievement as precious as it is rare. Selfishness blinds one to one's true motives. The bribe, which is the private goal, the elemental or refined ambition, 'perverts the just words,'[9] the false motive perverts speech or action. The voice of conscience is drowned by the clamorous argument of selfishness. It takes a brave person to listen to the stern judgment of his better ego, to see through the web of lies covered by the net of pious protestation.

Normal people are shocked by ingratitude, yet it may be due less to wickedness than to a person's unconscious – or half-conscious – willingness to recall the time of his dependency on somebody else's aid. On similar grounds, some may be willing to forgive wrong inflicted upon them by others, but will maintain a feeling of hatred towards those they themselves have abused. It requires real *gevurah*, strong courage, to see oneself objectively.

III

There is the courage of physical power, of spiritual strength, of moral steadfastness. The enemy within defeats not only a man's or woman's good intentions, often he robs them even of common sense. In our own days, we have seen a man of undoubted ability misled by his evil desire into the folly of thinking that his wrong actions will escape public scrutiny. The politician whose addresses, just published, contain a mass of utterly unacknowledged quotations from other people's writings, proved the wisdom of the Talmudic saying: 'No man sins unless the spirit of folly invades him.'[10] He reaps eventually his punishment: the contempt of the righteous, the scorn of the wise, the angry rejection by yesterday's faithful flock. This, indeed is the message of the Great Sabbath. Based upon the historical fact in the long ago, of our ancestors' brave attitude as they were about to be redeemed from Egypt, it bids man in all ages and climes to beware of the insinuations of the selfish, of the temptation which sees but the beckoning goal and ignores the pitfalls of wrong means on the way. We must collect wits and energies to fight oppression and malice whether they affect our own position or that of our neighbour. We must overcome, courageously, a spirit of weakness in the face of great handicaps. We must be on the alert to fight any desire to gain our ends by deviation from His way of righteousness and compassion.

Courage is the indispensable basis of political freedom. Courage is the indispensable basis of moral freedom. Through courage, the triumph of our will over fear, weakness, and evil, we become God's partners in our common task: the attainment of freedom in all its blissfulness for all His children all over His world.

Notes

1. *Or. Hayyim* CCCCXXX.
2. Ps. CXVIII, 11, in S. R. Hirsch's famous version.
3. Exod. XVII, 8; *Midr. Tanhuma Beshallah* 25.
4. The lowest enemies of Israel have come from apostates who defamed the flock they had abandoned.
5. Deut. IV, 4.
6. *Babli Berakh.* 5a.
7. *Pirke Abot* IV, i.
8. *B. Megillah* 15b.
9. Exod. XXIII, 8.
10. *B. Sotah* 3a.

Margin for Safety

When the Lord said to Moses: 'Speak to Aaron and his sons . . . "Thus shall ye bless the children of Israel,"' the latter pleaded: 'Lord of the Universe, we need Thy blessing, must there be human beings to mediate between Thee and us?' And He answered: 'The priests shall but pronounce the blessing, putting My name upon the children of Israel. It is I who will bless them.'[1] The blessing is to be pronounced by priests who have genuine affection for their flock. They are to pronounce it, says Rashbam, not as a casual, mechanical greeting, but fully conscious that the three lines, in their Biblical text, contain divine meaning, a power and fulness no human goodwill could convey.[2] Let us consider the text: 'Thus shalt thou speak unto them: "May the Lord bless thee and keep thee!"' The first words, say our Sages, refer to good health and prosperity. 'And keep thee' warns against *Mazzikin*, harmful influence of success: indifference to our fellowman's troubles: and – still worse – a feeling of superiority flowing from cocksure appreciation of our happy condition.

'May the Eternal bestow the light of His countenance upon thee,' that means: may He grant you full flowering of your mind, blessed use of your faculties. But 'May He be gracious unto thee', that you use those endowments and abilities for noble purposes, even the promotion of truth, justice, and peace. May you be protected by His mercy from abusing your talents for mean, low, selfish purposes, through deceit, half truth, and downright falsehood.

'May the Lord everlastingly turn His face unto thee and grant thee peace': Through abiding God-consciousness – seeing Him, as it were, ever in our mind's eye, – we derive guidance, strength, self-discipline, and nobility of thought, wish, and action, which are the ultimate sources of inward serenity and outward peace.

I

The message of these three lines has trenchant meaning in our life today. We are all under the impact of the assassination by an inflamed, immature fanatic, of Senator Robert Kennedy, a promising, dynamic leader of democracy. We are deeply shaken by a succession of such ghastly crimes. We see them as dreadful tragedy, personal, national, and global. All aspects of wealth and political questions lose meaning in the light of a wife who, in sudden bloody disaster, is robbed of the mate of her youth and maturity. As we think of the eleven children, who will stay deprived of their father's affection and guidance, of the image that kept their days bright with promise and joy, our hearts go out in profound sympathy to that house whose head and glory was in a moment destroyed. We are mourning for America, our blessed country, deprived of the benefit of his service, and suddenly become a place of reckless violence, with year after year darkened by political and racial murder.

Our *Torah* has taught us to inquire, with every calamity that visits us, whether in some manner, we may not have brought it upon ourselves.[3] Not indulgence in maudlin sentiment, but thoughful self-examination is vital so that we may discover the source of evil and plan ways and means of improving, together with own life, that of our fellow-man.

We recall the first line of the priestly words: 'May the Lord bless thee.' America has been amply blessed; ours is the richest country in human history. But, alas, we have not been protected against the *Mazzik* (the demon) of indifference to human woe. Throughout our fifty states, side by side with unimaginable riches goes indefensible privation. Heartless luxury is matched by heartbreaking poverty. A hundred years ago Abraham Lincoln, greatest American, issued the Declaration of Emancipation. But for a century it has remained to our dark fellow-citizens at best an idle dream, at worst a ghastly mockery. Thirty million Americans, mostly dark, but also in large numbers white, are suffering degrading lack of fundamental necessities from food, through decent housing, to economic opportunity. We do not condone the senseless violence now perpetrated all over the country. We do not approve of it, but we must learn to understand it. *Tout comprendre est tout pardonner*, means exactly this: we must forgive out of empathy, though we cannot have sympathy, with murder, mugging, and the spouting of racial hatred.

II

As we turn again to Holy Writ for a clearer view of past negligence and future commitment to social responsibility, the second line of the priestly blessing offers us its lesson: 'May the Eternal grant thee enlightenment'. Surely, that prayer has been answered. The growth of a host of universities, their classrooms, and their laboratories, has been miraculous. From the portals of colleges and research institutions hundreds of thousands of men and women have poured forth, whose total achievement staggers the imagination. More volumes of law, lore, and science, more learned magazines and other periodicals have appeared, more technical progress has been made in the last century than in hundreds of years before. But our major concern has been the enrichment and enjoyment of an upper and middle class. Our intuition, our genius, and our interest have stopped short at the border where the welfare of the common man, this century's most popular fiction, was involved. Our statesmen, our university leaders, the tycoons of industry and finance, not to speak of political leaders, have failed lamentably in the moral obligation to extend the pre-vision of a happier world to the tenant farmer and the slum dweller. Nor have the labour unions uniformly listened to the plea of those to whom admission to their ranks would have spelled economic, physical, and emotional salvation. Thus, hand in hand with stupendous harvest for those in position to reap the fruit of their endeavour, has gone a callous apathy to the misery of the underprivileged. In his comment on the sixth commandment ('Thou shalt not kill'), Ibn Ezra, one of the classic commentators of the *Torah*, observes: 'You may kill with fist or hammer, but you may destroy also by deadly indifference to your neighbour's plight!'[4] Whilst we gloried in conquering ever wider spaces of the world, in ever deeper penetration of the human mind, we have suffered increasingly from a shrinking of the national and individual conscience. There have been some voices in the wilderness, some sustained denominational protests, even some concrete enterprises to ameliorate conditions, but these efforts have been less significant than dogmatic or doctrinal principles. There has been neither thoroughgoing national awareness, nor honest congressional effort. America, the envy of the world and the magic formula for allies, or defeated enemies, has proved a moral failure and has reaped, in consequence, the resentment, the hatred, and the violence which now confuses as it rocks her cocksure citizenry.

III

We Jews derive no malicious joy from the fact that the reputed assassin of the lamented Senator is a member of an Arab state, whose murderous hostility has caused terrible trouble to its own people and endless pain to our brethren in the Holy Land. It is but another manifestation of the old truth: dictators feed on the empty stomachs of their misled followers. During two trips to Egypt, I was able to observe how poor, unwashed, and illiterate the average fellaheen are. Egypt, almost in literal documentation of the prophetic warning of Isaiah and Jeremiah,[5] plays again the role of the conscienceless ally and the ruthless, faithless enemy. The millions that could have gone to feed the children, to educate the peasants, to provide adequate housing and security, are being used for ever more frantic military adventures, for ever more savage propaganda. But Nasser is not the only culprit, blinded by his own undisciplined mind and ruthless ambition. When, a year ago, he proclaimed his intention to exterminate Israel, with clear emphasis on 'no mercy to be shown to men, women, and children', great America, whom he had insulted and betrayed before, had no answer, no warning, no determination to prevent another Mid-East bloodshed! The State department and many civic and clerical organizations exhibited amazing patience and too often an oil-inspired indifference. No wonder that the immature youth in Arab countries glories in the pre-vision of merciless victory over the remnant of our people, huddled for comfort in Israel. These slaves of the Dictator did not dream of the courage, the skill, and the total dedication of Israel's folk. Their disastrous defeat apparently did not teach the Arab masses a lesson. Soviet might and trickery prevented them from seeing the light.

Again, the United Nations, America, England, France, and other democracies, blessed by riches of assets and minds, could have come to the rescue not of Israel who, under God, single-handedly trounced the boastful Arab armies but of the whole Mid-East. Again there was blessing of resources, of natural and produced wealth, but the *ḥen*, the grace of wisdom was lacking and thus the clouds of the cold war are again forefelt and peace is as insecure as it is fervently prayed for.

IV

The decisive line of the priestly blessing is the last: 'May the Lord everlastingly turn his face unto thee and give thee peace.' Religion has lost its influence on youth and middle age in many, if not in most, of the countries of the world. Its texts are still used to inflame the unwary with hatred towards imaginary enemies and towards any outsider. Its teachers and officials have successfully defeated its true aims – brotherhood of man under the fatherhood of God – as they have eloquently quoted its message. Ours is the only monotheistic faith which does not claim a monopoly of salvation. Our *Torah* has proclaimed ethical universalism that allows every reverent soul, living the good life, acceptance by Our Father in Heaven and a share in the world to come. We hope and pray that Pope John's Ecumenical Vision, in word and deed, may become the record of the Christian world of tomorrow. Throughout our history, within the frame of our restricted possibilities, we have endeavoured to act in accord with Jewish law: 'to feed the non-Jewish poor, even as the Jewish poor, to cure the non-Jewish sick, even as the Jewish sick and, if there were none to attend to him, to provide a grave for the non-Jewish dead, even as we must do it for the similarly deprived Jewish dead.'

In this sad hour of the human conscience, we must dedicate our effort, enlist mind, heart, and means, in America and elsewhere, to improve human conditions, to provide sustenance, education, home, and above all, promote dignity, through sustained brotherly interest in every one of His children everywhere.

In this hour of supreme, universal agony, let us rise above our normal level, spread our hands to the merciful Lord of the Universe and pray to Him: 'Bless us Oh Lord, with good health and sustenance.' But guard us against the plague of indifference. Help us to stay dynamically active on behalf of all our fellowmen and women! 'Grant us enlightenment' and vision unlimited. But be gracious unto us that we may extend our gaze to those without light, warmth, or hope. Above all, bestow upon us the steadfast awareness of Thy justice and mercy, keep us God-conscious so that we may achieve the highest aim, the deepest yearning: *peace*. The world, because of selfishness, prejudice, or ignorance is full of fear, envy, and hatred. All over the globe cruelty and apathy have fostered cynicism; frustration has begotten hostility and blind fury.

We pray Thee, Almighty Father, turn our hearts towards goodness, truth, and beauty. Teach the man of faith that loyalty to his own creed is buttressed and ennobled by love for outsiders. Teach the men of science and those in the seat of power to be wiser, gentler, to those whom they can aid. It will underpin their own future and security. May the knowledge of the tragedies of yesterday and today help regain a vista of faith in Thee made concrete and blissful in the affairs of man everywhere, preventing oppression, heartlessness, and cynicism and commence to build up Thy kingdom of abiding peace for all, 'with none to make them afraid.'[6]

Notes

1. *Bam. R.* XI, 2.
2. a.l. *Bam.* VI, 23.
3. *Ber.* 5a.
4. Exod. XX, 13.
5. Isa. XIX, Jer. XV.
6. Lev. XXVI, 6.

Taking Religion Seriously (A *Shavuot* Sermon)

The beautiful flowers adorning the synagogue reflect the eternal freshness of our *Torah*. Their fragrance recalls the timeless spring in the heart of the believer who knows the beauty and power of our faith. They recall the greatest event in human history: the Revelation on Mount Sinai, the proclamation of the Ten Commandments, ever since engraved in golden letters in the annals of the human conscience.

I

The Ten Commandments, as has been pointed out,[1] are ten short statements, containing more than ten injunctions. But the very first does not, in most of the interpretations, read like a law. It sounds like the recording of a fact. It is the genius of Samson Raphael Hirsch which offered the clearest interpretation.[2] 'I shall be the Lord thy God', has as its meaning: 'Accept Me, and My laws as the code and order of your life! I am the Lord of freedom. I am the God, interested in every human being, determined to break every tyranny, from Pharaoh of old to the latest knave playing with human dignity and destiny. Accept Me as your God and your life has basis and goal. Accept Me as your God and your programme is clear and secure.'

'No other God beside Me.' Idols have a habit of changing form and purpose. From the crude figures of primitive man to the immoral deities of classical Greece, from the various gods of Hindu systems to the race theories of the ugly Nazis, there has never been a dearth of idols. Among the modern members of that clan we find ancient selfishness, greed, blind craving for social glory, and above all the pursuit of power. 'Accept Me as thy God,' says the Lord, 'shun every delusory substitute and you will be granted an everlasting, ever-expanding revelation!'

To take religion seriously, one must take one's personality seriously. One's word must be one's bond. Careless reference to God, or, in its worst form, perjury in the name of God, denies that acceptance, cancels that code of life, makes one that rootless vagrant in our life: the modern heathen. That type of man may be as low as Hitler, as cruel as Stalin, as senseless as the latest murderer. In every case he is a victim of insecurity and confusion. The oldest commentary on the *Torah*, the *Targum Onkelos*,[3] reads the third commandment thus: 'Do not take the name of the Lord thy God in vain; but I shall surely condemn him who takes it falsely' (*lemagana – leshikra*).

II

How can one keep on the high road of religion, as a system of thought, faith, and action to tie up man with God and with his fellowman?

To render such development possible, says the fourth commandment, there must be a weekly day of emancipation from business worries and from professional burdens: a day on which one will rise above the misery of money-making, the tensions of vocational jealousy, and the plague of urbanization removed from nature and deprived of family and friends. 'Remember the Sabbath Day to keep it holy.' Through their Sabbath rest, says the *Siddur* (the Hebrew Prayer book), the children of Israel 'sanctify Thy Name.'[4] The Sabbath day offers not only physical relaxation, but spiritual opportunity and moral challenge. That is 'the everlasting covenant with God.'[5] That emancipation includes 'man-servant and maid-servant,' even as it proclaims the animal's right to be spared ceaseless labour. Such a day, by its very nature, by the creation of a free mind, allows emotion its right, flows into family relations, encourages friendship and contact with park and garden, mountain and valley. The Sabbath community prayer, the Sabbath *Shiur* (attention to the study of

His Word), feed mind and heart and help Jew and Jewess regain the vision *sub specie eternitatis*, under the aspect of eternity. From such a day of rest comes a renewed physical, mental, and social energy.

Ancient humour recommends that we be careful in selecting our parents. It stresses the benefit of good background. Parents, wise and benign, provide both heredity and environment to the children of their love. Parents can draw not only on the timeless wisdom of the *Torah*, but also on their own life for useful lessons. They have gone through trials and disappointments, which have infused them with some precious wisdom. To honour father and mother, means, especially to adolescents, the obligation to listen to their advice. Not all parents are perfect examples of humanity or of Jewishness. But nor are young men and women the only ones blessed with universal wisdom. Too often they are swept off their feet by untrained emotions and hence prone to make decisions which land them in difficulties if not in disaster. Hence the relevancy of that divine direction!

Even as it is vital to an individual to benefit from parental advice, so is it essential to a people to read the records of its past. How many college students would be saved from inferiority complexes, from cocksureness on one day and cowardly self-condemnation on the other, if they were familiar with Jewish history, its precedents, our peoples' survival, honourable, proud, and fresh, after bitter experiences of prejudice, bigotry, or outright persecution! What we have given to the world from Moses to Einstein, from Hillel to Paul Ehrlich, outweighs a thousandfold the benefits we have received. A well-informed Jew, whilst traditionally dynamic in promoting human happiness, will retain self-acceptance and dignity under all circumstances. The cancer in interdenominational relations is the profound *am-ha-aratzut* (ignorance) of Jews and Judaism by the students and the general run of American Jews. To honour Father and Mother implies the privilege to honour and respect the great figures in our national gallery, our thinkers, dreamers, prophets, teachers, and workers on every battlefield of human history.

III

With such background, the text of the last five commandments acquires new meaning. The Hebrew form of prohibition is *Al*. *Lo* means simply 'not', *Al* introduces 'Do not!' This suggestion offers itself: if the man, or woman, has accepted the Lord as God, His law as the standard of conduct; if such acceptance is absolute, allowing for no idol of greed, passion, or other evil; if, hence, God's Name is holy enough to prevent careless or deliberate fraudulent use; if the Day of Rest brings the message of eternal verities, as above economic struggles and social activity, with a maximum chance for steady spiritual influence; if respect for parents prevents the normal heartaches of life, then, in consequence: 'Thou wilt not murder, nor commit adultery, nor steal, nor deprive your neighbour of life, possession, or honour by false testimony' – thereby will you ultimately reach the high level of religious life: 'Thou wilt not covet thy fellowman's house, wife, servant, or cattle, nor anything that belongs to your neighbour.'

IV

There remains but one question. Since the programme of the Ten Commandments is both so wide and deep, why, in the daily prayerbook, have they been placed at the end of the volume? In the Sanctuary of old it was cited whenever a sacrifice was offered, why then their removal from the main order of prayers? The *Talmud* answers that query:[6] 'outside the Temple people wanted to say the Ten Commandments, but they were prevented because of the insidious claim of the heretics (that only the Ten Commandments were essential in the Law).' It was part of the argument of the neo-Christians which would have reduced the validity of all other laws of our religion.

Reflect on this fact: the Ten Commandments do not include three aspects of the *Torah*: Dietary Laws, Marriage Laws, and especially the Laws of *Tzedakah*, without which Jewish life is unthinkable. The *Talmud* quotes several attempts to restore the Ten Commandments to their central place. But the danger thereby of endorsing the new heresy was important enough to cancel such effort.

In the great world the Ten Commandments established, at least in the minds of the noblest souls, a monument of morality. In the Code of the Jewish people, God's ambassadors to the world, the kingdom of priests, who were to teach by example,[7] appears the full programme, as conveyed by *Torah*, endorsed by the prophets, and applied by the Sages of the *Talmud*, and described in the literature of our noblest minds and hearts in the millennia of Jewish history.

This is the ultimate goal of religious affirmation: a life free from oppression, from wrong action, as from wrong thought. It endorses both love, and the honest acquisition of property as the enjoyment of anything acquired in integrity. It established the line between right and wrong. Enjoy what is rightly yours, but do not cast envious or predatory eyes on what belongs to others. Religion has never been defined more adequately than by the fact that the Ten Commandments commence with 'I shall be the Lord thy God,' and end with 'all that belongs to your neighbour.'

Notes

1. B. Jacobson, *Hazon Hamikra*, a.l.
2. In his comment on Exod. XX, 2.
3. *Ibidem.*
4. *Amidah* of *Minḥah.*
5. Exod. XXXI, 16.
6. *Ber.* 12a.
7. Exod. XIX, 6.

Spring as a Task

Mipne ḥata'enu galinu me'artzenu . . .[1] In a few minutes we shall proclaim again: 'It is because of our sins that we were exiled from our country,' to wander footsore through the centuries, from continent to continent, for almost two millennia. One of the tragic consequences of that tragic history has been: *Venitraḥaknu me'al admatenu* that we were removed from our soil. *Adam* and *adamah*, soil and soul, are meant to stay interdependent:[2] man to derive physical and spiritual sustenance from the soil, the soil to receive wise and loving care from man. When this blessed relation is interrupted, diminished, or destroyed, the earth languishes and man loses his spirit and his stature.[3]

Irreligious powers of organized religion did their best to speed that deterioration. The Church Council which forbade Jews to till the ground, to tend the vineyard, to work in the orchard, could not indeed destroy the creative impulse in the hapless people who had taught mankind about God, justice, and compassion. But as Jews were forced to move into ghettoes, huddled together for comfort in close habitations, they formed islands in a sea of enmity. Valleys and mountains, flowers and harvest, became mere objects of visions and prayers rather than sweet realities of daily life.

The study of secular disciplines, whilst not too flourishing among the Gentile majority, was deliberately and systematically impeded for our people. The urbanized Jews of the Ghetto concentrated on the Holy *Torah*. Self-government kept the community on a high level of social responsibility,[4] but life in the open spaces and interest in the beauty of nature became rare and unreal.

All that prevented a full living out of the *Torah*'s life programme. There were exceptional minds who found a way to overcome man's stupid discrimination against the alert minds and warm hearts of our people. There was third century Samuel, physician,[5] astronomer, and social reformer. There were individuals whose statements in *Talmud* and *Midrash* revealed constant and intimate study of God's creation and creatures.[6] But to the common man active interests in nature seemed unattainable, gradually becoming alien and undesirable. The recognition of such development, as contrary to the teaching of our tradition, caused an eminent Sage to exclaim:[7] *Kol ha-yodea laḥashov bitekufot uvemazalot ve-eno ḥoshev, alav hakatuv omer ufoal hashem lo yabitu*[8] – 'whosoever could study astronomy and fails to do so, concerning him does Scripture say: "They do not want to see God's work!"' – a strong and righteous rebuke!

I

The month of Nissan is 'the first of the months of the year,'[9] not only because it recalls the emancipation of Pharaoh's Hebrew slaves, but also because in nature winter is being conquered and spring with its promise is blessing man and challenging him. As soon as the first blossoms appear on the trees, our code bids us repair to the park, the garden, to the open spaces, take our family along and pronounce this prayer:[10] 'Blessed art thou O Lord, King of the Universe, Who hast made Thy world lacking in nought, but has produced therein goodly creatures and goodly trees wherewith to give delight to the children of man.' As soon as the trees invite us, we are to escape the noise and the gasoline-poisoned atmosphere of the street, and we are to capture a sense of the beauty and sheer sweetness of His world.

A new comradeship between parents and children, between man and his neighbour may be born from this joint enjoyment, from the awe and wonder of His world. Study of nature is part of the programme of the *Torah*, everything that lives, moves, flies, unconsciously forms part of the orchestra chanting His praises.[11] *Hafakh bah vehafakh bah dikola bah uvah teḥeseh*[12] (Turn it and turn it over again, for everything is in it, and contemplate it), refers not only to the Holy Scriptures, but to the timeless Book of Revelation, which is His world.

The imitation of God is a universally recognized principle or mandate of religion. Within the frame of human limitation the devout man or woman should contemplate His work of continued creation – *meḥaddesh betuvo bekhol yom tamid ma'asseh bereshit.*[13] His never-absent mercy is so trenchantly described in the concluding chapters of the Book of Job, His care for all life, so eloquent in the last line of the Book of Jonah. This imitation of His goodness and wisdom, at once challenge and promise, constitutes the programme of the man of faith. To be creative means to refine and improve one's mind and energies so that one's work, technical, moral, spiritual, in the realization of Jewish social idealism, will document one's attachment to the Source of all goodness, truth, and beauty.

II

To create works of art, opportunities for all decent men and women to earn their living, schools, playgrounds, housing that will make slums a matter of the vanishing past, centres of worship and institutions to take care of the sick and the blind, of old age and hopeless youth, is the translation into harmonious life of the moral behests of our Bible.

Modern life has seen the creation of wondrous buildings, gardens of pleasure, unimaginable programmes of luxury, undreamt-of entertainment, protection, and relaxation for the lucky possessors of fortunes, but far too little of these 'goodly creations and goodly trees' have been wrought 'to give joy to the other children of man.' Far too many suffer from lack of quiet and fresh air, two of the greatest assets of life. The 'Song of Songs' contains a much applauded verse:[14] 'Comfort me with flagons, for I am sick of love.' The word *ashishot* (flagons)[15] in rabbinic elaboration is rendered 'two fires,' the fire from above, the life-producing, life-promoting sun, and the fire from below – man's heart aflame with love of his fellowman. 'We are sick' with longing for the 'two fires' in abiding co-operation to create a world in which every one of His children will be blessed by the forces of nature, His gift to man, and by the wise helpfulness of other humans, keeping their full hands open for the benefit of all in need.

Twice during the *Seder* nights, near the end of the service, do Jews pray and hope: 'Next year in Jerusalem.' That prayer has sounded to us since the days of Nebuchadnezzar and furnished a remote hope for the families groaning under the heel of oppressive church, state, and neighbour. Almost two thousand years of forced separation from nature has made us a folk of perennial tensions, miraculously under control, but never absent from the fabric of individual and communal life.

Two decades ago the harvest of half a century of corporate effort began to create the miracle of modern Israel. The counting house, the college, the workshop, were supplanted by the green field, in which the back-breaking labour of dedicated *Ḥalutzim* was blessed by the beauty of spring and the glory of harvest. Again, as in Biblical times, the Jewish man, at night, after a strenuous day of labour, could sit under his vine and fig tree and be at ease. The *Ḥalutz* brought back the scene of classical memory, the happiness of goodly fruit, the peace of the man who loved his soil, worked, and guarded it.

It is good for Jews to escape the careless luxury of the metropolis and meet in Israel Jews and Jewesses who deliberately chose the less comfortable programme of *Kibbutz* life. It is wholesome for us, in ever larger numbers, to make a visit to the Holy Land a regular annual delight. It will be of profound therapeutic value for some to turn their back upon persistent bigotry and train their children in an atmosphere into which the mists, the meanness, and the ugliness, of prejudice cannot penetrate.

So let us go out into parks and gardens, absorb the beauty of buds and blossoms, inhale their fragrance, fill our lungs with fresh air. Then let us turn from the prayerful moments to our calendar of life, and share what we know, what we have, what we have cherished as good, true, and beautiful with friend and neighbour, with alien and stranger. Let us be ever creative of means for a better, happier life, ever planning our future for the bliss not only of ourselves but for the end 'to give delight unto all the children of all man.'

Notes

1. The Festival *Mussaf* Prayer (*Amidah*).
2. Gen. I, 26; II, 5; III, 19.
3. *Eccles.* V, 9.
4. L. Finkelstein, *Jewish Self-government;* A. I. Agus, in *Talpiot* VIII.
5. See W. Bacher, *B. Amoraim*, sub *Rav*.

6. Y. A. Kamelhaar, *Talmud U-Madae ha-Tevel.*
7. *B. Shabbat* 75a. See also Bruno Kisch, *Natural Science and Judaism* in *Israel of Tomorrow*, ed. by L. Jung, 2nd edition.
8. Isa. V, 12.
9. Exod. XII, i.
10. Daily Prayer Book, *sub* Special Blessings
11. *Ps.* CIII, CXLVIII.
12. *Pirke Abot* V, 26.
13. Morning Prayer.
14. II, 5.
15. See Gesenius and Briggs, Driver Bibl. Dictionaries, and compare with Jastrow, Talm. Dict. *ad hoc.*

Atmosphere

Atmosphere, the dictionary tells us, is a mass of gaseous fluids that surround the earth. In social psychology it is defined as the influence prevailing in the home, a club, or a meeting, local, national, or continental. That atmosphere, according to the teaching of the *Torah*, is to be based on holiness. Holiness[1] is the essential quality of the Lord, the Creator and Lawgiver, and the burden of our religious philosophy of life. It is composed of basic principles to be translated into the fabric of our daily programme in the family, in business or profession, even on the field of sport. Whosoever brings about such atmosphere, would in every situation or problem, consult his conscience and the guidance of the Divine Law. Loyalty to both of them produces an attitude of the imitation of God's ethical qualities as far as human beings can conceive and in their frame approximate them.

Our religion does not present us with a never-never vision of perfection, nor does it offer a pillow to rest on. Essentially it is a challenge, a task to perform throughout the opportunity which we call life.

I

In an atmosphere of the reverence, righteousness, and compassion which produces holiness, friendship is born. Its basis is mutual trust, a comradeship flowing from commitment to moral values and from consistent action on their behalf. Such friendship, beyond the cause which unites us, becomes a source of happiness. When we see the friend, living in the same moral atmosphere, our heart rejoices, our eyes shine bright with cheer, our lips spontaneously form fervent words of greeting. A friend is closer than a brother, avers the Book of Proverbs.[2] Faithful friends are the soil whence grows emotional stability and persistent determination to face and solve all problems in rectitude and wisdom. It is the test of friendship which blesses the relation. One accepts the neighbour's nobility as self-evident even as the bread which one eats and the breath which one draws. One believes in him and stays close to him in days of tension no less than in hours of triumph. One gives him the benefit of the doubt in twilight situations even as one feels sure of a similar attitude on his part.

Neither personal frustration nor any other trouble may change it. All that is the blessing of a good atmosphere. When it is invaded by untoward spirit, joy and peace depart and what was a source of serenity becomes a milieu of affliction. The good atmosphere is created and maintained by ethical personalities. Holiness, to pervade our life, requires not only righteousness and compassion, but genuine patience and sympathy.

II

There are few persons of perfect holiness – *lo nitnah torah lo-mala'akhe hasharet*[3] : – but he who meets them finds himself transported to rare nobility and unimaginable serenity. Jewish folklore knows of thirty-six such precious souls whose influence keeps the world steady and worthwhile.[4]

I have been privileged to see, meet, and observe one: He was this century's greatest man of our faith, Rabbi Israel Meir Hacohen of Radin, venerated throughout the Jewish world as the author of the work called *Ḥafetz Ḥayyim* (the Lover of Life). It was an unforgettable encounter. His eyes, his face, his voice, his words, never vanish from one's grateful memory. In Jerusalem, during the first third of this century, lived Rav Abraham I. Kook, the spiritual head of our people in the Holy Land. His neighbours were the pietists of old, men and women whose single goal was to serve the Lord in the Land of our Fathers. But there were also recent immigrants, who had fled from gruesome scenes of anti-Jewish barbarities and whose frightful experience had made them turn their back in despair on God and His *Torah*. Their atmosphere was one of stubborn determination to toil in the fields and vineyards of Palestine relying on nothing but their comrades and the harvest of their back-breaking toil. Religion to them was a sad illusion in the pogroms of Russia and Roumania. They swore deathless loyalty to each other and sang and danced and cheered in the fraternity they had forged. To them came Rav Kook. He divined their bottomless pain, he perceived the cause of their apparent irreligious ways, but he knew that atmosphere yields to consistent dedication. In that spirit he met them, listened to them, talked to them, danced with them. Little by little they yearned to dance with him, to chant his songs of friendship, understanding, of devotion. In the end they chanted the Psalms of our faith. For they heard him say and saw him write as his conviction: 'In the heart of the most "irreligious" *Ḥalutz* lives a divine spark, which needs but the breath of a brotherly soul to kindle it into a flame of Godliness. It needs but utterly selfishless endeavour, maintained in love and sustained in devotion, to restore in the brother the longing search for the lost treasure of faith and hope, to make him a comrade on the march towards the beauty of holiness, Jerusalem.'

This is the lesson the *Torah* offers *'el kol adat b'ne Yissrael* (to the whole congregation of the children of Israel).[5] For atmosphere is but rarely produced by a few, its strength and steadiness depend upon the spirit of the many. But: 'The more *Mitzvot* (commandments or good deeds)', says Rashbam,[6] 'the greater care must be taken to maintain the spiritual condition of heart, mind, and hand which bring about the atmosphere of His *Torah*.'

III

To the uninitiated, the nineteenth chapter of Leviticus may appear like a jumble of laws without order or system: the obligations recited therein – to honour mother and father, to shun idols, to include the stranger in one's harvest, not to lie, steal, or defraud, not to oppress the poor, not to sow mixed seeds, to eschew witchcraft, to love one's neighbour as oneself. What, superficially viewed, lacks meaning is but a panorama of the effect of holiness on human relations, pervading time and place and resulting in the atmosphere which shuts out evil and hails good.

Our age knows three types of Jews: some who are 'Jews at heart,' cardiac Jews, bereft of a sense of responsibility to faith and folk. We must not reject them completely. They challenge our wisdom even as our devotion and responsibility. They might be won back to a decent assumption of duty and to happy self-acceptance. Others are men and women who observe one part of the *Torah*, be it ritual or social. They are fragmentary Jews. A part of them never knew that the goal of the ritual is ethical, that there is no law and scarcely any *minhag yissrael* (general Jewish custom), without such motivation. The ritual trains the Jews in self-discipline, it helps to preserve Jewish identity through promoting group unity. Others again need to be taught that business honesty and charitable largesse, whilst great assets in the programme of Jewish life, have been the fruit of a timeless tradition and have a tendency to diminish when truncated from the tree of Jewish life. A truly Jewish atmosphere is the harvest of men and women who seek to know what the *Torah* teaches and who shoulder both the burdens and gifts of Jewish life.

IV

The Jewish atmosphere offers what the world needs and what we are sworn to present to our fellow men: the rousing, challenging, healing, and blessed example of a life based on reverence towards God and human personality, expressed by integrity and patience, and crowned by compassion. That Jewish atmosphere is meant to spread by its example, to encourage the best among mankind to form an orchestra, with various creeds and philosophies of life merging in a chorus, each voice, each instrument, each group, straining to offer its noblest for the achievement of a vibrant, powerful symphony which will merge the separate groups into a United Nations chorus of faith and brotherhood; the peoples, east and west, white and coloured in the end to become joint pillars of the building of enduring peace and security, in the atmosphere of brotherhood and co-operation, in the Name of God, all over His world.

Notes

1. Lev. XIX, I.
2. Prov. XVIII, 24.
3. *B. Berakh.* 28b.
4. Cp. *B. Succah* 45b.
5. Lev. XIX, I.
6. *ad locum.*

Ethical Sensitiveness

The hope for freedom is based on justice and mercy in inter-human relations. Ethical sensitiveness covers not only the facts of good and evil, but the nuances, an intuitive perception of what in German is called *Fingerspitzengefuehl.*

Why, in this modern, technologically ideal world, is there so much hatred to darken its horizon, threatening eventual universal annihilation and meantime erupting from East to West in endless riots, robberies and murder?

I

There are two causes of that hatred, one obvious, the other more subtle, but, in the long run, more pernicious. There is the resentment of the person or group who has been abused by neighbour or neighbours, all the way from discrimination in social, industrial, and civic life to outright violence and reckless killing. Even the mere memory of such suffering in the past builds up a powerful antagonism, an almost feverish passion for revenge, on every level of human relations. Yet, when yesterday's oppressor commences to mend his ways, endeavours to right the wrong, to make reparation in earnest, there is some hope that the hatred will abate, that the victim will begin to think of reconciliation, forgetting the past, and ready, once his quest for freedom, opportunity, and above all self-respect, is progressively granted, to join in co-operative labour with his erstwhile oppressors. The other cause is both more damaging and its effects are harder to overcome.

Why do so many Southerners hate Negroes? Why do so many Germans hate Jews? Why do so many Christian ministers, priests, and laymen have such concentrated illwill towards the people who gave them their Saviour, his apostles, and disciples, whose Ten Commandments they admire, whose Bible they quote, in both prophetic warning, the Psalmist's fervour, and the Sage's moral wisdom?

II

You may have heard of, or read, A. D. Morse's book *While Six Million Died, A Chronicle of American Apathy*, the incredible documentation of murderous indifference displayed not by heedless, incited mobs or drunken *mujiks*, but by men in high government posts in our own beloved America. It is true, there were exceptions in the world of the Thirties, both in our own country and in Europe, from most precious Denmark through kindly Sweden, to brave Bulgaria. But the average non-Jew either joined Hitler's hellhounds or did nothing to prevent their utterly ghastly extermination, their fiendish tortures, and every scientific devilry of affliction, of the million Jewish children, and five million Jewish adults. The Nazis caught them in carefully-prepared traps, reduced them in carefully-planned programme, by beating, starving, and overworking them to living skeletons in whom the will for survival was inexorably reduced, day by day, to the level of absolute hopelessness and a prayer for an end of the ghastly pain, even in the gas-ovens of Auschwitz and Majdanek. Why did the powerful Church remain indifferent or at best satisfied with pious proclamation in the face of that incredible mass murder, foretold and almost watched, conveyed by reliable messengers, Jewish and non-Jewish, to the heads of government in democratic countries, to their generals and lay leaders? Why was nothing done to destroy the death factories in Poland and Germany when their locations were known, when frantic cables gave every detail, geographic and other?

Again, why did the southern Americans, in spite of the blessed Constitution and the Emancipation proclaimed by Abraham Lincoln, allow the dreadful sufferings, the lynchings, the other nameless atrocities committed by Ku-Klux-Klan and their henchmen against our coloured fellow citizens?

III

The answer to all these questions becomes clear as we study the second cause. One who has committed wrong, carries within himself, in the occasional prompting of his conscience, a deep sense of guilt. His selfishness would fain drown that voice and his unredeemed arrogance renders all memories of past commission merely unpleasant. Hence the thought of his victim stirs rarely a sense of penitence but too often a feeling of resentment towards the very persons he has hurt. The people of Lessing, Goethe, Schiller, and Friedrich Wilhelm Foerster, normally vociferous about their 'national glory', are anxious to forget their insane hatred of the Jews from the days of Luther to the horrors of the Third Reich. To ease their easy conscience, they would deny or minimize the solid facts of Herrenvolk atrocities, invent all sorts of arguments to justify concentration camps, with their unimaginable barbarism, and, finally, unable to erase completely the hell of Himmler, Streicher, and other madmen from their memory, find it convenient to ignore those terrible years and to concentrate on vicious hatred of the people one third of whom, in their much-lauded plan for 'Final Solution', they reduced to mounds of corpses heaped up like sacks, to soap and ashes!

The New Testament is full of quotations from the Hebrew Bible. The Churches know the melody of faith from the twenty-four books of the Holy Writ. They have met Jews on every front of social advance. Jewish women in Germany pioneered social service, from nurseries for workers' children, to careful systems of aid to the poor, the sick, and the old. Liberalism in Europe knew Jewish leadership, self-sacrificingly promoting the welfare of every citizen.

IV

To Pope, Bishop, Minister, the knowledge of wellnigh two thousand years of Church atrocities committed against helpless Jews is unwelcome. The contrast between public assertion of Christianity as the religion of love, and countless expulsions, *autos-da-fé*, burning of Jews and their books, of deliberate defamation and inciting of loot-bent mobs, disturbs, at least occasionally, the usual story of triumphant glory in the cause of saving man, body and soul. Hence the consistent attacks on 'Pharisaism,' 'Deicides', 'Enemies of God,' and other convenient fabrications of Jewish 'sinfulness' to justify the ways of the Church to man. In our own times have arisen Travers Herford, George Foot Moore, Malcolm Hay, and, crowning them all, Pope John XXIII, rare protesters against the relentless chorus of slanderous malevolence. It has been more 'natural' and convenient to continue inflammatory orating on Christian pulpits than to face up to its inevitable consequence: the corrosive cynicism which encourages atheism, sovietism, and gangsterism everywhere in this world. It has been cheaper than it would have been to pay a millennial debt by a genuine endeavour of compensation, by aiding powerfully the growth of Israel, folk and republic, the single ray of joy in a bleak century of human conscience.

The prophet Obadiah excoriated Edom: 'For the violence done to thy brother Jacob, shame shall cover thee . . . in the day that thou didst stand aloof, as strangers would carry away his substance . . . even thou wast as one of them . . . but on Mount Zion there shall be those that escaped . . . and the house of Jacob shall enter upon their possessions . . . saviours shall come up on Mount Zion . . . and the kingdom shall be the Lord's.' But organized Christianity, very few friends excepted, listened as unmoved bystanders to Nasser's Hitlerite imprecations, watched indifferently his preparation for the extermination of men, women, and children of the new nation. No democratic army or navy, none of the statesmanship of the great powers were ready to protect the remnants of our people in the Holy Land. Deadly silence was the reaction of spiritual as of political leaders.

Did not the Psalmist plea foretell: 'Let the Lord help me against my friends, I shall look my enemies unafraid into their hate-filled face?' We had but one Friend above and a wondrous unity between Israel land and people that inspired the incredible bravery and total dedication of the Six Days' heroes!

Even individual histories show similar trends, and present an equal riddle. There are men who have risen to financial or professional success. In their lean years they had benefited from the favours of good souls. Yet they are often found prone to forget those kindnesses and to develop indifference mounting to hostility towards their erstwhile benefactors. Ingratitude is one of the saddest and basest indications of a selfish personality. Back of that phenomenon is the same moral deficiency: The pride of the 'self-made man' forbids him to recall the time when, for sheer survival, he depended on the advice, hospitality, or more substantial aid, of others. It goes still further: any evil corrodes, as it corrupts, the man or woman committing it. He who breaks a business contract, too often is found to hate the partner he had defrauded. He who would achieve success by climbing over his rival's body, speaks in defamatory tone about the man or woman whom he has injured. In my long life as rabbi I have met not only some of the finest persons one may hope to encounter, but alas, in endeavours to remove enmity, to make peace between relatives and strangers, I had to suffer the awareness of such unrighteousness, for which only the skilled psychiatrist or the dedicated man of faith may find interpretation and eventual cure. There is no ethical sensitiveness in a thorough-going egoist. He seeks no nearness of God, he fears His judgment.

V

Prevention, as you have read a hundred times, is a hundred times better than cure. What does our Holy *Torah* teach us to forestall all the evil which afflicts the modern world and which drives youth and adults towards moral and intellectual extremism? The third book of Moses offers the answer. Its major terms are *korban* and *Keddushah*, both victims of mistranslation. *Korban*, etymologically, does not mean 'offering,' or 'gift,' but has to do with the timeless quest for *Kirvat elokim*, nearness to Him. That is not a theological phrase, nor a mystic formula, but stands for the yearning to find the way to His mercy unobstructed by evil thought or action. The golden curtain leading to Him grows in power and beauty from the passionate awareness that only through imitating His qualities of justice and mercy can the Jews, even as all His children, attain peace of mind and soul, the salvation of a clear conscience, and physical security. Such 'nearness to God' was achieved by a moral sensitiveness. Even the wrong or sin committed by error plagued the faithful until he had offered, together with his penitent heart, the *korban ḥatat*, symbol of a passionate quest for His nearness. There was the *korban todah* offered as a symbol of gratitude, which the rabbis assert will never be out of date, even when other expressions seeking the *Shekhinah* (His presence) will have gone. There was the *korban shelamim*, of peace, when, together with one's family, in grateful happiness, one could find fulfilment in '*eating, drinking, and seeing Him.*' This never-ending effort to stay blessed by awareness of Him, love of Him, walking His way of mercy and equity, was to keep the voice of conscience ever more potent than the whispering of temptations, yea, in times of danger, stronger than the trumpets of a dreaded enemy. Indeed, through this abiding God-consciousness, the children of Abraham, Isaac, and Jacob, were challenged and promised, protected and warned towards the goal that Moses, again and again, had proclaimed to them.

Keddushah, usually translated as holiness, is a combination of three qualities or achievements, the three R's of our faith, harvest of both attitude and act. One reaches its level by Reverence towards God and human personality; by Righteousness in one's conduct and righteous indignation with every form of oppression or fraud; above all by abiding *Raḥamanut* (literally motherliness), an attribute of God as of any human whose love of the fellowman is unselfish and dedicated.

VI

The Tent of Meeting in the wilderness, even as the national sanctuary in Jerusalem, was meant to promote, through spreading general God-consciousness, both civic and moral freedom. In a classic interpretation, Rabbi Samuel ben Meir (known as Rashbam), found a significant message in the last verses of Exodus: 'The cloud covered the Tent of Meeting and the glory of the Lord filled the Tabernacle. But whenever the cloud was taken up from over the tabernacle the people of Israel marched forward . . .' onward towards the Holy Land.

Said that celebrated grandson of the immortal Rashi: 'By His grace, the cloud rested first on the Tent, then on the Ark of the Covenant.' From addressing itself to the whole congregation in the national sanctuary, the cloud moved to the Tables of the Ten Commandments in every heart which was aware of the Father in heaven and was to translate God-consciousness, even as the Cherubim taught it: For their faces 'were turned towards each other.' It is by facing our human brother in justice and love that we walk the way of the Lord. It is Ethical Sensitiveness which leads through Sinai towards the glory of *Torah* and the golden hope of the Messianic age – a hateless, warless, creative world, when, in the words of Maimonides, freedom from political and economic slavery together with the creative genius of Man, under the protection of God will provide sustenance, security, and happiness to Jew and non-Jew, all races, colours, and creeds for years without end.

Notes

Of the literature on the holocaust the most important books are:

1. Malcolm Hay, *Foot of Pride* (in paperback *Europe and the Jews*).
2. J. Wells, *The Janowska Road.*
3. A. Katsh, *Kaplan's Diary.*
4. J. Robinson, *And the Crooked Shall be Made Straight.*
5. Rolf Hochhuth, *The Deputy.*
6. Raul Hilberg, *The Destruction of European Jewry.*
7. Dagobert Runes, *The War Against the Jews.*
8. A. D. Morse, *While Six Million Died.*
9. Friedrich Heer, *God's First Love.*
10. Among a host of volumes and pamphlets mentioned in the notes and appendices of Robinson's above-named book.

Judaism and Old Age

There are three names in our sacred language for seniors: *yashish*[1] which means solid, substantial, significant.

The second word is *zaken* which, in the interpretation of our sages, means one who has acquired wisdom: *zeh shekanah hokhmah.*[2] The last word is *sabba* which, in general, means a hoary head, one whose strength and vision has shrunk; but it is also used for famous scholars above middle age. *Mipne sayva takum* – 'Before the gray head' of any man or woman does the *Torah* say that 'we should rise,' we should extend reverence to anyone who has gone through life and has faced its sun and shadow. To[3] any man or woman of that age our tender feeling ought to extend, no matter whether Jewish or Gentile. One of our sages never failed to greet an ancient heathen, saying to himself: 'How many troubles have come to him,[4] how much suffering has life brought him!' Our minimum recognition of that fact ought to be shown by courtesy and kindness.

I

To all of us is directed the commandment: *Kabbed et avikha ve-et immekha*[5] – 'Honour thy Father and thy Mother in order that thy days may be long upon the land which the Lord thy God giveth thee.' This recalls to me the memory of a sweet girl of adolescent age who used to attend my Sunday morning class. One day she suddenly confronted me with this statement: 'I don't like the fifth commandment.' Knowing her as an utterly fine human being, I expressed my astonishment at her words. But she explained: 'Father and mother have given me everything that I have, that I know, that I am. Why should I be rewarded for honouring them? One should serve them without expectation of special compensation.' I answered: 'The *Torah* does not say 'Love thy father and thy mother.' It is taken for granted that every normal child, on the grounds which you have stated, loves them. Honouring father and mother has to do with something different. Many an adolescent boy or girl think in their easy optimism that their own generation has garnered all the wisdom in the world. They look upon father and mother as very lovable, but in some respects as old fogies who are behind the times and whose advice, therefore, is not important enough for the profound problems of young people. Yet, father and mother have gone through life, have suffered trial and disappointment, and in the process have acquired a certain wisdom. They have learned not to be overwhelmed by appearances. Young people very often are carried away by superficial impressions and they easily make mistakes for which they pay heavily afterwards. If you honour father and mother by paying attention to their advice, you will not be swept off your feet by sudden emotion; you will thereby save yourself many heartaches, you will live happier and longer.'

II

As with all humans, senior citizens occasionally feel pain and are likely to be dismayed by it. It is good to remember that even pain comes from God's mercy. Pain reveals the fact that something needs attention. Pain serves as a warning that we ought to consult a physician and accept his direction as to a change in diet or programme of work. Intelligent care will prolong life and keep it pleasant.

Altogether, one should cherish advice of the sage:[6] As between the pressure of youth to rush into new movement or building and the advice of a maturer person to call a halt to headlong, reckless activity, it is wiser to stop building, which may lead to disaster, and to engage in work of enduring quality. Both in marriage, in business, as in politics, one may build up something on wrong foundations and invite only ruin. But one may hesitate to participate in rash enterprise and thereby eventually promote wholesome development, peace, and happiness.

III

'No man truly dies',[7] say our sages, 'except through doing nothing.' Wasting time is more tiring than laborious effort. The *Talmud* ordains that even a bride of rich background, bringing servants to her new home, must engage in regular work because[8] 'Laziness leads to idiocy.' Today we proclaim: 'A vacuum is a source of much trouble, real and imaginary.'

Above all, it is a problem for seniors what to do with life stretching out without a definite programme. To keep well and contented, they must keep alert. To continue in vitality, to remain physically and mentally on a good level they must have something definite to do every day. There was a time, before the days of Father Abraham, when old age met with utter neglect from the rest of the family and the community. For countless centuries, old age was at best ignored, at worst derided and treated with contempt by the heathens in all lands.[9] The horrible example of impatience with a long-lived father was portrayed, a hundred years ago, in Schiller's play, 'The Robbers': The scum of a son nails the coffin of his weak, old parent, calling out: 'Do you want to live forever?'

On the positive side: The programme of our sacred literature, offered to seniors,[10] is as varied as it is encouraging. The first advice is: every day study the *Torah*. It is never too late to acquaint yourself with its ideas and ideals, and especially with its programme of social righteousness. Read the immortal words of our noblest minds and hearts as they interpreted in thought and action the timeless life programme of Judaism! Let all great books give you joy! Read of the common sense, the vision, even the fancy and humour, of wise or benign authors from many ages and nations, from Cicero to Gandhi, from Mark Twain to Tolstoy, from Will Durant, to Reuben Dario, to Galbraith!

Immerse yourself in a study of the fascinating personalities of our history, from Moses, through dedicated and impatient prophets, pioneers of the spirit, to wise and efficient rabbis and lay leaders, men and women, down to the builders of Israel and Zion in our days!

Do not neglect the study of nature! Enjoy parks, mountains, oceans! Of one who has a chance to witness nature's revelation and who ignores it, says the *Talmud:* 'He belongs to the hapless group that will not look upon God's work.'[11]

By all means seek *Ḥabruta*, comradeship.[12] There are many fine folks whose fellowship and friendship you can enjoy. There are so many people whom you can help by your personal interest.

On a visit to a hospital a few years ago, I found an empty hour which I tried to fill by going to the wards. I asked the floor nurse whether there was any patient whom nobody visited. She pointed to a bed and said: 'The man with the beard stays all alone; he hardly eats, all day he lies with the sheet over his head,' I approached and called out: *Shalom Alekhem.* That greeting had a dramatic effect. Ten minutes later we were engaged in a spirited discussion of a rabbinic problem. The amazed nurse came over and said: 'What did you do to the rabbi, he seems actually alive?' His usually pale face was ruddy, his eyes were brilliant. I answered: 'I gave him a Hebrew pill, called *Gemilut Ḥassadim* (personal kindness).

Anyone of you could be of profound significance to a lonely soul at home, or in a hospital. Your kindness may accelerate recovery, and indeed it may prolong life.

IV

As a matter of fact, there should need to be no clear division between young and older folks. Abraham's Coin,[13] we are told, showed an old man and woman on one side, and a youth and maiden on the other. Their peace and happiness are interdependent. Young peoples' enthusiasm and older folks' maturity, in steady co-operation, will produce a happy group or community. The rabbis, in bold generosity, pronounced their conviction of the potential value of every individual by proclaiming that 'every school child is a potential Messiah.'[14] They also stressed the untold good that may come from wise, kind, patient seniors. The bridge between them and youth must be built by reverence towards God and human personality, by righteousness which can always repair breaches, and above all, by that unique quality of heart called in English 'compassion or pity' and in Hebrew *Raḥamanut*[15] or motherliness, unselfish love of one's fellow man.

V

To us Jews, life has been taught as every person's opportunity to spread light and warmth, to foster hope and cheer. It is not the number of years which matters, but the moral and spiritual contents of our record. 'Teach us to number our days!'[16] the Psalmist cried to God. 'We make our days precious through fine intention, steadfast effort, and above all, through noble action.'

Tzedakah, which means both justice and kindness,[17] is the life-long slogan of good Jews and Jewesses. We may perform that *Mitzvah* (commandment or good deed), no matter how young or old, how rich or poor, how strong or weak we are. All of you know from your own experience how endless the opportunities are for good work, for comforting the mourners, visiting the sick, and helping the friendless.

A Rabbi was once passing through a field when he saw a very old man planting an oak-tree. 'Why are you planting that tree?' said he. 'You surely do not expect to live long enough to see the acorn growing up into an oak-tree?'

'Ah,' replied the old man, 'my ancestors planted trees not for themselves, but for us, in order that we might enjoy their shade or their fruit. I am doing likewise for those who will come after me.'[18]

VI

One of the forms of *Tzedakah* has to do with the gift to the needy. In accord with Jewish law, we pronounce a *Berakhah* (blessing) before we perform any *Mitzvah*:[19] before the housewife lights the *Shabbat* candle, before we listen to the sound of the *Shofar*, before we sit down in the *Succah*. The one exception is the act of *Tzedakah*, when no blessing is proper although that *Mitzvah* is very great. The reason given by one of our luminous scholars is this:[20] 'Every act of charity has two aspects, one is the blessing of being able to give, the other is the shame or curse of having to accept, of being dependent for one's basic needs on the gifts of flesh and blood. Because of that embarrassment of our poor brother, we cannot be happy enough to pronounce a blessing.'

Finally, all of us seek *longe yohren* (longevity). *Leḥayyim* is a universal greeting and blessing. Long life is a Biblical promise for good conduct.[21] The *Talmud* records the question addressed to a sage long ago:[22] 'What did you do to live long?' He answered: 'I was anxious to create a happy environment, to remain ever conscious of my neighbour's dignity, I never called a man by an unpleasant nickname, I never listened to *Lashon Hara*, from careless chatter at a social occasion to any evil reference to his personality or conduct. I have always been liberal with my money. I have never seen a thoroughly bad man (most people are sick rather than wicked). There is hope for any one of God's children, no matter how far he had strayed before.'

One of the great rabbis, conscious of the enormous harm done by the common sin of the evil tongue, the lack of tongue control, went to a market place and called out:[23] 'Who wants life, who wants life? (I have a miracle cure).' Immediately many men and women were lured from the other booths to his own place. All looked at him expectantly for they all craved long life. Said he: 'To achieve it,[24] "Guard your tongue from evil and your lips from speaking guile."' The evil tongue has caused many a disaster and death. Careful control of our speech saves life and prolongs it.

VII

All the *Mitzvot* teach us to remain ever conscious of God, His justice and His mercy, and thereby to become fine, worthwhile persons. For thousands of years the Jewish life and lore has given us comfort, confidence, and a happy attitude. We have said, and taught our children to pray:[25] *Beyado afkid ruḥi* – 'In His hand I entrust my spirit, both when I sleep and when I awake. In God's hand, together with my spirit, also my body, God is with me and I am not afraid.' To the man or woman who is ever conscious of God, sounds the promise of our *Siddur*: [26]'Once I was young, now I am old, I have never seen a righteous, pious person who felt foresaken by God.' God stays with him or her challenging, encouraging, blessing, until the very setting of the sun.

This is what Judaism says to its senior citizens: 'As soon as possible, retire by all means from heavy work, lessen the burdens of your hand, mind, and heart imposed by private business. Engage in work for the common good and you will enjoy every hour of the day, every day of the year, *Leḥhayyim tovim u-le-shalom* good life and peace.'

Notes

1. Gesenius, Biblical Dictionary, Jastrow, Rabbinic Dictionary.
2. *Kidd.* 32a.
3. *Sabe de Pumbedita, San.* 17b.
4. *Rosh haSh.* 16a.
5. Exod. XX, 12.
6. *Meg.* 31b.
7. *Abot de R. Nathan* XI, 1.

8. *Ket.* 59b.
9. *Baba M.* 87a.
10. Joshua I, 8.
11. *Shab.* 75a.
12. Isaiah V 12.
13. *Baba Kama* 97b.
14. *Shab.* 119b.
15. The root is *Reḥem* – womb – motherliness.
16. *Ps.* XC, 12.
17. Throughout Hebrew Literature.
18. *Meg.* 28a *Baba Bathra* 11a. See also J. H. Hertz *Book of Jewish Thoughts*, p. 136.
19. *Pes.* 7b.
20. *Responsum* of *Adret.*
21. *Midr. Vay. Rabba* XIII, 3.
22. *Taanit* 20b.
23. *Abodah Z.* 19b.
24. *Ps.* XXXIV, 14.
25. *Ps.* XXXI, 6.
26. *Ps.* XXXVII, 25.

A Grave Problem

I

In one line, distinguished by clarity and timelessness, our Sages stated the total purpose of the Divine *Torah:* 'The sole goal of the *Mitzvot* is *letzaref et haberiyot,*[1] ('to purify human beings'). *Tsaref,* in Hebrew has three meanings: to ennoble,[2] to strengthen,[3] and to unite.[4] All the four orders, *Arbaah Turim,* were to be inscribed on the High Priest's Breastplate of Justice (the *Ḥoshen Mishpat*). God is holy because He is Righteous,[5] 'Abraham proclaimed Him by righteousness at every step.'

The highest merit attaches to righteous conduct. *Kiddush Hashem* (the sanctification of His name) is to be achieved *betokh bene Yisrael*[6] in the life of the Jewish community before endeavouring to convey it to the rest of the world. As the ritual law came from Sinai, on God's authority, so did moral principle, attitude, and action flow from His law.[7] If *Kiddush Hashem* is the greatest *Mitzvah,* so is *Ḥillul Hashem* (desecration of His name by evil conduct) the worst offence. The closer a man is to Him the sterner His judgment of moral wrong.[8] No earlier good deeds count for the man guilty of desecration of His name.[9] 'They who love the Lord must hate evil.'[10]

So far the teaching of Holy Writ, of *Talmud,* and *Midrash.* Throughout Jewish history the *mekaddesh Hashem* (one who sanctified His name) was the symbol of a hero, the shining example to fire the moral ambition of the youth. Throughout the millennia of our national record, the *meḥallel* (one who desecrated His name) was an object of utter contempt, to whom communal misfortune and national shame was attributed. *Kiddush Hashem* may be achieved by a single heroic act or by the noble pattern of one's whole life; so could *Ḥillul Hashem* be perpetrated by a single ugly action or by the low level of one's whole career.

The ideal and theory of the *Torah*'s way of life is clear enough. But the patterns of reality too often have a different story to tell. When they exhibit the personality of the *am ha-aretz*, the religiously illiterate, they are deplorable enough. When they reflect the character of persons pretending to be, or thinking they are, religious, these patterns become a source of intellectual confusion and moral cynicism.

II

For decades, we have had in this country the *Kashrut* jungle, in which predatory would-be rabbis and their lay confrères or employers abused the religious scruples of the loyal Jew for their nefarious greed. We have met men, known as *musmakhim* (endowed with rabbinic diploma) whose word none could rely on, whose deeds were execrable. One such *Ḥillul Hashem* is more damaging to the faith of the immature, to the image of loyalty to the *Torah* in American Israel, than a hundred dissenters or humanist deniers of the Lord of the Universe. The attention of the common citizen is drawn less to the sublime teaching of His *Torah* than to the evil odour created by persons claiming allegiance to its way of life. *Kashrut* endorsement, available to the highest bidder, has caused more deviation from the Holy Law than a multitude of sermons or articles against orthodoxy. Nor have such evil matters been too rare in our own days. In the thirty years of my chairmanship of the New York State government Advisory Board for *Kosher* Law enforcement, my colleagues and I have been more than once aghast at the moral imperviousness of men known for their learning, eloquence, and general astuteness. We have heard of scandalous vendettas and abominable battles by scholars in American Jewish houses of learning which have baffled pious lay members of their boards and disheartened if not disgusted the young student of *Torah*.

Other sources of much evil have been circles of extremists, insisting on going too far in the right direction in one aspect of the *Din Torah* whilst pursuing their private aims in clear violation of its ethical postulates; a plus conformity in ritual meant to cover up a minus in morals, and, by vociferous insistence on too much of the one endeavouring to silence the protest against too little of the other.

III

It seems to me that what is necessary to stem this evil trend is to emphasize the simple fact that none may claim loyalty to Judaism on a merely fragmentary basis. We must emphasize absolute conformity to the *Din Torah* as the *sin qua non* of loyal Jewishness. The *Din Torah* as the single timeless fortress of Jewish life and mandate for the right Jewish personality must be taught from Kindergarten to *Yeshivah*. As balancer of the various legitimate loyalties of Jews, the *Din Torah* must be emphasized again and again as a commitment not to one or two phases, but to the whole of Jewish law. The *Sidrah* of *Keddoshim* offers enduring teaching in this respect. The verses in chapters XIX and XX of Leviticus, to the uninitiated, may sound like a jumble of disconnected laws, including honour due to parents, prohibition of idolatry, attention to details about sacrifices, to rules about vineyards, followed again by honesty and charity, courtesy towards old people, and other rules. What is involved, however, is the key to Judaism: *Kedushah*, (holiness), which I have described as a synthesis, the three R's of Judaism: reverence towards God and human personality, righteousness in social relations, and *raḥamanut* towards the poor, the sick, the friendless – a principle to govern every aspect of the Jew's life, every hour of his day. To many of us these things are self-evident. To many more they stay unknown, undigested, or as merely subjects of sermons or poems.

What is required is a special emphasis in our schools: The student at *Yeshivah Ketanah* and at *Yeshivah* must be penetrated by the thought that uprightness of conduct is as basic as *Shemirat Shabbat*, that a lie, meanness, indifference to moral values, is as wrong as eating *Trefah* or neglecting to don *Tefillin*. Four times in the long *Vehu Raḥum* (prayer recited every Monday and Thursday morning) occurs the confession *Ki en banu ma'assim*, i.e., we lack the asset of good deeds. In the *Rosh Ḥodesh Tefillah* of *Mussaf* and in the *Neilah* of *Yom Kippur* we confess to *oshek*, (violence, fraud, oppression). These faults must be castigated not from the pulpit alone, but from first grades in Day Schools and *Talmud Torahs* to the graduation exercises of *Yeshivot.* Smartness, cunning, ruthless careerism must be held up to contempt, the character of a Jewish gentleman *à la* Psalm xv must be lauded, held up as the proper example of our faith with so much wisdom, consistency, and skill that they will forge the emerging personalities of our youth.

IV

We must train our adults, too, so that in communal life success will be measured not by wealth, nor by success in one's profession, but by the character of a man or woman. Biographies of our national gallery, in juvenile and adult literature, must lay stress not on intellectual achievement in the *pilpul* of ancient or modern dialogues, but on the beauty and power of noble personalities, rabbis, teachers, men of business or profession. It will be good to quote the Sage who named a comedian as worthy of the world to come because he cheered the unhappy; or the jailer who received eternal reward for protecting a helpless maiden. There are enough heroes and heroines of the spirit in the halls and corridors of Jewish history to fill a hundred textbooks, a thousand magazines, and to impress the maturing minds and hearts of tomorrow's adults in the Jewish camp.

V

Details, methods, curricula should be the task of conferences of expert pedagogues, removed from the limelight and normal competitive atmosphere. The world of *Ḥassidim* down to today's *Ḥabad* leaders and of *Mitnaggedim* including the modern *Mussar* schools, should be represented at such conferences. Pious educators and psychologists and laymen of fine principles and practices should be urged to attend.

Beyond classes, lectures, and publications, small intimate circles for training a moral *élite*, under the guidance of a strong, noble personality, may be found useful. His disciples would pledge themselves to definite missionary *Mussar* work among larger groups. Their dialogues would commence with a training in awareness of the great danger, a detailed programme and a library for juveniles planned *ad hoc.*

Such partnership of spiritual leaders and fine *Ba'ale Battim* might be crowned, eventually, by the harvest of a new generation, committed to *Hashem* by conformity to letter and spirit, to the programme of the good life, which Sinai taught us and which His genuine prophets of every age have been sworn to uphold, to preach, and to translate into the sustained reality of Jewish life.

Notes

1. *Vay. R.* XIII, 50.
2. Jer. VI, 29.
3. *Mishnah Makhsh* (V), 7.
4. *B. Nazir* 35b.
5. Isa. V, 16.
6. Lev. XXII, 32.
7. Rashi, *Vay* XXV, 1.
8. *B. Yeb.* 121b.
9. *B. Kidd.* 40a.
10. *Ps.* XCVII, 10.

Wilderness as Discipline

I

The Sages of old were translating their reverence for Holy Writ into minute attention to every word of the sacred text. This is how the Hebrew Bible remained an effervescent source of wisdom, reflecting the noblest thoughts of every generation of its loyal students. As they read between the lines, they found an amazing treasure, nuances and solid teaching, of intellectual, moral, and spiritual ideas.

The following may serve as example: The last verse of the third book of Moses (Leviticus) reads: 'These are the Commandments which the Lord commanded Moses for the children of Israel on Mount Sinai.' The first verse of Numbers, the fourth book, reads: 'And the Lord spoke unto Moses in the wilderness of Sinai.' Combining the two lines, the *Midrash Rabba a.l.* comments: 'Whosoever does not consider himself as insignificant as the ownerless (unattended) wilderness, is unable to acquire wisdom and guidance.' The *Talmud*[2] records: 'If a man looks upon himself as low as a wilderness, which humans treat contemptuously, his learning will stay with him.' The venerated Rabbi Jacob, author of the Code,[3] combines both sources in his statement: 'Unless you possess that humility, you will not understand either the *Torah* or its commandments.'

'Wilderness' may refer to a natural, historical, or personal condition. It always represents both a challenge and a promise. What it calls forth, is the skill and the devotion of the pioneer, the pathfinder, a type of human which to modern Jews is conveyed by the term *Ḥalutz*. In Hebrew etymology: *ḥalatz* means 'strike out', 'redeem', 'gird', 'relieve'; in modern usage: 'to tie', 'to blaze the trail', 'to pioneer'. Only the *Ḥalutz*'s stubborn devotion will transform the wasteland of the desert. Only his vision of its potentiality will stimulate his planning, blossoming into a programme of work, that will gradually cover naked rocks with vegetation, changing a spreading wilderness into gardens, fields, and vineyards.

II

There is a wilderness of history, through which the Lord's chosen people have been walking, marching, or driven, for two millennia. It is the story of our people, the world's most significant and almost smallest minority, battling, straining, against the incredible hostility, murderous hatred, and ruthless persecution of heathens, ancient and modern. How could we overcome all of that, what made us persist in what appeared a hopeless task? How could we survive against countless handicaps, organized madness, powerful armies? Says the *Midrash*:[4] 'Whenever the Israelites were marching, the Holy Ark was going in front of them. Two fiery sparks came out of the staves of the Ark burning up before them all the snakes and scorpions, destroying the haters of Israel.' It would have been impossible to continue on the march had it not been for these two powerful sparks, sources of inspiration symbolized by the Holy Ark. One, the faith in the Lord of the universe, Who redeemed our forefathers from the slavery of Egypt and promised them the Holy Land; the other, the growing conviction, in our people's heart and mind, of Israel's significance as His Ambassador, bringing the message of justice and compassion to a benighted world. The *Torah* reports: 'And it came to pass, when the Ark set forward, that Moses said: 'Rise up, O Lord, and let thine enemies be scattered; and let them that hate Thee flee before Thee.'[5] Out of that passionate faith came not only the assurance of His aid, but also the plea of Moses. 'But when it rested,' whenever his folk were moving from station to station in the wilderness, threatened by robber bands or the hosts of rapacious kings, he cried out, 'Return, O

Lord, unto the ten thousand of the thousands of Israel.'[6] When energy seemed waning, when courage failed the harassed Hebrews, it was His leading them back, it was their return to the Source of all life that brought them again encouragement, stimulation, challenge to carry on. In the wilderness of history, our people could survive only through the miracle of faith and determination: It was their faith in their ultimate salvation by the Lord of Sinai and their steely decision to espouse their religious cause to 'tie up' their life consistently, dynamically, wisely, and courageously with their timeless task: religion in the concrete, the practice of justice and kindness in private and public affairs. Clerical enmity will not readily admit those assets of the Jewish spirit. Envious illwill has been denying it. But whatever hope for the conquest of the human wilderness blesses modern mankind, is the fruit of two thousand years of our people's unbroken endeavour to substitute for stupid tyranny, ruthless national ambition, and the ever present temptation of spoil, the power of the light, the warmth, and the sheer humaneness which the *Torah* has taught us.

III

What applies to Israel collectively, applies to every Jew and Jewess, nay, to every human being individually. Everyone of us, in his or her undeveloped personality, resembles a wilderness. We know today that moral sterility, social fruitlessness, even as intellectual vacuity, can be overcome only by a growing, deepening *Ḥalutziut*, pathfinding, pioneering effort, We must start with the supreme quality of *Anavah* (humility) which recognizes the need for developing achievement of self-discipline, for acquiring knowledge, and using it to inprove our own life and that of our neighbours. Only through the inspiration of the *Torah* can we overcome the temptation to be driven by uncontrolled impulse, desire or passion which leads to the decay of all values. 'Teaching[7] is great' say the Rabbis, 'because it leads to good deeds; because it leads to reverence, to careful conduct.'[8]

But where shall one start? What should be the continued source of encouragement? Says the *Torah*:[9] Every man should be guided by the standard of his father's house. 'And the Lord spoke unto Moses and unto Aaron, saying, "The children of Israel shall pitch every man by his own standard, with the ensigns of their fathers' houses."'

If we are blessed by fine parental example, our path is easier. Otherwise we must learn to lay the foundation of the good life by our own effort, through acquiring a sense of our national memory, of the proud loyalty of our forefathers.

'In the wilderness of human history, the Lord found Israel.'[10] 'Even as a man goes through the wilderness and finds grapes, so did The Holy One, blessed be He, find Israel. The wilderness of mankind changed into a land of light when the Hebrews came to Mount Sinai and accepted the *Torah*.'[11]

Everyone of us has the power, hence the opportunity, to bring light and warmth into his own life and to spread these boons among his neighbours, his community, the nation. For us Jews in the diaspora, patriotism – the promotion of freedom, justice, compassion, and co-operation – is a religious obligation. Jeremiah proclaimed this duty:[12] 'And seek the peace of the city whither I have caused you to be carried away captive, and pray unto the Lord for it, for in the peace thereof shall ye have peace." In the statesman's cool prose, Rabbi Hanina, the Associate High Priest, urged: 'Pray for the welfare of the government, for were it not for the fear of it, men would swallow each other alive.'[13] In Israel, our duty is greater, deeper, abiding. Pioneering beckons to every generation. *Makom hinihu lanu lehitgader bo* (There is a broad margin left to us of the seventh decade to distinguish ourselves in).[14] There are enough challenges – human want, misery – and prospects waiting for the brave and worthy to conquer.

Only if we recognize the paramount obligation to study life as to its defects and its chances; only if we recognize the persisting evil in national and international affairs and are determined to pioneer for justice, peace, and security; only if we understand that life represents simultaneously opportunity and responsibility, shall we succeed in overcoming today's bleak outlook, the desperate rebellion of the youth of our time; only if we understand that each of us might become a source and achieve comradeship in a better age of goodness, truth, and beauty to ourselves, our family, and community, shall we have enough wisdom, energy, and devotion to promote our own worth and happiness, and through co-operation with steadfast fellowmen to work for the peace and prosperity of mankind.

Notes

1. *a.l.* I, 6.
2. *Erubin* 54a.
3. *Arba'ah Turim*
4. *Tanhuma a.l.*
5. Num. X, 35.
6. *Ibid.* X, 36.
7. *Kiddushin* 40b.
8. *Sifri, Shoftim,* XVII, 19.
9. Num. II.
10. Deut. XXXII, 10.
11. *Yalkut Shimeoni a.l.*
12. Jer. XXIX, 7.
13. *Abot* III, 2.
14. *Ḥullin* 7a.

THE EDITOR OF THE JEWISH LIBRARY

LEO JUNG – The Editor of the JEWISH LIBRARY is the Senior Rabbi of the New York Jewish Center; former President of the Rabbinical Council of the Union of Orthodox Jewish Congregations of America; Professor Emeritus of Ethics and Jewish Philosophy, Yeshiva University; Chairman of the J.D.C.'s Cultural and Religious Committee; translator of Tractates Yoma and Arakhin of the Soncino Talmud, and author of *Fallen Angels*, *An Essay on Comparative Folklore*, *Mistranslations as Source of Lore*, *Living Judaism*, *Crumbs and Character*, *The Rhythm of Life*, *Harvest*, *Heirloom*, *Human Relations in Jewish Law* and other books, pamphlets, and articles on Jewish Law and Lore.